CORRUPTION
IN AMERICA

CORRUPTION IN AMERICA

FROM BENJAMIN FRANKLIN'S SNUFF BOX
TO CITIZENS UNITED

ZEPHYR
TEACHOUT

Harvard University Press
Cambridge, Massachusetts · London, England

First Harvard University Press paperback edition, 2016
First Printing

Library of Congress Cataloging-in-Publication Data

Teachout, Zephyr.
Corruption in America : from Benjamin Franklin's snuff box
to Citizens United / Zephyr Teachout.
pages   cm
Includes bibliographical references and index.
ISBN 978-0-674-05040-2 (cloth : alk. paper)
ISBN 978-0-674-65998-8 (pbk.)
1. Political corruption—United States—History.   2. Judicial
corruption—United States—History.   3. Political culture—
United States.   4. United States—Politics and government—
Moral and ethical aspects.   I. Title.
JK2249.T43   2014
364.1′3230973—dc23   2014010417

To Aly, Waylon, Jed, Celia, Sargent,
Zoe, Dewey, Esme, Garth, Elise, and Elva,
my big-hearted, big-dreaming nieces and nephews

Contents

Introduction

WHEN BENJAMIN FRANKLIN left Paris in 1785 after several years representing American interests in France, Louis XVI gave him a gorgeous parting gift. It was a portrait of King Louis, surrounded by 408 diamonds "of a beautiful water" set in two wreathed rows around the picture, and held in a golden case of a kind sometimes called a snuff box. The snuff box and portrait were worth as much as five times the value of other gifts given to diplomats. One historian has called it the "most precious treasure in [Franklin's] entire estate."[1] It depicted the king with powdered hair and red cheeks, wearing white lace around his throat, two gold chains on his shoulders, and a blue robe with gold fleurs-de-lis.[2]

In Europe, gifts were socially required upon a diplomat's departure. A valuable gift indicated a regent's great favor and a job well done. But in the new United States, the snuff box signified danger. Such a luxurious present was perceived as having the potential to corrupt men like Franklin, and therefore it needed to be carefully managed. In Europe, in other words, the gift had positive associations of connection and graciousness; in the United

States, it had negative associations of inappropriate attachments and dependencies. The snuff box stood for friendship or old world corruption, respect or bribery, depending on the perspective. For the Americans it was a symbol of seduction, dependency, luxury, and a European confusion about the proper relationship between politics, power and intimacy, and friendship.

According to an idiosyncratic anticorruption rule in the Articles of Confederation, Franklin's present had to be approved by Congress, as did all gifts from foreign officials. By going through Congress, and requiring a congressional stamp, the direct relationship between the king and Franklin was complicated, made public, and partially reconstituted as a relationship between Congress and Franklin. It was no longer in the realm of private reciprocity and relationships, but was instead a regulated transaction. As I will describe later, this rule was initially taken out of the proposed Constitution but reinserted when some of the delegates to the convention worried that its absence threatened corruption.

The argument of this book is that the gifts rule embodies a particularly demanding notion of corruption that survived through most of American legal history. This conception of corruption is at the foundation of the architecture of our freedoms. Corruption, in the American tradition, does not just include blatant bribes and theft from the public till, but encompasses many situations where politicians and public institutions serve private interests at the public's expense. This idea of corruption jealously guards the public morality of the interactions between representatives of government and private parties, foreign parties, or other politicians.

The king's gift threatened *this* kind of corruption because it encouraged a positive tacit relationship between France and

Franklin, built on diamonds. This could interfere with Franklin's obligations to the country at large. No one charged the king's agent with explicit promises or threats. Instead, the worry was that intimate obligations that arise from large gifts could interfere with public commitments. Imagine anyone receiving a gift of 408 diamonds "of the best water," and then, a few hours later, describing the gift giver in unattractive terms. The recipient would sound rude, ungrateful, and ungracious; we expect that gifts lead to some warmth and generosity toward the giver, if not official favors. Such private generosity, however, could violate the posture that the diplomat is supposed to have toward the leadership of the host country—the allegiance ought be firmly to America. At the level of basic human intercourse, Franklin owed something to the king after receiving such a gift. These subtle sympathies threatened to corrupt Franklin because they could interfere with his responsibility to put the country's interest first in his diplomatic judgments, and cloud his judgments about French actions. The concern held even though Franklin never planned to return to his post.

Americans started their experiment in self-government committed to expanding the scope of the actions that were called corrupt to encompass activities treated as noncorrupt in British and French cultures. Disappointed with Britain and Europe, Americans felt the need to constitute a political society with civic virtues and a deep commitment to representative responsiveness at the core. They enlisted law to help them do it, reclassifying noncorrupt, normal behaviors from Europe as corrupt behaviors in America. During the revolutionary period, the Americans not only created a new country but crafted a powerful political grammar. The concept of corruption in Franklin's

America drew on old traditions but augmented them and gave them power. He and his cohort believed that if you don't take care to support public emotional attachments of those in power, you can't build a representative government. When they spoke about corruption, the framers focused on the moral orientation of the citizens and representatives, the most essential building blocks of the republican state. Other political traditions focus on the more material problems of stability, anarchy, inequality, or violence. The American one focuses on the virtues of love for the public and the dangers of unrestrained self-interest. As I show throughout this book, this commitment to a broad view of corruption stayed largely the same in the courts for the country's first 200 years.

Corruption is often equated with modern criminal bribery and extortion law, with kickback arrangements between mayors and contractors, and with officials who accept cash to change votes. But it plays a larger social and political role. The snuff box incident demonstrated the belief that temptation and influence work in indirect ways, and that corruption is not merely transactional, or "quid pro quo," as it is sometimes called.

The law that governed the portrait in a snuff box also exemplifies the founders' preference for a certain kind of anticorruption rule. These rules—which I call structural, or prophylactic—cover innocent activity as well as insidious transactions. They stand in contrast to laws that require corrupt intent to convict. They work through changing incentives before the fact instead of punishing activity after the fact. In the gifts clause and dozens of other constitutional provisions, the framers built their bulwarks against corruption through structural rules. For instance, the residency requirement in the Constitution limits the freedom of people to run for Congress to where they live but is a worth-while rule because it protects—imperfectly but practically—against "adventurers." Instead of requiring a jury to determine whether Franklin was *in fact* in secret communications with France, or whether there was *in fact* some whispered explicit deal, the only demand the prophylactic gift rule makes is that no gift be given without congressional approval.

✦ ✦ ✦

The particular word *corruption* has a long tradition of playing an important role in our country's political transformation. Charges of corruption and its variants were an essential force in the creation of the Constitution and part of almost every debate about governmental structure. In the first hundred years of the Republic the problem of corruption drove key decisions about how to structure government and business, and how to restrain self-interested legislators. Corruption rhetoric dominated the Jacksonian era. Corruption rallied people to pass several of the post–Civil War constitutional amendments, including the Seventeenth Amendment (allowing for the direct election of Senators) and the Twenty-Seventh Amendment (providing that congressional salary raises do not take effect until the beginning of the next session of Congress). Charges of system-wide corruption led to the 1880s antitrust statutes and the twentieth-century enforcement thereof. *Corruption, corrupt,* and related words were a major part of the grammar of the populists and the progressive reformers and were accusations that supported the rise of prosecutorial post-Watergate culture.

In its parallel life in the law, the concept of corruption has also been transformative. Legal disputes around the meaning of the concept of corruption—and in some cases the meaning of the words *corruption, corrupt,* or *corruptly*—have often been so vexing that they have forced courts to be inventive in other areas. This book focuses its attention on these moments of judicial uncertainty and ingenuity. A corruption case about land speculation in Georgia was the first case in which the Supreme Court invalidated a state law on federal constitutional grounds. The trail of corruption law leads to the public trust doctrine (an important environmental rule), the mail fraud statute, Watergate, and independent expenditures. This book follows land and debt scams through Tennessee and Chicago to the Oregon Coast. It follows lobbying as it shifts from a civic wrong to a First Amendment right. It explores legal responses to multicolored ballots and a late 1920s scheme to abuse the public trust in New Orleans. In bribery statutes, courts had to decide how to instruct juries about the meaning of "corruptly" in statutes. The relationship of corruption to law has led to a series of consequential questions that are inevitably entangled with political theory.

The meaning of the concept of corruption is now at the center of the most vital legal dispute in our democracy, one that threatens to unravel what the framers built. This dispute has its roots in *Buckley v. Valeo,* a 1976 case that struck down a law limiting campaign spending. While the *Buckley* Court recognized that there was a legitimate reason the public might want to stop corruption, it concluded that the provisions limiting spending did not have much to do with corruption. It did not define corruption or completely narrow it to explicit transactions—that came later—but it set up an awkward jurisprudential framework in which civic interests in blocking corruption are set up in opposition to First Amendment speech rights. *Buckley* also put the brakes on experimentation in the states, although it left some campaign finance rules untouched.

An aggressive misreading of *Buckley* that began in 2006 led to *Citizens United* in January 2010, when the U.S. Supreme Court made one of the most consequential decisions in American political history. *Citizens United* effectively gave wealthy individuals and wealthy corporations the right to spend as much money as they wanted attempting to influence elections and policy. The Court concluded that, as a matter of law, uncoordinated corporate spending was archetypal political speech and such spending did not corrupt candidates or the political system.

The crux of the *Citizens United* opinion is a claim about the nature of corruption and its historical role in American law. Justice Kennedy, writing for the majority of the Court, defined corruption as bribery, and bribery as quid pro quo. By quid pro quo he meant not the contract law phrase *quid pro quo*, which has traditionally meant equal exchange, but a particular understanding of quid pro quo that has developed in the corruption law context since *Buckley*. For Kennedy, quid pro quo meant explicit exchange of something of value for a specific, identifiable legislative or executive act. In applying this definition, he wrote that "independent expenditures, including those made by corporations, do not give rise to corruption or the appearance of corruption." He argued that "the fact that speakers may have influence over or access to elected officials does not mean that these officials are corrupt." In 2014, Justice Roberts's decision in *McCutcheon v. FEC* confirmed this analysis. The only constitutionally cognizable corruption, he wrote, is quid pro quo corruption.

This new legal order treats corruption lightly and in a limited way. It narrows the scope of what is considered corruption to explicit deals. It reclassifies influence-seeking as normal and desirable political behavior. It purportedly avoids difficult problems of definition. It attempts to wring the moral content out of the term *corruption* and tell a story about corruption that is consistent with a world populated by self-interested actors.

Such efforts are misguided. They do not really avoid the definitional problems, because quid pro quo, while sounding specific, is itself a contested term with a range of meanings. Most importantly, they are very dangerous to the health of the nation. The a-historical—and potentially tragic—mistake made by the Kennedy-Roberts model flows in part from a modern tendency to look at political-legal problems through the lens of the First Amendment, and in part from a belief that the corrupting influence of money is moot because everyone in politics is already on the take.

The justices have also likely been influenced by many political scientists and legal scholars who have adopted the selfish-man theory of human nature in the late twentieth century, an assumption that people will be self-interested in their behavior in all areas. As one theorist put it: "There is one human motivator that is both universal and central to explaining the divergent experiences of different countries. That motivator is self-interest." Such a theory of human nature is incompatible with the traditional American theory of corruption. The two most abrupt breaks with the historical meaning of corruption—*Buckley* and *Citizens United*—have occured when no politicians were on the Court. This suggests that biography may also explain the recent abandonment of old ideas. While lower courts and state courts have consistently expanded the scope of corruption laws, an opposite movement has happened on high. The Court has become populated by academics and appellate court justices, and not by people with experience of power and politics, who understand the ways in which real problems of money and influence manifest themselves. The lack of experience is compounded by a tendency to decide cases without full factual development.

* * *

The *Citizens United* decision was not merely bad law; it was bad for politics, and displayed an even worse understanding of history. Americans from James Madison onward have argued that it is possible for politicians and citizens alike to try to achieve a kind of public good in the public sphere. The traditional view is not naive—it does not assume that people are generally public-regarding. It assumes that the job of government is to create structures to curb temptations that lead to exaggerated self-interest. It certainly recognizes the power of self-interest; but instead of endorsing it, the traditional American approach makes it government's job to temper egocentrism in the public sphere. The traditional conception implicates difficult questions: What is self-orientation and public orientation, and what is the public good? But it does not discard these distinctions because they are difficult ones to parse. A classical American approach engages the complexity. Like liberty, speech, or equality, corruption is an important concept with unclear boundaries. It refers to excessive private interests in the public sphere; an act is corrupt when private interests trump public ones in the exercise of public power, and a person is corrupt when they use public power for their own ends, disregarding others.

Corruption in America is my effort to fill in the history that *Citizens United* ignored. It provides a previously neglected story of the use of the concept in American law and a much-needed account of the different kinds of meanings attached to it throughout the political life of the country. I show that for most of American history, courts remained committed to a broad view of corruption. The book draws primarily upon the texts used by lawyers: the Constitutional Convention, cases, and statutes. It shows how, starting in the late 1970s, everything began to change around this issue. The Supreme Court, along with a growing subset of scholars, began to confuse the concept of corruption and throw out many of the prophylactic rules that were used to protect against it. This rejection has led to an overflow of private industry involvement in political elections and a rapid decline in the civic ethic in Congress and the state houses. The old ideas about virtue were tossed out as sentimental, but the old problems of corruption and government have persisted. Interest-group pluralists who reject these ideas do not, I believe, have an answer to the problem of corruption and in fact have been part of the problem.

The contemporary era is full of proverbial diamond-encrusted gifts, although they are less likely to come from the king of France. Instead, they come from the lords of highly concentrated, monopolistic industries who, like the king of France in 1785, have an intense and personal interest in the political choices of the legislative branches and a casual disregard for the civic process. Candidates are dependent upon the gifts of wealthy individuals in the form of campaign contributions and businesses in the form of independent political expenditures. The impulse to resist these presents is a deeply American one, going all the way back to the founding. But in order to protect this resistance, we will need tools and approaches that are alien to the modern law and economic transactional understandings of corruption.

The book argues that prophylactic rules designed to limit temptations are not a backwater but a cornerstone of what is best in our country. In our modern prosecutorial culture, one might be tempted to think that white-collar bribery laws, which I categorized as "corrupt intent" laws, would be the appropriate tool for fighting corruption. But they are problematic. If a bribery statute is narrowly drawn (or interpreted), it covers only brazen, unsophisticated exchanges and does not actually solve problems of money being used to influence policy and undermine representative government. A narrow law will punish only clumsy politicians like William Jefferson, who hid his rolls of cash in a freezer. More broadly interpreted corrupt intent laws are troubling for the opposite reason: since they proscribe giving a "thing of value" with "intent to influence" governmental action, they can be used to punish political enemies. By their terms, they can even cover a politician's promise to help a teachers' group in exchange for an endorsement. A criminal law "War on Corruption" is arguably like the wars on drugs or terror—nearly impossible to win in arraignments. Corruption is far better fought through changing basic incentive structures. This might seem intuitive to anyone involved in politics, but the majority of the current Supreme Court openly prefer bribery laws to prophylactic campaign spending limits: one of their justifications for striking down campaign finance rules is that corrupt intent laws provide better protection.

I seek to enrich the way American judges, scholars, and citizens imagine the concept of corruption and its relationship to our legal system. The book challenges four commonly held misconceptions: that corruption law began in the post-Watergate era, that criminal bribery law is the dominant sphere in which corruption law plays out, that bribery law is coherent and consistent, and that quid pro quo is the heart of corruption law. A deeper understanding of the tradition of corruption can enrich our civic culture and our laws.

If the Supreme Court can better remember our past, it might overturn dozens of cases that have limited the capacity of elected legislatures to make their own experiments in democracy. And if we, as citizens, can remember our past, it could augment the way we think about our founding principles. What if we could add "anticorruption" to citizens' sense of national identity?

✦   ✦   ✦

We are a nation of dreamers and reformers, and in our struggle with corruption, tens of thousands of reforms have been offered up, some more colorful than others. In 1860 a correspondent of the *Chicago Press and Tribune* had a big idea about how to respond to the corruption he saw in Washington. The city, he said, was an

> out-of-the-way, one horse town, whose population consists of office-holders, lobby buzzards, landlords, loafers, blacklegs, hackmen and cyprian—all subsisting on public plunder. . . . The paramount, overshadowing occupation of the residents, is office-holding and lobbying, and the prize of life is a grab at the contents of UNCLE SAM's till. The public plunder interest swallows up all others, and

makes the city a great festering, unbealable sore on the body politic. No healthy public opinion can reach down here to purify the moral atmosphere of Washington.[3]

What reform did the writer advocate? Moving the capital to New York City. There, he argued, the office-jobbers would get swallowed up in a less corrupt culture. This book cannot describe all the reforms proposed and rejected or adopted. Instead, I use examples of different kinds of reforms in order to discuss the interaction of the courts with the law of corruption. In the Conclusion, however, I introduce two of the most important structural reforms allowed by current jurisprudence: public funding of elections and new antimonopoly laws.

For better or worse, American corruption law is so hydra-headed that my book cannot do its intrigues full justice. Therefore, after examining the founding era, I focus on cases in which there are powerful competing ideas about corruption, or competing ideas about who should define it. There are important areas of corruption law that this book only lightly touches on, like contracting rules, transparency laws, state and local government conflict of interest laws, administrative law, and judicial recusal laws. The great battle between machine politicians and reformers is for another day. Boss Tweed shows up only as an exception. His case violated the general rule that criminal bribery laws, for most of the nation's history, were a weak and rarely seen flank in the anticorruption fight.

As Jack Burden learns in the great American novel *All the King's Men*, there are no untainted men or women. His boss, the populist politician Willie Stark, charges him with finding something sordid about a seemingly completely virtuous father figure in his life: "I said, 'But suppose there isn't anything to find?' And the Boss said, 'There is always something.' And he said, 'Man is conceived in sin and born in corruption and he passeth from the stink of the didie to the stench of the shroud. There is always something.'"[4] A call for a return to traditional conceptions of corruption should not be confused with a call for a return to some golden era, or to a culture of moral purity. There is no such time.

Instead, I hope for a deeper understanding of the complex ways in which private and public morality intersect, and greater respect for the political dangers that flow from untethered self-interest. That understanding will lead to judicial support for clear rules that prevent us from succumbing to temptation. To borrow the lesson of one of the greatest works of political fiction, if we do not bind ourselves to the mast beforehand, we could end up in a graveyard alongside other former republics.

The book is divided into four sections. The first provides an introduction to corruption in the Constitutional period; the second examines the development of corruption law from the founding to the late nineteenth century in three different areas (criminal bribery laws, corruptly passed laws, and lobbying); the third traces campaign finance and bribery laws in the twentieth century; and the fourth addresses the revolution epitomized by *Citizens United*.

My passion for the book springs out of my own civic patriotism. To quote James Madison, "My wish is that the national legislature be as uncorrupt as possible." This is not a modest wish. But the United States has a profound civic culture, expressed all the time in the myriad ways in which people ask each other "what should we do?" instead of "what do I want?" when faced with public policy questions. If the structure of society stops being responsive, the latter question will inevitably overtake the former. I believe that the concept of corruption may be a difficult one, but we need it to survive. As the political theorist Hannah Arendt writes, no one in the classical tradition thinks that democracy is either the end of history or inevitable. In other words, democracy is always threatened. The point is not that it is easy, but that it is possible.

After the Philadelphia convention, a woman famously asked Benjamin Franklin, "What have we got, a republic or a monarchy?" Franklin allegedly replied, "A republic, madame, if you can keep it." His own gift to the country may have been his peculiar blend of persistent pessimism and persistent optimism, which inserted itself powerfully into the Constitutional Convention. Speaking before the convention in Philadelphia in 1787, Franklin said that the Constitution was "likely to be well administered for a course of years, and can only end in despotism, as other forms have done before it, when the people shall become so corrupted as to need despotic government, being incapable of any other." Franklin's political philosophy epitomized twin American desires to privilege private behavior *and* celebrate the precious nature of public-oriented government. In his youth he valorized thrifty private behavior; in his later years he turned outward and spoke about corruption in a deeply visceral way. Franklin's understanding of politics included a theory of power, and how power could be exercised through inveiglements and the promise of future employment. Franklin was at heart a practical politician and had spent decades abroad and decades in the politics that preceded the Revolutionary era. His own love of luxury and the good elements in life may have made him wary of the power of temptations. Temptation is a central theme of the book: as you will soon see, even the antiaristocratic Thomas Jefferson could not resist the temptation of hiding diamond gifts from the king when there were debts to pay.

What America now faces, if we do not change the fundamental structures of the relationship of money to legislative power, is neither mob rule nor democracy, but oligarchy.

CHAPTER ONE

Four Snuff Boxes and a Horse

A GIFT CAN BE A BRIBE. A bribe can be a gift. Whether a present counts as corrupt or simply generous depends entirely upon our cultural or political frame. Gifts are often part of what is best in society: they are a way of showing other people that they are seen and valued, perhaps even loved, and a way of providing rewards in a non-transactional way. They lead to amity and warmth in a way no explicit deal can. But gifts play a potentially dangerous role in both judicial and democratic practice. They can create obligations to private parties that shape judgment and outcomes. Part of designing a political system is separating gifts from bribes—that is, defining what gifts ought be categorized as corrupting. As Daniel Hays Lowenstein argued thirty years ago, a concept of corruption or bribery "means identifying as immoral or criminal a subset of transactions and relationships within a set that, generally speaking, is fundamentally beneficial to mankind, both functionally and intrinsically."[1]

In two recent cases—*Citizens United* and *McCutcheon v. FEC*—Supreme Court justices Anthony Kennedy and John Roberts wrote that campaign contributions—gifts—given with intent to influence policy are not corrupting. As they explained it, corruption requires more than intent on the part of the gift giver; it requires something like an explicit deal between the giver and receiver. When they made these pronouncements, they claimed to be merely following precedent. In fact, they were do-ing what Lowenstein suggested: identifying and circumscribing a small subset of activities as corrupt. Their circle was particu-larly small. In the early days of the republic, the new Americans took the opposite approach. They drew a large circle around gifts that they called corrupt. They were committed to treat-ing gifts as political threats, even when such treatment violated the law of nations and complicated vitally important interna-tional negotiations, and certainly when the gifts were not ac-companied by an explicit deal.

Plato's Republic in the New World

During and after the Revolutionary War the new Americans were driven by a fear of being corrupted by foreign powers, and a related fear of adopting the Old World's corrupt habits. The two national powers that dominated the colonies, France and Britain, represented two different models of corruption. Britain was seen as a failed ideal. It was corrupted republic, a place where the premise of government was basically sound but civic virtue—that of the public and public officials—was degenerat-ing. On the other hand, France was seen as more essentially corrupt, a nation in which there was no true polity, but instead exchanges of luxury for power; a nation populated by weak sub-jects and flattering courtiers. Britain was the greater tragedy, because it held the promise of integrity, whereas France was simply something of a civic cesspool. John Adams said of France, "there is everything here too which can seduce, betray, deceive, corrupt, and debauch."[2] As Thomas Jefferson—who adored Paris—wrote in 1801, the year he became president:

> We have a perfect horror at everything like connecting ourselves with the politics of Europe. It would indeed be advantageous to us to have neutral rights established on a broad ground; but no dependence can be placed in any European coalition for that. They have so many other bye-interests of greater weight, that someone or other will always be bought off. To be entangled with them would be a much greater evil than a temporary acquiescence in the false principles which have prevailed.[3]

This "hatred" of the European political culture and the fear of entanglement led to a problem. The new Americans wanted to be part of the international community, respect the laws and customs of nations as a matter of principle, and be respected as an autonomous new nation. But they also wanted to reject corrupt European customs. When it came to internal affairs, this was not a major conflict. But when it came to the customs of international diplomacy—like the custom of exempting ambassadors from paying duties—they wanted it both ways.

One of the customs of the international community was the giving and receiving of personal presents to ambassadors, as I described briefly in the Introduction. Expensive gifts—sometimes called *presents du roi* or *presents du congé*—functioned as "tokens of esteem, prestige items, and perhaps petty bribes,"[4] and were embedded in the culture of international relations. Gifts were typically given at the end of diplomatic tours. They were often very expensive, and were understood to be a supplement to salaries. In some cases the value of gifts constituted a substantial part of the income received by diplomats. The value of a gift might reflect the esteem in which a diplomat was held, or the importance of the relationship with his nation.

This practice was hateful to the Americans because it symbolized and embodied part of a particular culture they rejected. Jewels themselves signify luxury. They pointed to an old-world privilege that would not come easily to even the richest Americans. In the founders' minds, luxury represented a kind of internal corrosion—even in cases where there was no external dependency, a man could be tempted into seeking out things for himself, instead of seeking things for a country—he could, in some ways, self-corrupt. The diamonds of Franklin's gift would have seemed ostentatious to the founders.

The Articles of Confederation included this provision: "Nor shall any person holding any office of profit or trust under the United States, or any of them, accept any present, emolument, office or title of any kind." This ban on receiving gifts was perceived as severe and not a little eccentric. The provision was a close copy of a 1651 Dutch rule that their foreign ministers were not allowed to take "any presents, directly or indirectly, in any manner or way whatever."[5] The code was so far outside the normal state of affairs that it was ridiculed for its sanctimony. The Dutch political writer Wicquefort's analysis of the Dutch prohibition against receiving gifts was scathing: "The custom of making a present . . . is so well established that it is of as great an extent as the law of nations itself, there is reason to be surprised at the regulation that has been made on that subject in

Holland." Wicquefort went on to write about how so scrupulously observant they are that they refuse even the most trivial presents. He accused his countrymen of silliness for making a fuss over the smallest gifts, even a plate of fruit. "I cannot tell," he writes, "whether the authors of this regulation pretended to found a Republick of Plato in their fens and marshes," but "it cannot be denied" that they "condemn the sentiments of all the other kings and potentates of the universe."[6] He may have been referring to Plato because Plato had been rather severe about gifts. Not only did he recommend dishonor for judges who were bribed by flattery, but he thought that public servants who accepted gifts should die:

> Those who serve their country ought to serve without receiving gifts, and there ought to be no excusing or approving the saying, "Men should receive gifts as the reward of good, but not of evil deeds"; for to know which we are doing, and to stand fast by our knowledge, is no easy matter. The safest course is to obey the law which says, "Do no service for a bribe," and let him who disobeys, if he be convicted, simply die.[7]

The American founders did not advocate execution for gift-acceptance, but they might have taken Wicquefort's ridicule as a compliment—they *were* interested in establishing their own just republic. But their idealism quickly became difficult in the international context. The Europeans were not interested in complying with this new, self-imposed ban. During the early years of American independence, foreign princes generously loaded American emissaries with expensive gifts, and the Americans receiving the gifts had to figure out how to respond.

The first gift problem arose after the Declaration of Independence was signed. That was when American politician Silas Deane was charged with discovering whether France might be willing to aid the Americans with cannons, arms, and military clothing for the Revolution. Deane was a Yale graduate, a lawyer, a merchant, and politician who was known as "Ticonderoga" by some for his strategic role in the successful Ethan Allen capture of Fort Ticonderoga.[8] His first effort in France was not so much diplomacy as espionage. Under the name "Timothy Jones," he posed as a merchant trying to buy supplies for the rebels. When it became clear that France was open to trade with the colonies, he abandoned his disguise and established himself as one of the first formally commissioned representatives of the aspiring country. He was soon joined by Benjamin Franklin and Arthur Lee. The three men grew to hate each other, and the delegation was full of accusations and counteraccusations. Deane accused Lee of disloyalty, Lee thought Franklin was corrupt, and Franklin thought Lee was a lunatic.[9]

Deane's tenure was troubled from the start, as there were rumors about his loyalty. He was accused of using his public position to make a private fortune by manipulating the commissions he received on procured goods. His financial accounting was questioned, and he was generally thought of as ambitious and too tricky by half. Adams found him untrustworthy and distasteful. In 1778 Deane was recalled to Congress, charged with fraudulent account keeping and disloyalty.[10]

When he left France, Deane received a jeweled snuff box for his diplomatic service from the French court. King Louis loved these boxes and frequently gave them to foreign ministers. He allegedly called them *boîte à portrait* instead of snuff boxes: he disliked snuff, but liked the form and frequently adorned them with portraits of himself.[11] Deane apparently thought the gift would help save his reputation: he offered it as proof of the great work he had done for the new country. According to Arthur Lee's account, Deane "expected, from the effect of a French Fleet, of which he was to claim the sole merit, the brilliancy of a diamond snuff box, and complimentary letter," that he would return to the United States with sufficient proof of his loyalties.[12] John Adams was dismissive of the use of evidence, remarking that "unthinking men may be amused with a golden snuff box."[13]

Deane's acceptance of the snuff box led to Lee accusing him of violating one of the core laws of the Confederation. In his papers on the matter, Lee wrote: "Deane knew that it was one of *the fundamental laws of our Union* that no person in the service of the United States should accept from any king, prince, or minister any present or gratuity whatsoever . . . yet in the face of this fundamental law, Mr. Deane accepted of a gold snuff, set with diamonds, from the King of France."[14] The disloyalty and accounting accusations against Deane were never proven, as the French did not disclose their accounting. Deane would eventually return to France, disgraced but not sentenced. But the question of the appropriate relationship to foreign gifts remained.

It turns out it was far easier to criticize the gift acceptance than to resist it: the next snuff box went to Lee himself. Lee, along with Franklin, had negotiated the 1778 treaty with France. When Lee returned to the American states in 1780, he carried with him a new jeweled snuff box, also given to him by King Louis XVI, with the king's portrait set in diamonds. Lee was understandably concerned about the appearances of accepting the box—in part because Deane had countercharged him with disloyalty. But Lee was also worried about offending the king. He wrote to a friend that the snuff box might "excite some murmurs" and thought that the Articles of Confederation might prevent accepting the gift.[15] Like most humans, he found the ethical proscriptions of others easy to understand but when he was placed in the same situation as Deane, he was less sure about what to do.

As Lee was then embroiled in accusations that he had given offense to the French court, the gift also served for him as "proof of the untruth" of the accusations against him.[16] The French liaison, Vergennes, "warned his adjutant in Philadelphia that an unscrupulous politician like Arthur Lee might employ the King's portrait . . . to give the impression that he (Lee) held the king's confidence and thus could speak freely on matters of French foreign policy."[17] Lee wrote to his brother, "as you can imagine, I was embarrassed about receiving or refusing it." He explained that he had told the court that receiving such a gift was against the rules of those he represented, but the court insisted. Lee ultimately gave the gilded box to Congress to determine what to do with it. He wrote to the Committee of Foreign Affairs on January 19, 1780:

> I thought it my duty to decline accepting it, upon which his excellency told me it was a mark of his majesty's esteem, and was never refused. After this it appeared to me improper to persist in the refusal, and I received it with a determination to leave it to the disposal of Congress. . . . His majesty's portrait is graven upon my mind by the justice and virtue which constitute his character, of which gold and jewels can not enhance the value.[18]

Congress eventually allowed him to keep it.

The next gift that excited internal discussion was not a *bôite-a-portrait*, but a horse. John Jay, as the ambassador to Spain, was negotiating over navigational rights with Spain's representative Don Diego de Gardoqui on behalf of the Americans.[19] He had asked for a permit to buy a Spanish horse for breeding, but de Gardoqui told him that the king of Spain wanted to give him a horse instead. "His majesty, instead of granting a permit, ordered a horse to be sent from me to you," a horse that, by the time the letter reached Jay, had already been chosen and sent to a port where it only awaited the arrival of a vessel that would transport the horse to Jay. Jay responded with some trepidation. He knew, of course, of the prohibition against gifts, and likely knew of the public attention that accompanied Lee's and Deane's acceptances of their boxes.

A few days later, he wrote back, thanking his correspondent for the honor of having a horse purchased and exported for him. However, he said that he did not "consider himself at Liberty to accept the horse without the previous Permission of Congress."[20] Two days later, after he shared the letters with Congress, they gave him permission to keep the horse.

The final notorious gift in the post-Revolutionary period was the snuff box and portrait given to Benjamin Franklin. This ostentatious, diamond-decorated gift was troubling in general, but Franklin's place in the American imagination, and his well-known affection for the French, likely made it an especially worrisome gift. Franklin was notoriously adored by the French court. He was well loved in the United States as well, but not above the suspicion that other diplomats were subject to. Many of Franklin's cohorts did not trust him. Franklin had spent most of the post-Revolutionary years in France and had fallen in love with it. His veneration of France was such that even Sam Adams was concerned that he had turned Tory.[21] Two unsuccessful recall efforts had been launched against him by some republicans, concerned about his close connections to the French royalty. William Lee called England "the old mule," and Franklin "the old fox," a sly way of calling him too sly by half. Arthur Lee called Franklin "the most corrupt of all corrupt men."[22]

Franklin's diamonds embodied a whole set of fears about patriotism in general, loyalty in a republic, and the particular, time-sensitive concerns about how extremely elaborate gifts might sway Franklin's attitude toward his semi-permanent residence—Paris—and against his American home. Given Franklin's outsized role in the American political landscape, and France's wealth, this particular gift portended more than warmth and friendship. It was a show of power. France loomed large and threatening in American political life. The Franco-American relationship was halfway between troubled and passionate—the Americans deeply admired France and hoped for their continued alliance against the British, but at the same time feared that France aspired to slide into the colonial role from which they had violently ejected Britain. Newspapers were full of suggestions that the French government had designs on the country. In 1785 Franklin turned the portrait over to Congress and asked for approval to keep it, which, in the spring of 1786, they granted.[23]

At the Constitutional Convention, many parts of the Articles of Confederation were changed, but the framers kept the portion that would become Article I, Section 9 of the Constitution. It is one of the more strongly worded prohibitions in the

Constitution: "No person holding any office of profit or trust under them [the United States], shall, without the consent of the Congress, accept of any present, emolument, office, or title, of any kind whatever, from any king, prince, or foreign state." The initial draft of the new Constitution that was circulated and debated throughout the summer of 1787 did not include this provision, but merely prohibited titles of nobility. On August 23, however, delegate Charles Pinkney "urged the necessity of preserving foreign Ministers & other officers of the U. S. independent of external influence" and moved to reinsert the radical Dutch clause.

The gifts section softens the prohibition of the Articles of Confederation, inasmuch as it allows for gifts and emoluments if they are approved by Congress—the initial version declared a complete ban.[24] However, the softening may have merely adjusted the language to the contemporary meaning as it had been interpreted in both countries. According to John Quincy Adams, when he asked a Dutch friend about how they enforced their similar provision, the friend explained that a gift was almost always allowed when it was first presented to the government for approval.[25]

The clause was not extensively discussed in the Constitutional Convention, but there is some evidence that it was actively contemplated in connection with the corrupting potential of one of the snuff boxes, possibly Franklin's.[26] Virginian Edmund Randolph, describing the clause to the Virginia delegates as they were deciding whether or not to ratify the Constitution, explained:

> This restriction was provided to prevent corruption. . . . An accident, which actually happened, operated in producing

the restriction. A box was presented to our ambassador by the king of our allies. It was thought proper, in order to exclude corruption and foreign influence, to prohibit any one in office from receiving or holding any emoluments from foreign states.[27]

The lack of an exception for small tokens in the gifts clause is striking. The clause does not merely stop at "no gifts," but emphasizes the prohibition through the use of "any kind whatever," underlying the extreme importance of the prohibition.[28] Moreover, it forbids presents—not bribes. No exchange or agreement is required to bring it within the ban. That fierce rejection "of any kind whatever" reveals a commitment to transforming the political culture that persisted from the Revolutionary era to the Constitutional era. It was a ban on a culture of gift giving.

Jefferson's Brilliants

The last Constitutional-era snuff box never made it in front of Congress. When Thomas Jefferson, after the Constitution was ratified, took his own turn as a diplomat to France, he thought at first that he could be free from the custom of receiving gifts, which he found distasteful. As one of his biographers put it, "Jefferson thought it mercifully prohibited by the Constitution."[29] Nonetheless, the French court gave him a snuff box at the end of his tour, embedded with "brilliants" surrounding a portrait of the king. It was valued slightly less—but only slightly—than the one given to Franklin. He wrote to his assistant William Short, asking him to let the appropriate parties know that the gifts clause meant that he could not accept the customary present from the king. "Explain to them that clause in our new constitution which [says] 'no person holding any office of profit or trust under the U.S. shall accept any present, emolument, office, or title of any kind whatever from any king, prince or foreign state.'" Jefferson recognized that he could go through Congress for approval but told Short he did not choose "to be laid on the gridiron of debate in Congress for any such paltry purpose," so he should not even let the relevant parties know about it. "Be so good as to explain it in such a manner as to avoid offence." The difficulties attending the gift caused Jefferson "considerable anguish," but he eventually accepted it.

Instead of going through Congress, he asked his secretary to take the gilded frame, remove the diamonds, catalogue and value them, sell the most valuable, put the money toward Jefferson's own private account, and not report it. Literary historian Martha Rojas describes his response as "both calculated and tortured," and argues that it may have been driven by concerns about money. His letters to Short on the matter were written in cipher. He asked him to take out the diamonds and sell them, and then safely return the portrait, doing whatever was necessary to keep attention away.[30] Upon Short's instructions, the banker extracted the diamonds.[31] The money raised from the sale of the diamonds was put into his own account and used to pay for the diplomatic presents and embassy debts. When it was done, Short wrote: "I send you . . . the remains of what I received for you, agreeably to your desire. The secrecy you requested is fully observed."[32]

Whether Jefferson did not want to offend the French or could not resist the temptation of a chance to pay off debts, we cannot know. But his simultaneous disdain for European gifts and his inability to resist them foreshadow a long American practice: our desire to reject and accept the old practices simultaneously; our inability, at a deep level, to wrestle with how to allow wealthy presents and politics to coexist. The fate of the "dismembered" portrait of France is unknown.

The new political process envisioned by the new Americans gradually took hold. Congress appears to have taken its job seriously. A relative of Charles Pinckney was given gifts after his tours in Madrid; while the Senate approved receiving the gifts, the House did not, saying that it was against public policy. In the following years, horses, lions, and medallions were submitted to Congress for approval.[33]

In Joseph Story's 1829 commentary on the Constitution, he found great importance in the gifts clause. He argued that there "cannot be too much jealousy in respect to foreign influence. The treasures of Persia were successfully distributed in Athens; and it is now known that in England a profligate prince and many of his venal courtiers were bribed into measures injurious to the nation by the gold of Louis XIV." He argued that the clause should be extended to cover all citizens (an amendment circulating at the time would have had that effect). His proposed solution? "Disfranchisement, or a deprivation of all the rights of a citizen, seems the most appropriate punishment that could be applied, since it renders the seduction useless to those who were the authors of it, and disgraceful to the person seduced."

Was Franklin corrupted by his gift? Were Lee, or Deane, corrupted by their boxes or Jay by his horse? The constitutional gifts provision does not provide an answer, but it does announce an attitude toward corruption and a way of thinking about it. The clause was, as Lee called it, "fundamental," in part because it expressed a new view of the appropriate way to be a public representative of a country. It reflected a broad view of what constitutes corruption, a broad view of the importance of protecting against even the slightest temptation, and a commitment to using absolute, prophylactic rules to support a civic society in which people put public interests first in their public roles. The work that it took to change a culture highlights the strain of a country attempting to reject old traditions and replace them with their own, and to declare unconstitutional that which was only recently "good diplomacy."

In retrospect, all the fuss about diamond boxes and horses may seem like an amusing footnote to the larger discussions about redefining liberty and ambitions of true self-government. But they were not amusing to a country living in fear of the fate of all republics.

CHAPTER TWO

Changing the Frame

A REPUBLIC FLOURISHED POLITICALLY and culturally for centuries, until a slow corruption of public life by private concerns destroyed it. This republic sustained itself for as long as it did because of the moral habits of private men in their public roles, not because of the brilliance of individual leaders. Its decline, according to a famous interpreter, came from the power and increasing corruption of an elite group who had the power to remove its most powerful citizen. These guardians became increasingly involved in intrigue and abuse of power, lost a sense of civic virtue, and in so doing, lost the republic.

This republic is not America. It was Rome, as analyzed by Edward Gibbon. In 1776, the same year that independence was declared, Gibbon published volume 1 of *The History of the Decline and Fall of the Roman Empire*. It was a popular success. In a literary letter to Benjamin Franklin, a friend referred to the first volume as one of only two recently published books worth mentioning, along with Adam Smith's *The Wealth of Nations*.[1] In 1781, the year the Articles of Confederation were ratified, Gibbon published the second and third volumes. In 1788 and 1789, as the Constitution came into effect, Gibbon published his last installment of *The Decline and Fall*, the fourth, fifth, and sixth volumes. For the avid reader of that generation, Rome collapsed while America was born.

Gibbon covered 500 years of history, a remarkably minute description of petty and profound arguments, scheming, and treachery, and the battles at the edges of the collapse of the great empire. But he did not merely stick to the past. Gibbon argued that representative bodies, structured wisely and fairly, could allow liberty to survive. He contemplated how the right constitutional forms could have allowed the golden era of Roman culture to persist. He argued that if "an institution, which gave the people an interest in their own government, had been universally established by Trajan or the Antonines, the seeds of public wisdom and virtue might have been cherished and propagated in the empire of Rome." Representative assemblies might have prevented the "abuses of an arbitrary administration" and foreign invasion.

"Under the mild and generous influence of liberty, the Roman empire might have remained invincible and immortal; or if its excessive magnitude, and the instability of human affairs, had opposed such perpetual continuance, its vital and constituent members might have separately preserved their vigour and independence."[2]

Gibbon both reflected and influenced the intellectual currents of eighteenth-century intellectuals, with a particular message for the new revolutionaries trying to build sustainable political architecture. The Americans read the story of Rome as a direct analogy to the corruption in the British Empire and a caution for the future. Gibbon's blended tones of caution and hope were evident throughout the American elite around the time of the Constitutional Convention. The Roman narrative held a strong grip on the imaginations of the framers. After he borrowed it from a friend, Benjamin Franklin was "quite absorbed" in Gibbon, so much so that repeated requests to return it were unavailing.[3] Jefferson had his own copy of *The Decline and Fall*. In one section he transcribed in the margins a poem attributed to the fictitious Irish warrior-poet Ossian:

> I have seen the walls of Balclutha, but they were desolate.
> The stream of Clutha was removed from its place by the
> fall of the walls. The thistle shook there its lonely head.
> The moss whistled to the wind. The fox looked out from
> the windows: the rank grass of the wall waved round his
> head.

He, and the other framers, were haunted by the spector of future desolation.

But Gibbon was not the only source of the preoccupation with Rome. The pamphleteers and letters of the time show that the most important activists and intellectuals read the Roman writers directly.[4] They cited Plutarch, Sallust, and Cicero—each of whom pointed to corruption as the core reason for political decline. Jefferson thought Tacitus was the greatest writer of any generation, and John Adams emotionally embraced the writing, saying that it was as if he were reading a history of his own political times.[5] The founding fathers' "scrutiny of the late Roman republic resembled an autopsy."[6] Throughout the Constitutional Convention and the ratification debates, the framers refer to Roman and Greek corruption. The names Brutus, Cassius,

Cicero, and Tacitus were cited everywhere, barefaced nods to the great Roman orators.

Republic meant something very particular to the readers of Gibbon: a society dedicated to liberty in which people are not subjects, but rather participatory citizens infused with civic virtue. Eighteenth-century Americans were heavily influenced by republicanism, and understood their country to be living on the verge of either great flourishing, or a fatal sickness. Their bleak outlook, combined with the equally powerful optimism, proved fertile soil for extraordinary ambition. Corruption is inevitable, and corruption defeats liberty, but corruption's worst dangers may be overcome by structure and culture: versions of these three ideas showed up everywhere. Entrepreneurialism and pessimism were bound together. The Irish philosopher Edmund Burke thought this came from the deep infusion of law in the colonies. Men were "prompt in attack, ready in defence, full of resources." Americans were both more hopeful and risk-taking— therefore open to structural experiment, and more wary— therefore anxious to trust no individual with power. "Here," wrote Burke, "they anticipate the evil, and judge of the pressure of the grievance by the badness of the principle. They augur misgovernment at a distance; and snuff the approach of tyranny in every tainted breeze."[7]

Rome held such sway because it resembled Britain, which they knew well and perceived as a failed polity. Corruption in Britain was embodied by the king and his *placemen*, the term used to describe subservient political appointees. The king used wealth and patronage to gain influence over British parliamentarians, undermining constitutional government. This perception existed on both sides of the Atlantic. British reformers were quicker than the Americans to call Britain corrupt. When Benjamin Franklin arrived in Britain in the mid-eighteenth century, he found that many of its citizens believed England was "universally corrupt and rotten from head to foot."[8] Franklin himself found England less corrupt than he had been told but still worried that it might be a lost cause. Franklin later came to believe that America had sufficient elements—primarily of character—to protect itself against the rotting of civic virtue. His late-century transformation reflected a transformation in the country as a whole: in America in the years leading up to the war, references to Britain became increasingly accompanied by charges of corruption. At the same time, the corruption anxiety shifted focus: public writers in the American colonies in the early part of the eighteenth century were more likely to be concerned with private or religious corruption. But once the conflict with Britain began, American public intellectuals became more worried about *civic* corruption in their own country.

Britain was the best example of structured self-government that the framers could imagine; therefore it was a tragedy, wracked by a culture of pandering and angling. Even the most radical of American patriots, like Patrick Henry, held up Britain as a great aspiration gone awry, writing, "Look at Britain: see there the bolts and bars of power: see bribery and corruption defiling the fairest fabric that ever human nature reared!"[9] Britain provided both the model government and the harbinger of doom because of its current corrupt government. Small features of the British government were examined closely, to see if they held a fatal flaw. South Carolinian delegate to the Constitutional Convention Pierce Butler said:

We have no way of judging of mankind but by experience. Look at the history of the government of Great Britain, where there is a very flimsy exclusion—Does it not ruin their government? A man takes a seat in parliament to get an office for himself or friends, or both; and this is the great source from which flows its great venality and corruption.[10]

To compound their fear of impending corruption, charges of corruption at home bedeviled many states after the Revolution. Several of the states sent their delegates to the Constitutional Convention with statements of purpose: the Virginia Act appointing delegates to the Constitutional Convention explained that the states were "giving way to unManly Jealousies and Prejudices or to partial and transitory Interests."[11] "What led to the appointment of the convention?" John Francis Mercer, a Virginia delegate to the Constitutional Convention, later asked rhetorically. His answer was corruption, "the corruption and mutability of the Legislative Councils of the States."[12] To be sure, some of those charges simply represented upper-class distaste for democracy, but some involved real concerns that legislators were using power for plunder.

The founders were not worried that their government would become nonrepresentative in form (like contemporary France). However, they were worried that it would become nonrepresentative in fact (like contemporary Britain) because of structural dependencies that would transform self-government into oligarchic or despotic rule. In the 1960s, a group of historians—including Gordon Wood, Bernard Bailyn, and J. G. A. Pocock—began to painstakingly detail the ideology of the founding era.

They showed that the framers were "perpetually threatened by corruption."[13] Corruption fears—fears of a "conspiracy against liberty . . . nourished by corruption" "lay at the heart of Revolutionary movement."[14] The fear of corruption was "near unanimous" and there was a sense that corruption needed to be "avoided, that its presence in the political system produced a degenerative effect."[15] While liberty was not the opposite of corruption, corruption precluded liberty, and corruption encompassed not merely leaders but society as a whole. The Americans were anxious about the "torrent of corruption, which 'like a general flood, has deluged all.'"[16] As the Constitutional Convention got under way, George Mason, a strong Anti-Federalist from Virginia, said, "If we do not provide against corruption, our government will soon be at an end."[17]

By corruption, the early generations meant excessive private interests influencing the exercise of public power. An *act* was corrupt when private power was used to influence public power for private ends. A *system* was corrupt when the public power was excessively used to serve private ends instead of the public good. A *person* was corrupt when they use public power for private ends. There was no way for government to work without virtue, and "no substitute for good men in office."[18] A successful political society needs to create, in Jefferson's words, an "aristocracy of virtue and talent" instead of an aristocracy of power and wealth.[19] They saw their job as designing conduits for ambition and instilling dams to slow greed and limit abuse of power. "Controlling and channeling the overweening passions of these extraordinary men . . . seemed to many to be the central political problem of the age."[20] For John Adams, for example, patriotism and corruption were opposites; a patriot was one who puts the country's interest "in his care," whereas a corrupt courtier is one who puts his own interests in his care when in public service.[21] Adams had come to reject the king because he saw the role as leading to nothing but private interests and therefore not worthy of governing.[22]

Early American conceptions of what corruption meant flowed from two related but distinct sources. The first was Aristotelian and republican, embodied in the thinking of the French political philosopher Baron de Montesquieu; the second was Christian, puritanical, and intertwined with theories of natural law, embodied in the theories of the English philosopher John Locke. In both traditions, the core metaphor of corruption was organic and derived from disease and internal collapse. Corruption was a rotting of positive ideals of civic virtue and public integrity. It "most often brought to mind a fuller, more coherent, and more dreadful image of a spreading rot. A frequent metaphor compared corruption to organic cancer, eating at the vitals of the body politic and working a progressive dissolution."[23] In the republican tradition, corruption was the cancer of self-love at the expense of love of country. It existed at a personal and structural level. The individual was a metaphor for the state, and the state was the metaphor for the individual; both were complex psychological institutions that could fall prey to weaknesses that would corrode them from within. In the Christian tradition, corruption was the loss of personal virtue and expressed itself through hedonism, sloth, arrogance, and laziness at the expense of the love of God and the good. In both traditions, systemic corruption occurs in political/ethical structures that create temptations and encourage private-seeking behavior over public-seeking behavior. Republicans believed it was was society's job to channel those temptations.

Montesquieu

The framers were well-read and drew on many sources. However, as historian Bernard Bailyn persuasively argued, the "chief authority" for the Constitutional framers was the eighteenth-century French political philosopher Charles-Louis de Secondat, Baron de La Brède et de Montesquieu. *The Spirit of the Laws* was written just thirty years before the Constitutional Convention and was a foundational part of their political education. Montesqueiu's name "recurs far more often than that of any other authority in all of the vast literature on the Constitution. He was the fountainhead, the ultimate arbiter of belief; his ideas were the standard by which all others were set. The framers reverted to his authority at every turn."[24] Therefore, understanding the way that Montesquieu thought about human nature, government, and corruption enriches our own understanding of the meaning of corruption during the Constitutional era.

Montesquieu is most known for his support of different branches balancing powers against each other. But his advocacy for mixed government was a direct outgrowth of his beliefs about human nature. Montesquieu's approach was Aristotelian. Aristotle set out six ways a government can constitute itself: three kinds of governments, and three perversions. The rule of one is monarchy or tyranny; the rule of a few is either an aristocracy or an oligarchy; and the rule of the public is either a polity or mob rule. The fundamental difference between the good and perverted form of government, or good and corrupted state, is the psychological orientation of those that govern. The "deviation from monarchy is tyranny; for both are forms of one-man rule, but there is the greatest difference between them; the tyrant looks to his own advantage, the king to that of his subjects." A tyrant is a king who "pursues his own good"; an oligarchy is an aristocracy that pursues its own good; mob rule is a publicly governed polity whose constituent parts each pursue their own good.[25]

Following this view, Montesquieu wrote about the "calamities" that can befall "human nature" because he argued there are potential changes between one way of being (self-oriented) and another (public oriented). He believed that people *can* be self-interested but can also be public interested. Virtue, for the baron, was necessary for good government, and good structure was necessary for virtue. For Montesquieu, corruption and love of country were opposites. His methods were institutional: he supported a legislative, executive, and judicial branch with mixed government in the legislative branch as between the house representing people and the house representing the aristocracy. His final goal, however, was representative government, and for him representation depended in part on the civic attitudes of citizens.

His idea of civic virtue is not reductionist, but intimate. "Virtue," for Montesquieu, is "the love of the laws and of our country." The love is a "sensation, and not a consequence of acquired knowledge: a sensation that may be felt by the meanest as well as by the highest person in the state." His definition of the nature of this love is demanding:

Such love requires a constant preference of public to private interest, it is the source of all private virtues; for they
are nothing more than this very preference itself. This love
is peculiar to democracies. In these alone the government
is entrusted to private citizens. Now a government is like
everything else: to preserve it we must love it. Everything
therefore depends on establishing this love in a republic.[26]

Thomas Jefferson copied these passages into his common-
place book, where he recorded his literary interests. Jefferson,
like the other framers, believed that one cannot be dispassion-
ate without risking corruption; there is a necessarily intimate,
emotional role for the state in our hearts. The love must be greater
than a mere identification along the lines of nationalism. Instead, the nature of the love must extend to a love of the ideal
form of the country. "A love of the republic in a democracy is a
love of the democracy; as the latter is that of equality."[27] Montesquieu believed that love is more likely to spring from the "common people" and most likely to be eroded by elites. "It is very
rarely that corruption commences," he argued, with "the common
people," compared to "those whom we call gentlemen." The common people have a "stronger attachment to the established laws
and customs."[28]

Because Montesquieu returned again and again to the problem of public virtue, he was understandably equally focused on
its opposite, which he called corruption. Corruption for Montesquieu lay in the erosion of this love. Again, he described it in
emotional, romantic, and necessarily imprecise terms. For him,
corruption was the erosion of the love—passionate, sensible
love—for one's country and the rules of the country. The pas-

sionate, sensational love of the rule of law, and love of the spirit of law itself, is the basis on which a country can govern itself.

If Montesquieu established the thesis of government and citizenship for the framers, the English philosopher Thomas Hobbes represented the antithesis. Hobbes rejected the idea that people should or could be virtuous. He dismissed the "babbling philosophy of Aristotle" and argued that there is no difference between monarchy and tyranny, or between a corrupted democracy and an uncorrupted one. They are just the same things, he said, by different names: the word *monarchy* is used by those who like a particular leader, and *tyranny* by those who hate him. In the eighteenth century, Montesquieu picked a fight with Hobbes. Hobbes saw entirely self-interested citizens as inevitable human nature, whereas Montesquieu saw them as the greatest threat to political society. Montesquieu set out to wrest realism from Hobbes: in his view, not only was Hobbes's psychological portrait inaccurate, but his political science would lead to more unstable governments. He directly attacked what he saw as Hobbes's falsely dark, and possibly naive, description of human nature. Simone Goyard-Fabre calls him the "anti-Hobbes."[29]

Hobbes—like some modern justices—believed that people are fundamentally egoist. Corruption was an incoherent idea for Hobbes—a view we find dormant for hundreds of years, but then recurrent in late-twentieth-century Supreme Court doctrine. The founders read Hobbes, but most of them also rejected him and his view of human nature. Adams thought he treated men "like cattle" and misunderstood the role of context, reason, and law.[30] Jefferson "lamented" that a contemporary was going to adopt Hobbes's view of human nature. Hobbes saw no justice or injustice, but "only convention."[31] Jefferson believed that systems supported or undermined justice. The only significant contributor to the Constitution who was deeply influenced by Hobbes was Alexander Hamilton, and even Hamilton rejected the amoralism of Hobbes. And at the Constitutional Convention, his monarchist plans for the country largely failed.

John Locke and similar influential writers who were more focused on property rights and individual freedom brought a non-Hobbesian theory of corruption as well.[32] A Unitarian and moralist, Locke was deeply concerned with virtue and the "moral implications of political action."[33] Corruption and virtue were also part of Locke's grammar. For Locke, corruption was often more associated with a loss of innocence and a fall from a natural state of virtue. One can be corrupted by "education," or "custom" or "fashion," or "common opinion."[34] There was a sense of individual corruption that is unconnected with the state. But he also had a very traditional public sense of corruption. In his discussion in *Of the Dissolution of Government*, he argues that it is a violation of trust to use

> the force, treasure, and offices of the society to corrupt the representatives and gain them to his purposes, when he openly pre-engages the electors, and prescribes, to their choice, such whom he has, by solicitation, threats, promises, or otherwise, won to his designs, and employs them to bring in such who have promised beforehand what to vote and what to enact.

This kind of corruption "cut[s] up the government by the roots, and poison[s] the very fountain of public security."[35] Another influential scholar associated with the liberty school, German jurist Samuel Pufendorf, also used corruption as a central concept. Historian Barry Alan Shain cites a widely read publicist of the time, explaining that common good was the proper goal of government: "If the authority of Locke, Montesquieu and natural reason are not sufficient to prove this position, and if anyone desires further satisfaction . . . we would refer them to Pufendorf."[36] He argues that citizens have duties to the state that depend upon their position, and that failure to perform those duties is, within his structure, corruption. Individuals, to be virtuous, must attempt to put the state's interest first; to remain free of corruption they must guard against efforts to influence them.[37] He was particularly concerned with those tempted by foreign interests: "Those whose services the state employs in foreign countries, should be careful and circumspect, skilled in distinguishing the unreal from the real, the true from the fictitious, very tenacious of secrets, persistent in the interest of their state as against corruption in any form."[38] Pufendorf also argued that the corruption of states can be located either in individuals or in the systems themselves.

Inasmuch as Locke and Pufendorf were drawing from Christian tradition, they drew on Christian notions of sin and corruption. Public corruption is not the sine qua non of corruption, but a variation of the epicenter of corruption: moral corruption. The Christian understanding carried with it a more clearly dichotomous understanding—the corrupt is opposite to the noncorrupt, and corruption is personal. The Christian vision of corruption, like the secular vision of corruption, is psychological and moral, not transactional. However, when in the public realm, the Christian notion took on republican overtones. In Noah Webster's 1832 *History of the United States,* he argued that the Christian tradition was fundamentally entangled with republican theory. Citizens have a duty to elect "principled men" or "the government will soon be corrupted; laws will be made not for the public good so much as for the selfish or local purposes," which will lead to the "rights of the citizens" being "violated or disregarded."[39]

Corruption and Self-Interest

One of the most famous passages of the *Federalist Papers*, the widely circulated essays written in favor of state ratification of the Constitution, can be found in Federalist No. 51: "If men were angels, no government would be necessary. If angels were to govern men, neither external nor internal controls on government would be necessary." This passage is sometimes referred to as support for the argument that James Madison believed that human beings are fundamentally selfish.

This might seem to create a contradiction. An essential self-interest thesis is, on its face, incompatible with the founding-era grammar of virtue and corruption. Madison clearly believed in virtue, and in other speeches he appeared to put his *entire* faith in the virtue of the people; "no theoretical checks," he said, "can render us secure" if the people are without virtue. This is the "spring" of "virtue" that Baron de Montesquieu described as necessary for a popular state in his *Spirit of Laws*: "It is the spring that moves republican government, just as honor is the spring that moves monarchy."

In short, we have two thoughts: (1) men are not always angels, and therefore structures must help us; and (2) virtue is necessary, and structures alone cannot help us. The reconciliation between these two Madisonian beliefs holds the key to understanding the moral psychology of most of the framers. These can both be true if one perceives a dynamic relationship between constitutional structure and political morality. Because men are not always virtuous, structures must be enacted in order to discourage self-serving behavior in public life. The public orientation that flourishes in these structures in turn helps maintain the structures, which in turn helps maintain the virtue.

The task of structuring political society is to align self-interest with the public interest, not because people will *only* be self-interested, but because people will *often* be self-interested, and incentives can reduce both the damage of the first and the likelihood of the second. Corruption cannot be made to vanish, but its power can be subdued with the right combination of culture and political rules.

Moreover, as Montesquieu was translated into the Constitutional framing discussions, his highly demanding vision of citizenship and public office was somewhat tempered. Whereas the most extreme civic humanists believed that one should submerge oneself in the public good, the Madisonian modification was that one should not *suppress* or *override* private interests, but rather pursue them in congruence with the public good. The virtuous citizen will not see the two interests in conflict, whereas the corrupt citizen will both perceive and act on the conflict. There is a space for a private realm, but in the execution of public duties, the public good ought to be sought first. The citizen should and *can* be both self-regarding and other regarding. Historian Lance Banning synthesizes it this way:

> [The citizen] was expected to contribute to political decisions precisely on the basis of his independent understanding

of his needs, choosing what was good for him as well as for the whole. He was not expected to surrender his particular self-interest. Instead, he was thought of as pursuing his particular desires while still remaining conscious of the interests of his peers and participating in a collectivity of equals.[40]

This belief in flexibility—that man can be either good or bad, but incentive structures will have an impact—is a profoundly American belief and part of our national ideology. The nature of a person is not fixed. This belief has also led to the American devotion to education, and to our collective belief that a person can rise from rags to riches and transcend inherited circumstances.

The framers' virtue focus creates another question: Doesn't that mean that people are corrupt most of the time, because we normally care about ourselves, and only rarely devote ourselves to the public? No. Even the most expansive concept of civic corruption did not include everything that was not public and virtuous. Instead, corruption was invoked only in the worst instances of private interests trampling on public ones. Corruption was invoked in a variety of ways, but with a limited range—it tended to refer to situations in which a public officer or set of public officers were systematically using public resources for their own enrichment or advancement. Corruption was not, as Justice Scalia would later claim, an unbounded word describing every kind of "moral decay." A corrupt political actor would either purposely ignore or forget the public good as he used the reins of power.

The relationship between corrupt acts and corrupt thoughts— between faith and works, to crib from Christian doctrine—was not always clear. There are no debates about whether a *good* outcome derived from a corrupt mental state would be classified as a corrupt "act" or merely a corrupt actor. It was, however, clear that the framers believed that corrupt mental states tended to lead to corrupt actions, and therefore fixing structures to encourage certain sympathies was a primary job of Constitutional design. Again, they perceived a dynamic relationship between acts and thoughts.

In Federalist No. 55 Madison wrote about how corruption might "subdu[e] the virtue" of senators.[41] Pennsylvania delegate Gouverneur Morris spoke about how "wealth tends to corrupt the mind & to nourish its love of power, and to stimulate it to oppression."[42] Morris was clearly talking about a transformation in "the mind," a fundamental corrosion of the interior life that would then lead to a corrosion of practices (stimulating it to oppression). When Madison, in Federalist No. 10, puzzles on the problem of bias in self-government and notes by analogy that "no man is allowed to be a judge in his own cause, because his interest would certainly bias his judgment, and not improbably corrupt his integrity,"[43] he is making a claim about the interior life of the mind—the moral attitude taken by an individual. He is claiming that exterior forces have the power to shape the moral orientation of a person, just as a powerful flow of water might shape the soil around it. Money has an alchemical effect—not just leveraging action, but in so doing, changing the nature of the agent that it works upon. The language is both technical and moral.

A set of actions were treated as archetypal corruption, regardless of the mental state. The king's use of his power to bestow offices to create allegiances among parliamentarians was corrupt.

(On this, the outlier was Alexander Hamilton, who argued that the king's using offices to create "attachments" was not corrupt, but merely influence. His belief in the legitimacy of such influence was entangled in his monarchism. For the rest, the king's use of power was treated as implicitly corrupting, whether or not the parliamentarians would have supported the king without the promised offices.) Bribery and extortion were likewise considered per se corrupt, but such crimes were rarely punished criminally, so invocations of bribery were rarely in reference to criminal law standards and were more often in reference to the use of a gift, political office, or flattery to persuade someone to change a course of action.

One thing shines through all the usages: the way corruption was referred to at the time was rarely in conjunction with violations of criminal law. There were relatively few criminal laws of corruption at the time, as I'll show. Gouverneur Morris explicitly said that the corruption concern encompassed lawful abuses of power, not merely unlawful abuses or usurpations.[44] Morris argued, as an example of predictable legal corruption, that legislatures might want to print money in ways that enriched them personally, using legitimately granted public power for private gain. Though the word *corruption* was used hundreds of times in the convention and the ratification debates, only a handful of uses referred to what we might now think of as quid pro quo bribes.[45] That constituted less than one-half of 1 percent of the times corruption was raised. In direct contradiction to the interpretation of corruption in *Citizens United*, the concept of corruption encompassed, but was not equated with, explicit exchange or explicit embezzlement.[46]

Citizens and Institutions

The framers rarely attached corruption to individuals separate from their institutions: parliament could be corrupt, or boroughs could be corrupted. The collective, and the institution itself, could become a servant of private, instead of public, ends. But corruption was not limited to officials. The framers believed that a citizen could be corrupt: he could use his public roles for private gain instead of public good, he could be extractive instead of supportive of the polity. A citizen has several public functions: the vote, the jury, and public speaking about matters of public importance. When a citizen is petitioning the government, he is acting in his public role. Citizens are the foundation and fabric of the country and are fundamentally responsible for the integrity of their government. All citizens—especially powerful citizens—are responsible for ensuring that public resources generally serve public ends. Historian Bernard Bailyn writes that the framers "never abandoned the belief that only an informed, alert, intelligent, and uncorrupted electorate would preserve the freedoms of a republican state."[47] The electorate—not just the elected—must be dissuaded from corruption. Because the new government was founded on the authority of the people, the people themselves must have integrity and be publicly minded in order for the nation to thrive.

But, as with the institution of parliament, citizen corruption was often seen collectively. Montesquieu put citizens at the center of the thriving republic. For him, the true danger in a republic is mass disaffection with public life, when society turns away from trying to influence government and citizens instead turn toward their own preoccupations and examining how they can personally benefit from particular laws. Montesquieu argued that government breaks down when citizens do not care about it: "The misfortune of a republic is when intrigues are at an end; which happens when the people are gained by bribery and corruption: in this case they grow indifferent to public affairs, and avarice becomes their predominant passion. Unconcerned about the government and everything belonging to it, they quietly wait for their hire."[48]

Citizens are collectively virtuous inasmuch as they have the kind of attention to a love of country and the public good, and corrupt inasmuch as they use their public role for private ends. A virtuous citizenry will put private goods ahead of other, public concerns, and will not primarily perceive government as a potential source of personal gain but as a source of collective gain. Good citizens may be self-seeking in other areas, but in their public functions they will eschew the pursuit of wealth for the pursuit of liberty—a public, political liberty, a statewide freedom from oppression. Citizens as governors are not consumers but holders of a public trust. George Washington wrote to the Marquis de Lafayette about the threat of "corruption of morals, profligacy of manners, and listlessness for the preservation of the natural and unalienable rights." "So long as there shall remain any virtue in the body of the people,"[49] he wrote, the country might not decline into an oppressive regime. Without the virtue of the people, Madison argued, "no theoretical checks, no form of government, can render us secure. To suppose that any form of government will secure liberty or happiness without any virtue in the people is a chimerical idea."[50] Wilson reinforced this idea in his claim that the opposition to Britain was not against the king but against "a corrupt multitude."[51]

Dependency

One of the most dangerous structures, one that was likely to lead to corruption, was the dependent one. The language of dependence and corruption was so intertwined at the founding that in some cases, corruption and independence could sound like opposites. Contemporary theorists sometimes used "corruption" and "dependence" together, indicating that they saw corruption as the natural result of dependence. Scottish philosopher David Hume, for example, in discussing the relationship of the Crown to the kind of public offices that were frequently given out as rewards for loyalty, wrote that "we may give to this influence what name we please ... we may call it by the invidious appellations of corruption and dependence."[52]

The Declaration of Independence was in part a declaration of freedom from corruption. While modern rhetoric often treats *independence* and *liberty* or *freedom* as interchangeable, *liberty* referred to either a Christian conception of rationally limited human action or a set of substantive privileges and immunities, or freedom from enslavement.[53] *Independence*, on the other hand, was not invoked in the discussions of liberty and was more related to the rhetoric of corruption. Independence is the absence of (*in*) a power relationship (*of the pendant*). *Independence* was at its core a relational word, which symbolized the rejection of a kind of relationship. Dependence could refer to a kind of structural dependence (where a person is actually dependent upon others financially and therefore must do their bidding) or a psychological dependence (where a person's character is corrupted by another's influences to think and act differently), but most often it referred to the situation where financial dependence led to psychological dependence. It could be a direct kind of dependency, where a representative's well-being and financial income depended upon a salary paid by the king, or a subtler kind of dependency, where people's mental independence could become soft—corrupted—because they rather liked the gifts bestowed on them, the flattery given them, or other trinkets and phrases that obscured their independent judgment and capacity to think and decide as truly free men. In each instance, though to varying degrees, the dependent figure would shift his actions to align himself with the desires of the person who had power over him. A contemporary commentator claimed that Virginia's executive had "not a single feature of Independence" because the executive was "paid, directed, and removed by the Legislature."[54] A man might become dependent upon another because the other had provided him a job, so he could not live—or live as well—without the other's favors. Lawrence Lessig argues that an essential form of corruption for the framers was "dependence corruption."[55]

Dependence did not define corruption, but it was a part of the cluster of structural relationships that led to corruption. One of the clear goals of the Constitutional Convention was freedom from a political culture where dependence was the primary mode of advancement. The job of political architecture was to discourage dependencies and temptations that might lead to corruption. The most rigid view held that the citizen should be "free from dependence and from the interests of the marketplace. Any loss of independence and virtue was corruption."[56] A dependent relationship with the king, or with a wealthy foreign sponsor, could lead citizens or representatives to misunderstand themselves and believe, falsely, that their own ends were more valuable than the public ends. But other reasons—narcissism, ambition, or luxury—could lead people to place private gain before public good in their public actions.

All the writers of the era also believed that luxury tended to move people away from the love of democracy.[57] As Gouverneur Morris stated, "wealth tends to corrupt the mind & to nourish its love of power, and to stimulate it to oppression. History proves this to be the spirit of the opulent."[58] In Morris's view, the fact of wealth causes internal distortion, and the "spirit" of wealth becomes antagonistic to the spirit of republicanism. Luxury seeking perverts a culture of civic virtue. "An avaricious man might be tempted to betray the interests of the state to the acquisition of wealth," wrote Hamilton in Federalist No. 75.[59] Perhaps because he understood the appeal of luxury, the "most corrupt of all corrupt" old men—Benjamin Franklin—was well placed to insist on a radical vision into the Constitutional Convention, floating on a sedan chair, carrying a prepared speech.

CHAPTER THREE

Removing Temptations

IN THE EARLY SPRING OF 1787, Benjamin Franklin, eighty-one years old, wrote an old friend from France about pigeons, lightning, mutual friends, and the "art of ballooning." Showing off both his enthusiasm and his sense of a declining body, he wrote about his dream of having a French balloon that was large enough to lift him, "being led by a string held by a man walking on the ground."[1] Franklin, as ever, believed in the possibilities of progress but wanted to be sure that his flights—into electricity, politics, and air travel—were grounded. A little more than six weeks after writing his letter, Franklin attended the opening of the American Constitutional Convention, not lifted by a hot air balloon but carried on a sedan chair. He was too weak to walk. But he was not only aware of his own body's degeneration. Rather, he saw how the body politic could degenerate if given a chance.

Franklin's first speech—his major contribution to the convention—was about money, power, and the inconsistencies of the ambitious human heart. At stake was short-term stability, but also the nature of the new country. Would it be able to justify its violent separation from England, or would it become another corrupt failure?

The convention had begun a week earlier, on May 29, 1787, with delegates from seven states (New Hampshire arrived later) dedicated to reconstituting the political society and power relations among the newly independent colonies. It was meant to enable a major revision to the Articles of Confederation, which had been adopted in 1781 as a collective coordination security pact. The thirteen states had agreed to provide for shared defense in case of attack, to maintain basic sovereignty in other matters, and to allow for freedom of movement between the states. The Articles were passed "for their common defense, the security of their liberties, and their mutual and general welfare, binding themselves to assist each other, against all force offered to, or attacks made upon them."

Chaos and domination, outside power and internal insurrection: this was the context of the event. The fifty-five delegates were worried about the disagreements between the states, the threat of foreign powers that might use military force to overrun the country, and growing friction between creditors and debtors. But the big fear underlying all the small fears was whether they'd be able to control corruption as England and France had not. Alexander Hamilton eventually described the Constitutional Convention this way: "Nothing was more to be desired than that every practicable obstacle should be opposed to cabal, intrigue, and corruption."[2] In Madison's notebook from the summer of 1787, the word *corruption* is scrawled in longhand fifty-four times. Corruption, influence, and bribery were discussed more often in the convention than factions, violence, or instability.[3]

Many of the delegates had "Shays' Rebellion" in the backs of their minds. In 1786, Daniel Shays, a former officer of the Continental army, led a violent protest of farmers in response to growing foreclosures, high taxes, and deflation that had enriched elite bondholders at the expense of farmers. Shays was able to assert control of part of western Massachusetts for almost half a year, terrifying politicians and elites elsewhere in the country. The revolt was particularly jarring because Massachusetts had been viewed as a relatively stable political community. And its policy predicament was not unusual: the early years of the confederation had been extremely trying, and many states were burdened with debt and wracked with economic insecurity. States owed bondholders money from the war. They tried different tactics to relieve the debt, including printing more money and raising taxes. Real income shrank, and many people called for nonpayment of bonds to the wealthiest Americans. The national government had financial trouble of its own, due to the unanimity requirement for raising funds in the Articles of Confederation. The parchment power to raise a navy and to defend against these incursions seemed meaningless without the practical ability to raise the money and resources needed to do so. At the same time, European powers occupied parts of the continent that infringed on the confederation—Spain in the south and Britain in the northwest. Early negotiations with foreign states led negotiators to feel weak.

In the first few days of the Constitutional Convention, the conversation was framed around these sets of threats: what could foreigners and farmers do to us? But it shifted during the convention to a more introspective question: what could we do to ourselves? During the long, notoriously hot summer of 1787, the framers of the Constitution began building more of a psychological document: their radicalism lay in their belief that passions, like water, could be redirected, not merely contained.

The "unique and universal crisis" of corruption as experienced by the framers drove their thinking during the convention.[4] Unlike Hobbes, they did not see human nature as uncontrollable, or self-interested behavior as irreducible. But they did see a polity destroyed by corruption as the most likely outcome. The question that haunted the convention was this: would these men manage to wrangle the worst impulses of rulers and ruled and transform them into representatives and citizens? If so, for how long?

The Problem of Placemen

On May 29, 1787, Edmund Randolph, a well-to-do lawyer and governor of Virginia, opened the convention with a prepared speech. Randolph described the reason for the convention in terms of the external and internal threats of violence facing the confederacy. He argued that there was no security against foreign invasion, because Congress had no power to punish treaty infractions and because states might, on their own, cause foreign conflict. In the case of a full-scale war, neither a draft nor militia would be successful; the country would need to enlist soldiers, and such enlistment would be very costly and beyond the financial capacity of the Continental Congress. Moreover, there were potentially great commercial advantages to joining: states could collectively bargain better with other nations. For the next few days, the discussion generally followed Randolph's framing. The delegates debated whether or not the states should join into a federal government and submit to a supreme government at all.

But a few days later, Franklin intervened with his own prepared speech, which was read out loud for him.[5] Franklin's biggest concern was a version of the modern revolving door between Congress and well-paying lobbying jobs: the problem of people going into office not to represent the public but in order to get a well-paid job. They called this the problem of "placemen." Randolph had proposed to pay salaries to members of the executive branch. Franklin disagreed: he thought officials should work for free and the expenses be merely defrayed. His speech expressed a peculiar—and rather wonderfully radical—American contribution to thinking about government and corruption. Just as the Articles of Confederation had taken "gifts" from the category of diplomacy and put them in the category of corruption, Franklin was trying to take "payment for offices" out of the category of "practices of governing" and put it in the category of "corruption."

Franklin presented a model of human behavior in which men are flexible and can be "good" and virtuous in one setting, yet destructive and corrupt in another. Franklin's speech was full of broad claims about human nature and its relationship to power: delegates ought to watch carefully the powerful influences of ambition and greed, or what he called "the love of power, and the love of money." Power and money can spur action, "but when united in view of the same object, they have in many minds the most violent effects." One cannot "place before the eyes of such men" jobs that have both honor and money in them. If a "post of honor" is "at the same time a place of profit," then men "will move heaven and earth to obtain it." He wrote that the disorder and troubles in Britain had come from the existence of lucrative executive posts. These could lead to factions that then divide the nation, distract the government, and encourage "fruitless and mischievous wars" and some dishonorable terms of peace. When the twin temptations are joined, moderates will not seek office. The temptations will create so much heat and contention that "men of strong passions and indefatigable activity in their selfish pursuits" will become "your Government and be your rulers." Even these bold, violent men will be disappointed, he promised, because the system will perpetually be creating an engine for more faction, dissension, and tearing down, and be motivated to "distress their administration, thwart their measures, and render them odious to the people."

He imagined ever-growing salaries, because there would always be some reason proclaimed and groups who would speak in favor of increasing salaries. For him the question of the scope of payment represented a fundamental struggle that appeared between rulers and ruled, which could lead to "great convulsions, actual civil wars, ending either in dethroning of the Princes, or enslaving of the people." In these struggles, the "ruling power" generally wins, and the "revenues of princes" just continues to increase. The greater increase in the power of princes leads to greater dissatisfaction, which in turn leads to a greater need for a well-funded police force. His particular fear was the tendency of governments to become monarchic. Without serious intervention, those in power could control elected representatives in a way that would lead them away from public service. He claimed he saw the seeds of the monarchy in the mere existence of any government. His goal was to delay the onset by making sure that "posts of honor" are not "places of profit."

Government inclines toward centralized executive power, he argued, and that tendency is exaggerated when people who would be servants of the state get paid well to do so, because they then become dependent upon the centralized power that pays them. As James Madison noted, the proposal was not taken seriously. But it may have shifted the terms of debate.

In these two prepared speeches—Randolph's and Franklin's—there is a difference in the framing of the problems leading to the convention and the framing of the solutions coming out of the convention. For Randolph, the concerns were specific to that point in history and a response to short-term difficulties. For Franklin, the concerns were universal and related to human nature and power. For Randolph, the natural starting place was the states as actors; for Franklin, the natural starting place was the individual and his passions and motivations. The baseline of the discussion was money, power, politics, personal corruption, and human nature. By mid-June, they no longer spoke of niggling, particular problems, but rather of the universal dilemma of people's relationship to power. Debaters defended their positions by using corruption as a villain; and during ratification debates, Madison and Hamilton, who started from different ideological premises, used corruption to explain their final proposed solutions to the public. They saw their task this way: how could they create a system that would be most likely to be filled with men of civic virtue but avoid creating temptations that might corrode that virtue?

James Madison—diminutive and weak, having all the presence of "half a bar of soap" according to some accounts—was the greatest intellectual force behind the Constitution. Though he may have dismissed Franklin's proposal for free executive branch labor, he was deeply concerned about the powers of appointment and the creation of posts, places, and perks. The problem of offices—and who should appoint them—led to some of the most passionate discussions at the convention. Madison's theory of government derived from Montesquieu's: "If there is a principle in our Constitution, indeed in any free Constitution more sacred than another, it is that which separates the legislative, executive and judicial powers." That principle had its most difficult application in deciding who had the power to appoint officers to governmental positions.[6]

Government depended on officers appointed to carry things out. In Britain, these offices had become the great prize that others sought after, and legislators and the king had used the power of appointments to enrich themselves and their friends. There seemed no way to avoid the problem of placemen. If Congress was given the power to give offices, the framers worried that members of Congress would use their position to enrich themselves and their friends and would see public office as a place for gaining civil posts and preferences instead of as a public duty.[7] George Mason worried that if legislators were allowed, they would "make or multiply offices, in order to fill them."[8] Elbridge Gerry argued that if the Senate had the power to appoint ambassadors, they would "multiply embassies for their own sakes," akin to "nurseries" where infant ambassadors could be coddled.[9]

The other option was equally dangerous. If the executive had the power to appoint, it would aggrandize his power and lead to a return to British corruption. Franklin had argued that if all profitable offices are given to the executive, "The first man put at the helm will be a good one. No body knows what sort may come afterward. The Executive will be always increasing here, as elsewhere, till it ends in a Monarchy." Thomas Paine's *Common Sense* put it this way: "That the crown is this overbearing part in the English constitution needs not be mentioned, and that it derives its whole consequence merely from being the giver of places and pensions is self-evident."[10] Even Hamilton, the strong advocate for vesting appointment power in the executive, was concerned that the power of appointments might corrupt both the Congress and the president. He disliked a model that would have given the Senate a role in selecting the presidency because it would lead to the president using his power of appointments to curry favor with Senators.[11] In other words, a would-be president would promise senators appointments in exchange for their support of his candidacy.

The main proposal was that representatives should be banned from holding elected and appointed office simultaneously. But some objected that the prohibition would lead to the best people refusing the job. Mason replied: "Are gentlemen in earnest? Are we not struck at seeing the luxury and venality which has already crept in among us?" The structural task of the present, he said, was to

> remove the temptation. I admire many parts of the British constitution and government, but I detest their corruption. Why has the power of the crown so remarkably increased the last century? A stranger, by reading their laws, would suppose it considerably diminished; and yet, by the sole power of appointing the increased officers of government, corruption pervades every town and village in the kingdom. If such a restriction should abridge the right of election, it is still necessary, as it will prevent the people from ruining themselves; and will not the same causes here produce the same effects?[12]

Representatives, it was feared, would be seduced to ignore their duties by the promises of future offices. "A man takes a seat in parliament to get an office for himself or friends, or both; and this is the great source from which flows its great venality and corruption," Butler said.[13] Some proposed a one-year revolving door, or an absolute ban on office holding for all senators and members of Congress.

The appointments power "was thrown into different shapes"[14] before it was adopted as it is in the Constitution, giving the president the power to appoint, with the advice and consent of the Senate, the "Ambassadors, other public Ministers and Consuls . . . and all other Officers of the United States, whose Appointments are not herein otherwise provided for." At the same time, "Congress may by Law vest the Appointment of such inferior Officers, as they think proper, in the President alone, in the Courts of Law, or in the Heads of Departments." The founders hoped they blocked "the avenues by which corruption was most likely to enter"[15] by parceling power between the president and the legislature. Part of the appointments were given to the legislature to keep the executive from developing dependent placement. An accompanying clause prevents elected officials from simultaneous appointment as civil officers. It also prevents legislators from taking jobs when they are out of office that they created while in office, or for which they increased the salary while in office.

It was not universally loved. Charles Pinckney sought to strike the proposal and Mason satirized him. As Madison's notes reflect:

Col. MASON ironically proposed to strike out the whole section, as a more effectual expedient for encouraging that exotic corruption which might not otherwise thrive so well in the American Soil—for compleating that Aristocracy which was probably in the contemplation of some among us, and for inviting into the Legislative Service, those generous & benevolent characters who will do justice to each other's merit, by carving out offices & rewards for it. In the present state of American morals & manners, few friends it may be thought will be lost to the plan, by the opportunity of giving premiums to a mercenary & depraved ambition.[16]

Maryland delegate James McHenry summarized the debate as one of "division in sentiment" but finding compromise around the principle "to avoid as much as possible every motive for corruption."[17] Later, Mason described these clauses as the "cornerstone" of the new republic.[18]

Some of this discussion, and Madison's later reflection on it, demonstrates that much of what we think of as "separation of powers"—applied to the revolutionary context—can be understood as a set of concerns about dependency and corruption flowing from the problems of who should be able to appoint officials:

The Executive could not be independent of the Legislure [sic], if dependent on the pleasure of that branch for a reappointment. Why was it determined that the Judges should not hold their places by such a tenure? Because they might be tempted to cultivate the Legislature, by an undue complaisance, and thus render the Legislature the virtual expositor, as well the maker of the laws. In like manner a dependence of the Executive on the Legislature, would render it the Executor as well as the maker of laws; & then according to the observation of Montesquieu, tyrannical laws may be made that they may be executed in a tyrannical manner.

Separate branches without independent capacity to fund are not truly separate, as Madison argues. In his mind, separation of power is the key, not separation of function—and the key power that needed to be separated was the power of appointment, to prevent corrupt officers and the corruption that attends civil offices as institutions.

Two hundred years later, a different problem of placemen arose, as I explore later. The founders' fears that legislators would go into public office in order to get a job became realized when lobbyists starting hiring over half the members of Congress and many of their staffers after they left office.

Elections

Madison described the essence of good government this way:

> It is essential to such a government that it be derived from the great body of the society, not from an inconsiderable proportion, or a favored class of it; otherwise a handful of tyrannical nobles, exercising their oppressions by a delegation of their powers, might aspire to the rank of republicans, and claim for their government the honorable title of republic.[19]

Elections are necessary to create this relationship. Without elections, nobles can be tyrannical at whim. But elections are not sufficient in themselves; an elected body could become its own cabal and plunder the resources of the country. Virtue, James Wilson argued, is an inadequate protection for the legislature if all the legislative authority resided in one place.[20] Therefore, the framers split power between two different legislative bodies.

The framers brought a range of views about whether the Senate or House would be more corrupt: some, like Mercer, worried about excesses of democracy; others worried about aristocracy. The majority view was that the Senate was more inclined to corruption—Randolph argued that "the Senate will be more likely to be corrupt than the H. of Reps."—and the House to irrationality or supporting projects of the lower classes that hurt elite interests. While Morris, among others, expressed a fear that senators had shared interests that were not the interests of the people, he hoped the Senate might be resistant to corruption because the elites have some dignity. The House of Representatives' resistance would derive from its size: the supposition was that it would be impossible for various representatives to all have similar interests that could be similarly exploited.[21]

Both, according to Madison, were likely to engage in "schemes of usurpation or perfidy"—without a check, each on the other, a single body could come under the sway of "ambition or corruption" and government would betray the people. The difference between the two bodies would make corruption across both highly difficult. "The improbability of sinister combinations will be in proportion to the dissimilarity in the genius of the two bodies."[22] In order to protect the legislature from self-corruption it had to be divided.

What about size? The argument for a large House of Representatives and the argument for a small House of Representatives were both based on the same foundational principle: each,
it was claimed, would lead to less corruption. The argument for
a large body was that it would make it harder for representatives
to coordinate and intrigue for their own gains. Massachusetts
delegate Elbridge Gerry (best remembered for his association
with the "gerrymander") argued that small groups of people who
came together would shift their alignment from those they represented to the new small group, finding similar personal interests
within the small group that would override their other obligations. "The larger the number, the less the danger of their being
corrupted," Gerry argued. "It is a lesson we ought not to disregard, that the smallest bodies in G. B. are notoriously the most
corrupt."[23] If this is the starting point, one would want to give
the smaller legislative body less power, because of the many opportunities for intrigue, thus the Senate was more prone to corruption because of its size. "The Senate are more liable to be
corrupted by an Enemy than the whole Legislature,"[24] and "The
Senate will be more likely to be corrupt than the H. of Reps.
and should therefore have less to do with money matters."[25]
Magistrates, small senates, and small assemblies were easier to
buy off, and it was easier for small groups to find similar motives and band together to empower themselves at the expense
of the citizenry. Larger groups, it was argued, simply could not
coordinate well enough to effectively corrupt themselves. "Be-
sides the restraint of integrity and honor, the difficulty of acting
in concert for purposes of corruption was a security to the public. And if one or a few members only should be seduced, the

soundness of the remaining members would maintain the integrity and fidelity of the body," Madison said.[26]

George Washington's only contribution to the Constitutional Convention arose in the context of a debate about the size of the House of Representatives. He argued that it should be larger, so as to ensure accountability to the people.[27] With a large body, differences between legislators would lead to factional jealousies and personality conflicts if the same corrupting official tried to buy, or create dependency across, a large body: the sheer size and diversity of the House would present a formidable obstacle to someone attempting to buy its members. Madison explained that the framers had designed the Constitution believing that "the House would present greater obstacles to corruption than the Senate with its paucity of members."[28] Several delegates noted that Holland was a small state, and its smallness was one of the reasons it was easily corrupted by French influence.

Related to size was the vast geography of the country. Distance and inconvenience were seen as good defenses to corruption. Hamilton argued in Federalist No. 68:

> The business of corruption, when it is to embrace so considerable a number of men, requires time as well as means. Nor would it be found easy suddenly to embark them, dispersed as they would be over thirteen States, in any combinations founded upon motives, which though they could not properly be denominated corrupt, might yet be of a nature to mislead them from their duty.

But the roads were too bad, the distances too great, and the numbers too formidable to allow for the concerted redirection of the minds of men to private gain and the interests of the state to private or foreign interests. While traditional republican theorists had always argued that only small countries could be republics, Madison and the founders argued that larger countries, among other attractions, provided better protections against corruption.

The frequency of elections was also tied up in corruption. How to use elections to make each branch dependent on the people instead of on a different branch? The problem, as later explained by Madison, was that in Britain, members of the House of Commons were elected for seven years, and only a small number of people participated in the election.[29] The longer terms strengthened the legislators' bonds with the executive and weakened them with the people. Two-year periods would not lead to the same kind of corruption. But if the political terms were too short, the legislature might be too erratic, as the body itself would constantly change. If terms were too long, however, legislators would come to entrench themselves and use their offices for their own advantage. Madison argued that election enabled "an immediate dependence" and "intimate sympathy" with the people. Frequent elections were "the only policy" that secured this kind of psychological tie to the public. A short term would ensure accountability and make it difficult to run too far on the public purse. But a long term, Williamson argued, would make it more likely that men of good character would undertake the commitment to service—that is, a short term would attract only weaker men, whose characters were capable of corruption.[30]

The framers were also vexed about the Senate selection process. Pinckney wanted to replace the method of selecting the Congress, switching its selection from "by the people" to "by the legislature." Gerry objected because he thought it would lead to dependency flowing both ways, between state and national legislatures, instead of to the people. He had a pessimistic view of the capacity of state legislatures: "If the national legislature are appointed by the state legislatures, demagogues and corrupt members will creep in."[31] But these arguments failed, at least for the next hundred years. Over a century later, the Seventeenth Amendment allowed for direct election of senators, motivated because the people thought the process corrupt. Hamilton explained the final compromise between direct elections and state legislative elections: senators would bring with them a virtuous attitude toward government, something deemed less likely in the democratic rabble. But inasmuch as power and wealth could corrupt them, too, the elections would ensure that those corrupted would not be reelected.[32] Of course, Hamilton believed that corruption would still follow—leading members would become corrupt and then in turn, through "arts and influence," convince the majority to follow them in policies that are "odious to the community." However, "if the proofs of that corruption should be satisfactory," the public resentment would show itself and the leading members would be sacrificed at the next election.

Rotten Boroughs

Above all, the framers didn't want representatives who did not work for the public but rather worked for themselves or for a powerful patron. They saw how rotten boroughs had enabled that in England. In the New York state convention, Alexander Hamilton explained that "the true source of the corruption which has so long excited the severe animadversion of zealous politicians and patriots" was the way in which these boroughs were "in the possession and gift of the king."[33] The term *borough* referred to a municipal region with a right to have representation in the British House of Commons. A rotten borough existed in England when a disproportionately small number of voters had outsized political power, which they often sold. The elected representative of the borough would then be directed by a wealthy member of the elite. They were often controlled by the same family for many generations, and the votes were directed by people who had no interest in what was actually happening in the borough. Revolutionary writer Thomas Paine, in *The Rights of Man*, complained of rotten boroughs when he said:

> The county of Yorkshire, which contains near a million souls, sends two county members; and so does the county of Rutland which contains not a hundredth part of that number. The town of Old Sarum, which contains not three houses, sends two members; and the town of Manchester, which contains upwards of sixty thousand souls, is not admitted to send any. Is there any principle in these things?

The name *rotten borough* was arguably both a technical term for a borough with exaggerated representation and a moral description of a borough that was fundamentally in the "possession and gift" of the king. A young John Dickinson claimed it was thought that there was "not a borough in England in which [bribery] is not practiced."

In England, commentators of the day would mock the empty parks that were well represented in Parliament while the huge cities had no voice.[34] In March 1776, the Whig John Wilkes, who later supported the Americans, made a forceful speech demanding the end of the rotten borough system. He detailed borough after borough—each with only a dozen people, yet represented equally in Parliament. Because these parliamentarians had so few voters to contend with, they were easily bought by the Crown: the king would give offices to the representative, who would in turn pay off the voters. Wilkes thought the rotten boroughs were the primary cause of corruption and that "the disfranchising of the mean, venal, and dependent boroughs would be laying the axe to the root of corruption and treasury influence, as well as aristocratical tyranny."[35] In England, however, the reformers felt stuck in a system with no release: those in power were not likely to give it up.[36]

In the United States, they had a chance to start fresh. The census provision became the constitutional protection against rotten boroughs and the corrupting influence of disproportionate power. There were two census protections in the original Constitution. The first required that legislators (and taxes) be tied to the number of people in each state—or, more precisely, tied to the number of white people and three-fifths of all other people, but not including untaxed Indians. The provision required a new census every ten years and provided a set of formulas for determining representation, starting with one representative for every 30,000 people. The second provision, later amended by the Sixteenth Amendment, prohibited Congress from imposing direct taxes that are not in proportion to the census. The debate at the convention over these provisions was largely a debate about slavery, and not the reasons for the census.

Age and Time

Corruption concerns also led to the constitutional provisions that limit who can run for office. Representatives need to be American citizens for seven years and at least twenty-five years old; and senators need to be residents of their state, at least thirty, and American citizens for nine years. Inhabitancy in the represented state was included as a requirement for House members in part because it protected against corruption. The framers feared that wealthy nonresidents would purchase elections. George Mason argued that "if you do not require it—a rich man may send down to the Districts of a state in which he does not reside and purchase an Election for his Dependt. We shall have the Eng. Borough corruption."[37] After extensive deliberation—some wanted even greater protection, including a term-of-years residency requirement in the particular area in which the person was seeking election—the word *resident* was switched to *inhabitant* to clear up confusion, and the residency requirement, with no time requirement, was kept.

The clause demanding seven years' citizenship in the United States for House members also stemmed from a concern about corruption. Mason, who introduced the bill, said he was all "for opening a wide door for emigrants; but did not chuse to let foreigners and adventurers make laws for us & govern us."[38] One of the meanings of *adventurer*, then as now, was someone who seeks out wealth or power through illegal or unscrupulous means. As the passage indicates, Mason was wary of people who would take advantage of democratic forms to pursue their own ends. The distinction between "emigrants" and "foreigners *and* adventurers" shows that the baseline anxiety for Mason was not that people came from elsewhere but that they exploited the system and did not truly belong to or intend to respond to the residents. The parallel nine-year citizenship requirement for senators was also heavily debated—Mason again taking the charge and telling stories of cabal and adventurers—but they ultimately settled on nine (instead of three, fourteen, or thirteen) as fittingly more than that for the House "because they would have more power."

The age requirements for federal office come from an effort to limit the power of family dynasties. The age limits make it harder for one to come into power just by being a child of a wealthy or political family. The provisions were "aimed to prevent wealthy candidates from gaming the system."[39] Those most affected by age limits would be the wealthy sons of a political dynasty—not those without means. As Mason said, "If residence be not required, Rich men of neighboring States may employ with success the means of corruption in some particular district and thereby get into the public Councils after having failed in their own State. This is the practice in the boroughs of England."[40]

Accounting

Giving the legislature the power of the purse was supposed to stop corruption.[41] The founders were concerned that an executive with the power of appropriation would use it to create dependency by giving out money to political leaders.[42] The Constitution required that the treasury be accounted to ensure that money was not stolen from the national treasury.[43] All military appropriations were limited to two years. The appropriations clause also ensures that this happened by including a requirement that funds be appropriated transparently. The transparency requirement gives the public a tool with which to govern the elected representatives, because they can identify—and then refuse to reelect—those who spend money in a way that is self-serving instead of public serving. Likewise, the journal clause requires accountability, such that secret intrigue cannot occur.

Takings and Givings

The initial Constitution did not protect citizens from having their property taken by government. But one of the amendments, ratified in 1791, elaborated that any private property that was taken should be, in some sense, paid for: "Nor shall private property be taken for public use, without just compensation." This has become known as the "takings clause," and the reason it was included in the amendments was unclear, as no state requested it.

The takings clause is sometimes treated as a pure expression of property rights, although most historians who have reviewed the evidence conclude that it is less about property law and more about protecting against process failures, including corruption. Legal historian William Treanor's masterful history of the takings clause concludes that the most likely source was a set of political process failures—situations in which the system would not work, and therefore individuals should have the right to demand fair compensation. William Fischel has argued that the use of the word *just* compensation—instead of the compensation demanded by the property owner—shows that something more than simply asserting property rights was driving the law. Malla Pollack argues further that the takings clause was partially James Madison's version of a proposed antimonopoly clause. The ability to grant monopolies (or other special privileges) and to take private property were intimately related. They are both forms of state power susceptible to corruption.[44] For hundreds of years, the English Crown had used its power to grant special privileges to businesses—sometimes called monopolies—in exchange for fees. The Crown got payments from companies, and those companies would then be able to make profits from their special privilege. The middlemen—agents of the Crown who operated like early lobbyists—would get some fees. The monopoly privileges tended to corrupt because they bypassed the public scrutiny that follows taxing and spending. The House of Commons denounced monopoly patents as corrupt, and lucrative patents frequently went to courtiers. In 1599, the famous jurist Sir Edward Coke held that the grant of exclusive right to sell was against the fundamental public commitments of English law. Monopolies "do not conduce to the public weal." Some of the anti-British sentiment two centuries later was against the use of monopolies by the Crown. The riot in Boston where tea was dumped into Boston Harbor—the original Tea Party—was in part a protest against the British East India Company's monopoly on the importation of tea. Monopolies often enriched the Crown and private interests at the cost of the public. Several states asked for an antimonopoly provision in the Constitution, which Thomas Jefferson also supported. Many Anti-Federalists—and some of the delegates to the convention—ultimately refused to sign it because the convention refused to adopt proposed antimonopoly provisions.

Pollack argues that the takings clause—taken in hand with the copyright and patent clause—was intended as at least a partial limitation on the power to corruptly sell special property privileges. Most of the argument is speculative—there is no record of why Madison included the takings clause or why he refused to support an antimonopoly clause that was twice introduced by Massachusetts delegate Elbridge Gerry. However, Madison's later expression of his theory of property suggests that government may not take away the power of a merchant to do something (which a patent effectively does):

> That is not a just government, nor is property secure under it, where arbitrary restrictions, exemptions, and monopolies deny to part of its citizens that free use of their faculties, and free choice of their occupations.... What must be the spirit of legislation where a manufacturer of linen cloth is forbidden to bury his own child in a linen shroud, in order to favour his neighbour who manufactures woolen cloth; where the manufacturer and wearer of woolen cloth are again forbidden the economical use of buttons of that material in favor of the buttons of other materials!

Furthermore, some Federalists, criticizing Gerry's final rejection of the Constitution for its failure to include an antimonopoly provision, suggested that the patent and copyright clause implicitly limited the scope of congressional monopoly power. That clause gives Congress the power "to promote the progress of science and useful arts, by securing for limited times to authors and inventors the exclusive right to their respective writings and discoveries." By the principle that what is not expressed is not granted, there is evidence that at least some contemporaries believed that this grant of power was intended as the *sole* grant. The "limited times" part of the clause showed that the framers wanted monopolies (which both represented corruption and led to temptations) to be carefully constrained.

Treaties

While most of these provisions related to internal governance, the specter of foreign power was always present. In one proposal, treaties could be approved with half of the Senate's approval. Gerry, however, "enlarged on the danger of putting the essential rights of the Union in the hands of so small a number as a majority of the Senate, representing, perhaps, not one fifth of the people. The Senate will be corrupted by foreign influence."[45] The delegates, in turn, enlarged the requirements, demanding two-thirds of senators to agree to a treaty. As Lawrence Lessig puts it, "The Framers didn't want a Congress that was a farm league for the French Riviera."[46] The executive was given the treaty-making power after much disturbed debate.

CHAPTER FOUR

Yazoo

IF YOU WERE a politically active American in the 1790s and early 1800s, you would have had an opinion about Yazoo. Alexander Hamilton was pro-Yazoo. John Randolph, the powerful speaker of the U.S. House of Representatives, was anti-Yazoo. Patrick Henry and Supreme Court justice James Wilson were both tainted by their relationship to Yazoo. James Madison was (as described below) both pro- and anti-Yazoo, depending on whether you were asking him about law or policy. Joseph Story was pro-Yazoo. Jefferson disdained Supreme Court justice John Marshall for his Yazoo leanings. People sometimes called themselves "Yazoo men." Others called Yazoo "marked with fraud, injustice and villainy" and akin to "perjury and murder, and every other species of villainy."[1] Opponents accused supporters of "Yazooism."[2]

What was this controversy with a funny name? Superficially, it was a big bribery scandal where speculators paid legislators to sell state land for much less than it was worth. But at heart, it was a case about power and politics. Your view on Yazoo depended on your view about who gets to decide when something is corrupt: courts or legislatures. Back in the 1780s the Constitutional Convention had defined the republic as a nation preoccupied with corruption. A decade later, corruption was still a national fixation. In this case, it circulated around the relationship of state legislators to land sales rather than the relationship of kings to parliamentarians.

The scandal happened in Georgia. Land speculation flourished in early America, and some of the cheapest land deals were in state houses. States barely knew their own borders, so the public might not even notice that land was sold, or how much. Successful speculators were well connected and used personal influence to persuade their political friends that selling land was good for all parties: the state would get income, speculators would get land, and the public wouldn't miss it. Some investors would buy land from the state with little evidence that it even existed because it was so cheap, hoping for big profits from natural resources.

Georgia was particularly ripe for this kind of speculation because it claimed jurisdiction over vast masses of land that the state did not control. Members of several Native American tribes lived in those regions—and were resistant to colonization— while other sections were deserted. Georgia's governor had the power to give small tracts of land to people who tilled it for at least twelve months, a system designed to encourage homesteading. In practice, neither the small tract rule nor the tilling rule was closely followed. Instead, millions of acres—some of them nonexistent—were given away in tracts as large as 50,000 acres to people from all over the country who had no intention of working the soil.

The politician Patrick Henry is best known to history for his provocative speech to the 1775 Virginia convention in support of the American Revolution, where he allegedly shouted: "Give me liberty or give me death!" In 1789 Henry led a coalition of companies that successfully secured an agreement with the state of Georgia to buy thirty-five million acres of land close to the Yazoo River (mostly within what is now Mississippi). When word of the deal leaked, the public reacted angrily, and the Georgia government quickly modified the contract to appease them. It was a move worthy of Shakespeare: the state promised to keep to their bargain, but insisted that the land be paid for only in gold or silver. Henry and his associates lacked the precious metals, and the modification successfully killed the deal.

But he was not dissuaded. A few years later, new companies were created with the same goal. The Virginia Yazoo Company, the South Carolina Yazoo Company, and the Tennessee Company joined in the "Combined Society." This time they were more prepared. Henry and his associates made sure that Georgia's legislators were invested in the commercial associations. When the bill came in front of them, they would want to support a sale.[3] The companies' records showed that "every member of the legislature—with a single exception—who voted for the bill was a shareholder in the purchases."[4] It was no surprise, then, that the first bid of $250,000 for thirty-five million acres passed the legislature. But the governor vetoed it. The next offer for $500,000 again passed the legislature and was this time accepted by the governor. Some acres sold for less than one cent.[5] It has been called by one commentator the "greatest real estate deal in history."[6]

These actions laid the groundwork for legal disputes about how courts would struggle with the concept of corruption for the next 200 years. The voters in Georgia were at first stunned and then outraged. "Anti-Yazooist" factions sprang up and people held meetings around the state. James Jackson, one of Georgia's great politicians, rushed back from Washington to lead the protests. In the next election, according to one account, "the only issue was Yazoo and anti-Yazoo." The public threw out every lawmaker who had voted for the deal, and once the new legislature was elected, "there was no other business before the General Assembly until this matter was disposed of. The body was flooded with the petitions and remonstrances that had been sent to the convention."[7] The new anti-Yazoo legislature immediately created a committee (with Jackson at its head) to investigate the Yazoo sale. It took them less than a month to come to a conclusion. The committee reported that the initial act was unconstitutional and had been fraudulently passed. In response, the new legislature passed a law declaring the act void and a nullity. But revocation was not enough for the betrayed Georgians. They needed to actually set fire to the prior act:

> The feeling of the Legislature was so strong, that, after the Yazoo act had been repealed, it was decided to destroy all the records and documents relating to the corruption. By order of the two Houses a fire was kindled in the public square of Louisville, which was then the capital. The enrolled act that had been secured by fraud was brought out by the secretary of state, and by him delivered to the President of the Senate for examination. That officer delivered the act to the Speaker of the House. The Speaker in turn

passed it to the clerk, who read the title of the act and the other records, and then, committing them to the flames, cried out in a loud voice, "God save the State and preserve her rights, and may every attempt to injure them perish as these wicked and corrupt acts now do!"[8]

For some individuals, the legal battle ended with the new legislative act. Several people who had purchased Yazoo land from the initial companies voluntarily gave up their titles and got their money back. But the corruption controversy didn't die in the fire. The Yazoo companies, in defiance of Georgia, continued to sell claims to the land throughout the country. According to the sellers and buyers, a deal is a deal, even if it is a bad one, and the land was no longer owned by the State of Georgia. Through these proliferating land sales, the local issue quickly became national.

Pro-Yazoo and anti-Yazoo divisions largely—but not completely—reflected the lines between the early parties: Federalists (who favored strong central governments) and Democratic-Republicans. Political pamphleteers got in on the act and distributed screeds about the sale. The Yazoo scandal became a political litmus test for politicians outside of Georgia.

Yazoo supporters argued that the sale could not be nullified. From their point of view the state was bound by the contract to sell the land. It didn't matter if the motives of all the legislators were obviously self-interested, and it didn't matter whether or not it reflected the will of the people. Their vision of a republic depended on stable property rights: whether or not the purchasers were exactly disinterested or innocent, purchasers needed assurance that what they bought wouldn't be snatched away from them by the whimsy of state houses. Their ideology reinforced their interest: many Federalists came from the upper classes of society and were closely associated with businessmen, the speculators of the time. But race and attitudes toward slavery also percolated through the Federalist concern—many of the most prominent Georgian anti-Yazooists were slaveholders. Therefore, being pro-Yazoo was associated with anti-slavery sentiment: by the time Yazoo became a national scandal, all of the northern states had either abolished slavery or taken steps to abolish it. To support the slaveholders, even if they had a legitimate democratic complaint, was to support men who had embraced a deeply corrupt and self-serving theory of democracy.

The anti-Yazoo faction—largely Democratic-Republican— thought that the Georgia legislature clearly had the right to void a corrupt contract. A leading Republican newspaper, Philadelphia's *Aurora*, denounced Yazoo as "melancholy proof of the depravity of human nature" and as one of the worst examples of unchecked land speculation.[9] Some of the debate was on "small-d" democratic grounds (the people have the right not to be saddled with corrupt choices). Some of it was on contract law grounds. The anti-Yazooists tended to be very wary of the national government and the elite institutions of the Supreme Court, which they did not trust. For them, the Yazoo repeal was a case of a state using its powers of self-government to self-govern. The initial act was illegitimate, and the revocation was legitimate. In contract terms, the anti-Yazooists regularly reminded their adversaries that every company that sold Yazoo lands refused to give a warranty against a defect in title. This should have put a purchaser on notice of the problems with the sale.

John Randolph was a Jeffersonian republican, the Speaker of the House, and perhaps one of the most extraordinary orators of his time. The scandal that bothered him the most—in a long career in politics—was Yazoo. It seemed madness to him that a group of confidence men could take over the government, give land to themselves, and then walk away scot-free, losing only their elected positions, nothing more, and taking with them the full value of the property they had given themselves. "At his coolest moments the word Yazoo was to him what the sight of a bodkin was to Sir Piercie Shafton," his biographer wrote. At other times "the effect was beyond all measure violent."[10] Randolph kept insisting that the citizens of Georgia had acted exactly as they should and in the only way in which they could: they had elected representatives, they had paid attention to their representatives' actions, and then, when their representatives had betrayed them, they had immediately and forcefully ejected them from office. From his point of view, the voters of Georgia "had instantly, publicly, violently disavowed those agents and repudiated their act, calling upon all the parties who had meanwhile paid value for lands, under the obnoxious grants, to receive back their money and surrender their titles. What more could they have done? What more should they be required to do?"[11] He proudly proclaimed anti-Yazooism the project at the center of his heart, and committed that he would "never desert or relinquish till I shall have exercised every energy of mind and faculty of body which I possess in refuting so nefarious a project."[12]

Yazoo made for clear political positions, but complicated legal ones. In this, it prefigured campaign finance law cases today, where it is easier to identify corruption as a political incident than make sense of it legally. In the heat of the public debate, the legal status of the land remained unclear. The anti-Yazooists said that Georgia retained the title to the land; the pro-Yazooists said that the purchasers had the title. In response to the crisis, President Jefferson appointed three commissioners, including then–Secretary of State James Madison, to resolve the legal questions surrounding their claims to the land. Madison and the other commissioners unequivocally concluded that the initial sale was void. Their report to Congress stated that they "feel no hesitation in declaring it as their opinion, that under all the circumstances which may affect the case . . . the title of the claimants cannot be supported."[13]

The Georgia lands commission *also* concluded that it was in the best interest of the country to come to a compromise with the claimants. As the U.S. government had bought the disputed land, they were in the position to pay the claimants some portion of what they thought they were owed. Their recommendation was vilified by angry populists as being a compromise with corruption, and rejected by the certificate holders as too weak. But Congress adopted the report and in a federal act provided a method for claimants who had received lands under the "act or pretended act" to sell their purported interest in the lands and release their legal claims to the United States.[14] The report led to a split in the Democratic-Republican Party, much to the Federalists' delight. Randolph was furious about the Jefferson-Madison compromise and broke with the party over it, starting a party called "quids"—the first third party—that harked back to old republicanism as against the federal tendencies of the government.

Some claimants took the opposite view: they considered the compromise insufficient and pursued legal remedies to get the full value of the land, which is how the struggle ended up in the Supreme Court. The new Court, testing its own powers, had to make sense of this constitutionally weighty concept and who had the power to enforce it.

The Concept of Corruption in the Court

In 1810 the third presidential succession—from Jefferson to Madison—had gone smoothly, resolving the last doubts that the United States would persist as a unified, federal nation. Sixteen years had passed since the initial Yazoo land sale. The Supreme Court's capacity to judge corruption was litigated for the first time. A New Hampshire citizen, Robert Fletcher, bought some Yazoo land from Massachusetts citizen John Peck and then sued him for violating the warranties of good title. Peck hired first John Quincy Adams, then Joseph Story, to defend the good title of the land he sold. The case quickly went to the Supreme Court. The case was about corruption, but it arose under dubious circumstances, calling into question the integrity of the Court itself. Many commentators—then and now—believed the Fletcher-Peck sale was merely a pretense for initiating the lawsuit. The land claimants were itching for a case and saw a possibility of winning in the Supreme Court while the federal payouts stalled.[15] This suspicion that Fletcher was put up to the task clearly troubled some justices—it violated the principle that courts should not address theoretical questions but actual legal disputes. Justice Marshall scolded Joseph Story from the bench for representing a case that was "manifestly made up." Justice Johnson concluded that it was a "feigned case."

It was hardly an equal match-up. Peck's attorney, Joseph Story, was a famous Massachusetts lawyer. Fletcher's attorney, Luther Martin, was considered brilliant and principled, but he was also a notorious alcoholic or "Lawyer brandy bottle." An acquaintance explained wryly that "his potatoes may sometimes perhaps coagulate, but they will never acidify the fluid with which it is so well replenished."[16] His once great oratory was declining. In the Yazoo appearance in the Supreme Court, Martin was too drunk to make any sense, and the case was suspended while he sobered up.

But perhaps the most troubling aspect of the case was the appearance of conflict on the part of the most powerful decision-maker. The Chief Justice of the Supreme Court, John Marshall, had a history of land speculation that closely resembled the Yazoo speculators'. Biographer R. Kent Newmyer describes how, after the war, he became a lawyer for many officers, and in that role

> Marshall was well placed to garner a sizeable piece of the action; to buy at a discount and sell at a profit, or to sell a part to pay for the rest. Judging from his dealings with Arthur Lee and James Monroe, he was not only successful but aggressive. As he confessed to Monroe regarding his various land dealings, "If I succeed I shall think myself a first rate speculator."[17]

As a congressman from Virginia ten years earlier, he had argued to the House of Representatives that the federal commissioners should not investigate the legitimacy of the claims to the western lands of Georgia. His personal and political history cast a pall over his role as the final arbiter in the case. When the Yazoo case came before him, he had become a speculator of a different sort, one of the most important justices in U.S. Supreme Court history.

The technical issue before the Supreme Court was whether Peck had breached the terms of his contract with Fletcher by selling land he didn't own. But that legal question turned on deeper questions of political design: Was the initial act a nullity because it was procured by corruption? And, if not, was the *second* act valid in its revocation of the first act?[18]

These are hard questions on their own, but consider the intellectual difficulties posed by these questions in the context of the Revolutionary philosophy of the founding era. Francis Hutcheson, a Scottish Enlightenment philosopher who greatly influenced the framers of the Constitution, argued that when the governors of a state act corruptly, the trust they have been given "is violated, and the Grant thereby made void."[19] Richard Price, an English supporter of the Revolutionary War, wrote that governments "possess no power beyond the limits of the trust for the execution of which they were formed." Government, he wrote, dissolves itself when it attempts to exercise power that it has not been given by its constituents.[20] Or, as Locke argued, the "legislative constituted" by society "can never be supposed to extend farther than the common good,"[21] implying that when it extended beyond that, it ceased to exercise legislative authority. A representative is imagined as an agent or fiduciary of the public. Just as an agent has no authority to act if she stops acting as an agent of those who hired her, a representative lacks authority if he is no longer accountable to his constituents.[22] All of these theories helped build the theoretical justification for the Revolution. But what happened when the same dynamics played out on a smaller scale? Could corruption in a legislature justify a state "overthrowing" a law passed by a bribed body of representatives?

When state-level protections against corruption failed spectacularly, the Supreme Court had to confront the legal version of the Revolutionary claim: that a law could be so tainted with bribery accompanying its passage that it was not a law. The Courts had three options: The first was Yazooism. This approach would forbid either judicial or legislative review of whether a law was passed corruptly. A law is a law, and the process by which it was passed is irrelevant. The second was a judicial review of corruption. The Court could void laws passed because of bribery. This approach requires courts to determine when a law is corruptly passed and distinguish those cases from the routine case of a law being passed with some private reasoning done by legislators. The third was a democratic review of corruption. The Court could treat the initial law not as void but voidable— capable of repeal. This approach gives legislators wide latitude to reverse their policies and grants of power. Which way would the Court go? As with many later corruption cases, the decision would impact legal history in cases outside of corruption law.

Luther Martin argued that the initial act was void because it was corrupt. He also argued that the second act (destroying the contract) was within the power of the people of the state to change laws. His argument depended on how one imagined the legislature's relationship to the people of the state of Georgia. If one treated the principal to the contract as the *people of Georgia,* the legislature was like an agent acting outside its authority in selling the people's lands. To continue the analogy, it would be like a company (the public) hiring a lawyer (the representatives) to negotiate, but the lawyer making deals far outside what the company hired him for. In general, an agent's actions outside the scope of a contract aren't enforceable as against the principle.

Story and the Yazooists argued that it didn't matter if the initial act was corrupt. "The grossest corruption will not authorize a judicial tribunal in disregarding the law" because "this would open a source of litigation which could never be closed. The law would be differently decided by different juries; innumerable perjuries would be committed, and inconceivable confusion would ensue." As to Martin's second argument, the Yazooists argued that the Georgia legislature was the party to contract, not the people. In voiding its own law, the legislature had done something entirely unacceptable: entered into a contract and then later pronounced its own action invalid. To continue the analogy above, it would be as if a company directly negotiated with someone to buy an order of chairs, and then, after leadership changed hands, unilaterally announced the initial contract was void. Such an action would be against the basic principles of contract.

In the opinion deciding the case, *Fletcher v. Peck*, Marshall concluded that in the abstract, a legislative act *might* be void if secured by bribery, but the posture of this case did not allow for that examination. He concluded that the corruption challenge to the law could not be brought in that particular way, "collaterally and incidentally" to a case about a private contract. It would be "indecent, in the extreme, upon a private contract, between two individuals, to enter into an inquiry respecting the corruption of the sovereign power of a state." However, he strongly indicated discomfort with the idea that a court could ever explore the corruptness of legislation as a process matter, even if the subject was not a private contract. He wrote that it would be very difficult to find a process violation based on "the impure motives which influenced certain members of the legislature which passed the law." It would be hard to know what constitutes corruption and hard to create a rule that would allow for judicial review.[23]

Courts, he suggested, do not have the competence to examine the motives of legislators and determine corruption. How much can a court look into the "particular inducements" offered to form the contracts? Could it be possible that the "validity of a law depends upon the motives of its framers"? If so, how would one possibly look into the minds of the framers of the law, and would not the court become so entangled in motive that no law could withstand it?

> If the principle be conceded, that an act of the supreme sovereign power might be declared null by a court, in consequence of the means which procured it, still would there be much difficulty in saying to what extent those means must be applied to produce this effect. Must it be direct corruption, or would interest or undue influence of any kind be sufficient? Must the vitiating cause operate on a majority, or on what number of the members? Would the act be null, whatever might be the wish of the nation, or would its obligation or nullity depend upon the public sentiment? If the majority of the legislature be corrupted, it may well be doubted, whether it be within the province of the judiciary to control their conduct, and, if less than a

majority act from impure motives, the principle by which
judicial interference would be regulated, is not clearly
discerned.

His language was less positivist or Hobbesian than despair-
ing. For a positivist—someone for whom there is no moral content to law—corruption is a very troubling legal idea because it
is so deeply intertwined with a moral idea, or a baseline attitude
toward what constitutes "good" politics. In Marshall's rejection,
he did not reject the possibility of corruption but was clearly
troubled by the idea of law (the judiciary) having anything particular to say about corruption, because it would mean that the
act of law giving would be the act of assessing the good or evil
about a particular kind of political behavior. Marshall was also
bothered that corruption lacks precise definition as a matter of
law. Because it has no clear bounds, setting aside a law on the
grounds of corruption opens up all laws to similar charges. This,
then, could undermine law itself, as it would leave ambiguous
what laws were legitimate expressions of authority and what
laws were illegitimate expressions, depending upon a later judgment by a subjective court.

Marshall's decision sided with the Yazooist: the legislature is
the principal because the people *never* act except through the
legislature. The public is unlike individuals, who can act directly,
without agents. Because this is the sole mode in which "the people"
exist and enter into arrangements, to dispute the legitimacy of
one agent (one legislature), the only way to do it is through a subsequent agent (another embodiment of that legislature).

As Marshall saw it, if a legislature could revoke its own corrupt prior actions, it would either be either acting as a judge in

its own tribunal, or, if not acting as a court, "exerting a mere act of power in which it was controlled only by its own will." Since he did not want to give the legislature the authority to act either as a judge upon itself or as unconstrained mere power, he concluded that the only way to examine the revocation is through the traditional common-law lens of contracts—with the legislature (not the public) as the relevant actor. Within the realm of contracts, then, he turned to the public policy goal of making sure that titles are secure and the importance of keeping open "the intercourse between man and man." It was of utmost importance to protect innocent third parties.[24] While initial conveyances might be set aside because they were procured by corruption, once they had passed into an innocent third party's hands, they became enforceable.

Marshall reasoned that Georgia was asking for legislatures to get special treatment in contract law. To treat the legislature as a special category for purposes of these kinds of conveyances would lead to the legislature being able to "devest any other individual of his lands, if it shall be the will of the legislature so to exert it." In order to support the right of the legislature to revoke its own grants, Fletcher would have to argue this principle: "That a legislature may, by its own act, devest the vested estate of any man whatever, for reasons which shall, by itself, be deemed sufficient."

In some ways the most radical move was Marshall's characterization of the land grant as a contract.[25] This allowed Marshall to place the case in the context of the contracts clause of the U.S. Constitution, Article I, Section 10, which says that no state may "pass any Bill of Attainder, ex post facto Law, or Law impairing the Obligation of Contracts." According to Marshall, this clause was designed as a limit on emotional democracy and excessive democracy:

> Whatever respect might have been felt for the state sovereignties, it is not to be disguised that the framers of the constitution viewed, with some apprehension, the violent acts which might grow out of the feelings of the moment; and that the people of the United States, in adopting that instrument, have manifested a determination to shield themselves and their property from the effects of those sudden and strong passions to which men are exposed. The restrictions on the legislative power of the states are obviously founded in this sentiment; and the constitution of the United States contains what may be deemed a bill of rights for the people of each state.

The effect of the second act on Fletcher would be, according to Marshall, like the effect of an ex post facto law. In his reading of an ex post facto law, the legislature is "prohibited from passing a law by which a man's estate, or any part of it, shall be seized for a crime which was not declared, by some previous law, to render him liable to that punishment." Without this prohibition, emotional actions and excessive instability would be forthcoming. Therefore, the purchasers of the land were entitled to the full value. However, Marshall was also moved by a sense of natural law that protected the sanctity of property.

There is no evidence that most of the framers intended the contract clause to operate this way. To be fair, the reason for the contracts clause is unclear—it seems a redundancy. It is likely that its sole purpose was to limit state interference with private contracts—unless it was snuck in by Alexander Hamilton, as one historian speculated.[26]

The ideological underpinnings of the case undermined any democratic check on corruption. In Marshall's way of thinking, the scope of government largely ought not extend to the ability to transfer property:

> It may well be doubted whether the nature of society and of government does not prescribe some limits to the legislative power; and, if any be prescribed, where are they to be found, if the property of an individual, fairly and honestly acquired, may be seized without compensation. To the legislature all legislative power is granted; but the question, whether the act of transferring the property of an individual to the public, be in the nature of the legislative power, is well worthy of serious reflection.

Marshall's logic leads to nonreviewable giveaways and takings, because he perceived democratic review as destabilizing. A legislature that could take back what it has given would leave property rights uncertain, which could limit economic growth and development. The passions that excite citizens in a democracy would be too fickle, according to Marshall, and must be restrained by the contract clause and common law of contracts, or commerce would not be allowed to develop in a stable way.

Democratic Power to Fight Corruption

The impact of *Fletcher* was enormous, and largely unanticipated. The *Fletcher*-created contract clause "served in the antebellum era as the most significant constitutional limitation on state power to regulate the economy."[27] After *Fletcher*, the Marshall Court followed the same logic and declared a tax repeal unconstitutional, and modifications of corporate charters unconstitutional. The doctrine became a radical restriction on the scope of legislative supremacy. *Fletcher* was the first time that the Supreme Court struck down a state law on constitutional grounds. It set in motion a generation of cases in which courts invalidated legislative actions. Scholars have questioned Marshall's motives, his logic, and his use of the impairments of the obligations of contract.

The contract clause reading created a barrier to electoral restraint of corruption because the capacity of the legislature to reverse policy in one direction acted as an invitation to corruption in that area. Any time a legislature corruptly granted water rights, a monopoly in bridge building, land, or reduced tax rates for a certain class of companies, the public was stuck. For the democratic theory of corruption control to work, the people must be able to throw out the legislature and elect a new legislature to revoke the water rights, revoke the monopoly, revoke the corporate charter, revoke the land grant, and change the tax rates.

Thomas Jefferson and James Madison were not pleased. Two months after the decision came down, Jefferson wrote to Madison: "Really the state has suffered long enough by having such a cypher in so important an office, and infinitely the more from the want of any counterpoise to the rancorous hatred which Marshall bears to the government of his country, & from the cunning & sophistry within which he is able to enshroud himself."[28]

According to Jefferson, "His twistifications in the case of Marbury, in that of Burr, & the late Yazoo case, shew how dexterously he can reconcile law to his personal biasses."[29] They used the word *Yazooism* as shorthand for Marshall's reasoning and the reasoning of anyone who supported the certificate holders over the power of the state legislature. Jefferson later advocated for a candidate for the Supreme Court, noting that he had been "interested in Yazooism" but was now "clear of it."[30] President Madison, however, rejected the candidate on the grounds that he was still "infected with Yazooism."[31] Madison's impulse toward federalism was greater than his impulse toward judicial review. In 1788 he worried about too much judicial power and argued that it was neither intended nor proper that the judicial department be paramount to the legislature.[32] Nor did he call upon judicial review as a check on legislative powers in the *Federalist Papers*. While he supported some scheme of national federal review, he never suggested judicial review of state laws. If he had believed in judicial review, it is almost certain—especially given his own review of the Yazoo scandal as a commissioner— that the review would not extend to invalidating an act of a state legislature on contract clause grounds.

Marshall's opinion in *Fletcher v. Peck* foreshadowed some of the central intellectual disagreements in corruption cases 200 years later. The first disagreement is over how abstract to be. Can corruption make sense separate from the particular political context? Justice Marshall described the case in general terms, not in terms of the particular wholesale bribery and theft. That enabled him to use the difficult meaning of corruption as a way to avoid the particular issue, arguing that the specificity of the facts ought not obscure the abstract issue. This prefigured the move in the campaign finance law cases, where modern justices describe corruption in purely abstract terms and therefore narrow its meaning.

It also foreshadowed the modern corruption nihilism of the kind we see again in Chief Justice John Roberts. Determining what corruption is constitutes neither a judicial nor a legislative task. Judicial intervention will lead to instability, and legislative intervention will lead to instability. The legislature should not have complete freedom to upend settled property laws on the mere charge of corruption, but the judiciary should not intrude unnecessarily in the workings of the legislature because it would lead to a troubling intervention in political activities. Marshall noted with sorrow and condemnation that "corruption should find its way into the governments of our infant republics, and contaminate the very source of legislation." But his answer, in effect, was that nothing can be done about it. As we turn to bribery laws, we peer into the precise shape of that nothing.

CHAPTER FIVE

Is Bribery without a Remedy?

IN THE EARLY 1850s in Britain, Sir John Eardley Eardley-Wilmot, Second Baronet, a prolific writer, dedicated himself to two topics: cold water baths and political reform. In this, he followed Benjamin Franklin, who also loved reform and frigidness (Franklin was partial to cold air baths). Sir John's successful *Tribute to Hydropathy* went through three editions—the final one in 1855—as he detailed the wonders of plunging oneself in cold water and covering oneself in a wet sheet while taking the "Water Cure." He described being treated by a bath-man (a "bad man," in Sir John's words), who, "in a novel and vehement process of pushing and pulling, tugging and tightening" left him "like a chrysalis, incapable of motion."[1]

These dousings and massages freed him of recurrent sickness, reinvigorated him, and allowed him to pursue his passion for law. In 1853 he published a long open letter to Lord John Russell, the leader of the House of Commons. The letter, or tract, was called *Is Bribery without a Remedy?*, and it addressed itself to the bribery of and by parliamentarians. Sir John approached the sickness of the body politic—and its potential cures—as he had analyzed the sicknesses and cures of the body. No one, he argued, could ignore the "cancer" that had been "slowly developing itself in the political body."[2] He detailed the proliferation of bribery in parliamentary elections and the absence of prosecutions. Unlike the bribery of judges, which had long been punished as a heinous act in Britain, bribery around parliamentary elections seemed barely criminal. Instead, legislators regulated themselves, holding the rare impeachment trial, and typically ignoring the problem.

Sir John could only find one instance of a member of parliament being punished for bribery. Why? He had two main speculations. First, serving in parliament had previously been seen more as a chore than a prize, so bribery had not been a problem because earlier generations of lawmakers would not bribe to get something so invaluable. Second, parliament jealously protected its traditional privilege to judge its own members through impeachment proceedings, and courts were wary of stepping into a different branch's internal affairs.

But the deeper reason likely lay elsewhere, in the history of extortion and bribery laws, which came into being when England was less democratic. Extortion occurs when a public official demands payment for something he is already supposed to do; bribery occurs when a private party pays an official for influence or a particular favor. While both kinds of law have come to apply to elected officials, neither began that way. Bribery laws largely grew out of judicial rules, whereas extortion statutes grew out of rules governing appointed officials.

The word *bribe*, according to the prominent seventeenth-century jurist Sir Edward Coke, "commeth of the French word *briber*, which signifieth to devour, or eat greedily, applied to the devouring of a corrupt judge."[3] The archetypal bribery occurred when a litigant paid a judge. The initial English bribery statute, put in force in the 1380s, prohibited judges from taking a "robe, fee, pension, gift, nor reward of any but the King, except reward of meat and drink, which shall be no great value."[4] Enforcement was potentially severe, but practically depended upon the whims of the Crown.[5] Even after parliament's power had expanded, the widely read jurist William Blackstone described bribery in relation to judges and those involved in the administration of justice.[6]

Extortion, on the other hand, applied to all public ministers. "For the difference between bribery and extortion is this," Coke wrote, "bribery is only committed by him, that hath a judicial place, and extortion may be committed by him, that hath a ministerial office." The oldest Anglo-American extortion rules were codified in 1275 in the Statute of Westminster, prohibiting an officer of the king from taking payment—except from the king—for his public duties. Blackstone, writing in the 1760s, described extortion as "an abuse of public justice, which consists in any *officer's* unlawfully taking, by color of his office, from any man, any money or thing of value that is not due him, or more than is due, or before it is due."[7] While the word *officer* might include elected officials, it typically referred to appointed officials, and the archetypal extortion involved a local functionary demanding extra money from a citizen.[8]

These crimes preceded the existence of a powerful parliament and were not initially designed to police the flow of money around elected representatives. Therefore, bribery seemed to have no remedy: the common-law crimes of bribery and extortion did not fit well, and parliamentarians—who reserved for themselves the "sole and exclusive right to punish their members for the acceptance of a bribe in the discharge of their office"[9]— did not seem inclined to punish their own. The common law did include crimes against what was called *treating*—giving food or drink to a voter—but they were also rarely enforced.

Confusions in the First Generation

But what about America, the country formed on anticorruption concerns? The baronet's anxious question—is there a remedy?— applied just as well to the United States. When the Americans inherited the English tradition of using criminal law to prosecute corruption in a republic, it was a weak inheritance. The Constitution may have been designed to protect against corruption by creating incentive structures, but when bribery slipped through the cracks, would criminal law provide a second line of defense?

The newly formed American federal government did not pass a general bribery or extortion statute, or any bribery statute directed at legislators. Instead, they passed an antibribery statute prohibiting the giving or receiving of bribes to certain judges, customs officers, and tax officers.[10] The punishment was a fine and imprisonment. The absence of a general federal legislative crime led to a series of early confusions about federal common law and the authority of Congress.

At the same time, federal prosecutors were not sure whether they had power to indict anyone for bribery who was not listed in the limited federal law. The issue came to the fore in the building of a lighthouse. Ten years after the Constitutional Convention, Congress gave the commissioner of the revenue, Tench

Coxe, the authority to select a builder for a Cape Hattaras light-house. An eager contractor, Robert Worrall, wrote Coxe describing his skill and suggesting that if he got the commission, he would share some of the proceeds with Coxe. Coxe promptly shared the letter publicly, and federal prosecutors indicted Worrall. In *United States v. Worrall*, the District Court of Pennsylvania had to decide a foundational legal question: does the United States have a criminal common law? Worrall argued that he could not be convicted of bribery because there was no relevant statute. A three-judge panel was split. Then Supreme Court justice Samuel Chase (riding circuit) concluded that Congress had power to define and punish crimes, but without congressional action, there was no bribery.[11] Judge Peters, disagreeing, believed that the capacity to prosecute bribery was an essential feature of what it means to be a government:

> Whenever a government has been established, I have always supposed, that a power to preserve itself, was a necessary, and an inseparable, concomitant. But the existence of the Federal government would be precarious, it could no longer be called an independent government, if, for the punishment of offences of this nature, tending to obstruct and pervert the administration of its affairs, an appeal must be made to the State tribunals, or the offenders must escape with absolute impunity.

In the absence of agreement—and an apparent lack of willingness of the defendant to appeal to the Supreme Court—they compromised: the defendant received a fine and three months' imprisonment. No meaningful precedent was set.

While it seemed there was no federal common law of bribery, it also was not clear whether the new country had inherited the English tradition of legislative bodies having authority to punish corrupting behaviors in their own halls. In 1795 two land speculators, Robert Randall and Charles Whitney, offered congressmen land and money in exchange for supporting their plan to buy nearly twenty million acres of land abutting Lake Erie. The lawmakers reported the attempted bribes, and Randall and Whitney were taken into custody at the House of Representatives and questioned by the Speaker of the House. Throughout the imprisonment and interrogation there was confusion about Congress's authority and the correct internal process, but a supermajority supported bringing corruption charges. Randall was found guilty of contempt of the body for "attempting to corrupt the integrity of its members" and punished by a reprimand from the Speaker and being held by the sergeant at arms "until further order." A week later, Randall successfully petitioned to be released. Whitney was absolved because he had offered a bribe to a member-elect, not a sitting member, and the offer occurred away from the scene of the House of Representatives.[12] It seemed that Congress had the power to make life annoying, but little else, for those who tried to bribe its members.

Twenty years later, the role of Congress in punishing bribery was still confused. On January 7, 1818, North Carolinian congressman Lewis Williams "laid before the house" a letter from a "John Anderson," who had offered him $500 as "part pay for extra trouble," in relation to help he was requesting regarding the Raisin River. Anderson was arrested by the sergeant at arms, but the House was split on its authority to punish him. Some members claimed that the 1795 Randall contempt hearing represented "high handed" "British notions" that predominated in Washington's presidency and should be abandoned. Others argued that contempt power was essential to protect the integrity of the House. A committee was constituted to manage the affair, and it resolved that Anderson should be "brought to the bar of the House and interrogated"; after extensive debate (and with several members adamantly opposed), the vote authorized the contempt proceedings. For two days, January 15 and 16, the Speaker of the House interrogated Anderson about his alleged bribe; Anderson had a lawyer and presented witnesses. He was found guilty of contempt and punished by being brought before the Speaker and reprimanded "for the outrage he has committed."[13]

Anderson promptly sued for assault, battery, and false imprisonment. His argument was that the Constitution did not vest in Congress the power to punish for contempt. When the case came before the Supreme Court, it concluded that while there was no explicit provision, the structure and purpose of Congress implied its power to protect itself. The case, *Anderson v. Dunn*, is remembered for establishing congressional authority to use the contempt power, but in a limited way—no imprisonment could exist past the adjournment of the legislative session.[14] And Congress seemed to still lack power to punish bribery that did not happen in the physical jurisdiction of the legislature.

In the states, on the other hand, a patchwork of statutory and common laws covered a small set of potentially corrupting activities. Extortion was more likely to be criminalized than bribery, perhaps because the power dynamic of an official extorting a citizen was more dangerous than a citizen bribing an official.[15] States recognized common-law crimes of bribery and extortion but rarely used them. To the extent there were bribery laws directed at elections, they tended to criminalize vote buying (a candidate paying for a vote) instead of law buying (paying a candidate to get a law passed). These laws, as I mentioned earlier, were called treating laws, covering election day bribery of voters with food and drink and cash. For instance, the Maryland rule in 1776 was that "if any person shall give any bribe, present or reward, or any promise ... to obtain or procure a vote ... or to be appointed to ... any office of profit or trust ... [he] shall be forever disqualified to hold any office of trust or profit in this state."[16] Georgia, in 1799, passed a law imposing a penalty of up to $100 for anyone caught bribing a voter. North Carolina passed an 1801 statute that prohibited giving voters meat or drink or anything else of value on election day. An 1825 Delaware law imposed penalties of $50 to $200 for the use of influence in getting a free elector to cast his vote for a particular candidate running for office. An 1823 Tennessee statute made it a crime "for any person offering himself as a candidate for any office of honor, profit, or trust, to treat the electors, for the purpose of obtaining their votes, with spirituous liquors."[17] In Virginia, candidates who gave money, meat, drink, or reward for elections would be expelled from office (if they held it) and not able to run for office for another three years, unless the food and drink was provided in the normal course of hospitality. The New York rule in 1787 was that any individual who would "directly or indirectly, attempt to influence any free elector of this state" would have to pay 500 pounds and be "utterly disabled, disqualified and incapacitate, to hold exercise or enjoy any office, or place of trust or profit, whatsoever within this state."[18]

For non-election-related crimes of bribery and extortion, punishments on the books could be quite severe. Michigan and

Maryland passed statutes with fairly heavy penalties in the first decade of the 1800s: Michigan allowed for a fine of up to $800, five years' hard labor, and disqualification from offices of honor, trust, or profit; and Maryland punished bribery with twelve years in prison. New Jersey in 1795 passed a statute directed at judges, with a punishment of up to five years of hard labor, an $800 fine, and permanent disqualification. Taking extra salary for ministerial and judicial offices was punishable by up to two years' hard labor and a $400 fine.

Most reported cases (typically, those in which there was an appeal) involved a bribed judge or juror, or local law enforcement.[19] In general—though the lines were not neatly drawn—bribery retained its historical association with judicial wrongs in the early republic and up through the late 1820s, whereas extortion was more associated with executive offices. The association was not absolute, but it reflected a general conceptualization of bribery punishments as primarily protecting the sanctity of trials, whereas extortion punishments were intended to protect the sanctity of governmental processes. In an early Virginia case from 1795, a lawyer could argue that bribery "can be committed only by a person in a judicial capacity. . . . Extortion may be committed by him who acts ministerially, but bribery cannot."[20] The argument was unpersuasive to the court, but its formulation shows how the language of bribery was still associated with the judicial sphere, and similar arguments show up in cases for the next few decades.

In the political arena, the punishment was primarily political, as the New York statute suggested. As in England, common-law bribery and extortion were misdemeanors, albeit serious ones. They were called "high misdemeanors." The "high" indi-

cated that they were within the category of wrongs that disqualified one from office or public service—regardless of the
size of the criminal penalty. Several states kept this tradition.
For example, the original New Hampshire constitution included
this provision: "No person shall ever be admitted to hold . . . any
office of trust or importance under this government, who in the
due course of law, has been convicted of bribery, or corruption,
in obtaining an election or appointment."[21] And of course the
U.S. Constitution retained this feature, making it an impeach-
able offense to commit "high crimes and misdemeanors." One
might not be jailed for extortion, but it disqualified one from
public office.

Neither corruption nor bribery nor extortion were uniformly
or clearly defined. A 1797 Delaware list of "indictable crimes"
described bribery broadly, as "an offense against public justice,"
constituted by undue reward for one in the administration of
public justice, in an attempt "to influence him against the known
rules of law, honesty, or integrity, or [constituted by] giving or
taking a reward for offices of a public nature. He who accepts
and he who offers the bribe are both liable to punishment."[22]
Because extortion cases were more frequently appealed than
bribery cases, we have a better sense of what constituted "corrupt" behavior in the extortion context in the early years of the
country.

Courts were split both on whether some kind of corrupt
intent was required to prove a violation, and on what kind of
evidence was required to show corrupt intent.[23] Criminal corruption law in Maryland was close to an absolute "bright-line"
rule—a rule in which the act is examined without regard to
whether there is corrupt intent—in that no officer was allowed

to take more than his statutory salary. The Maryland court held that intent did not matter—the crime was complete upon the illegal taking, even though, "No doubt he received the fee under an entire conviction that he had a right to it."[24] As the Maryland judge argued, if you needed to prove corrupt intent, there would be few convictions. In an 1827 Pennsylvania case, where a justice of the peace took money from someone charged with assault, the justice of the peace appealed a conviction of extortion on the grounds that there was no proof he took the money with corrupt intent. The Supreme Court of Pennsylvania rejected the appeal because of the danger that "pretexts would never be wanting." Therefore, "sound policy" led the court to conclude that "the absence of a corrupt motive, or the existence of an agreement by the party injured, furnishes no justification for doing what the law forbids."[25] In contrast, a Massachusetts court concluded that corrupt intent was an essential element of the extortion statute. "Unless the excess [fee was] *wilfully* and *corruptly* demanded and received, it was not within the statute."[26] Some courts held that corrupt intent could be deducted by circumstance. A 1796 North Carolina case included the indictment that the defendant "took eight shillings for a certain service by colour of his office, and for wicked gain sake." The defendant said that it was by mistake, but because the amount taken was above the legal fee, there was sufficient evidence of a crime and the wicked gains sake requirement was presumptively satisfied.[27] All of these issues return in later years to make bribery laws difficult to pin down.

One 1795 Virginia case foreshadowed another interesting question in bribery law: is it illegal if you bribe someone who does not have the power to make a difference? A candidate for county clerk promised one of the justices of the peace that if the justice of the peace would vote for his candidacy, he would share the profits he earned if elected. A judge puzzled over whether it was possible to say that corrupting one of a group of electors constituted bribery. He concluded no: one cannot be convicted of selling an office when only one of many of the electors is offered a payment, because the electing body is larger than the individual whose vote might be influenced.[28]

There is little case law evidence that these laws were broadly enforced.[29] Furthermore, bribery laws were not mentioned in the Yazoo scandal; they were treated skeptically in *Anderson v. Dunn*; and there are less than a dozen reported political corruption cases in the first fifty years after the ratification of the Constitution. One would have to conduct a study of trial records of the period to know more precisely how often they were used, but they were not a significant part of the discourse in the early republic.

Expansion of Corruption Laws to Legislative Activity

James Monroe's inaugural speech in 1817 reaffirmed the most basic principles of the Constitutional era, that the biggest threat to a democracy was the corruption of its people:

> It is only when the people become ignorant and corrupt, when they degenerate into a populace, that they are incapable of exercising the sovereignty. Usurpation is then an easy attainment, and an usurper soon found. The people themselves become the willing instruments of their own debasement and ruin. Let us, then, look to the great cause, and endeavor to preserve it in full force. Let us by all wise

and constitutional measures promote intelligence among the people as the best means of preserving our liberties.[30]

His language is Montesquieu's. The effort to stave off political parties had failed by this point, and politics was partisan, but the essential role of the citizen has retained its force.

In 1816, six years after *Fletcher v. Peck* annulled Georgia's effort to repeal a corrupt law, the state passed a broadly worded statute that directly addressed legislative bribery, unlike most of the prior laws. The Georgia statute provided a punishment of five years for any person who tried to "influence" the "opinion, judgment, decree, or behavior of any *member of the general Assembly*, or any officer of this State, Judge, or Justice."[31] Georgia represented the beginning of a new trend in corruption laws— the expansion to cover legislative activity.

After the 1820s, most states that passed new antibribery laws included bribery of legislative officers as a crime. For instance, a few years after becoming a state, Illinois passed a bribery law that covered judges and members of the general assembly. Bribery was punishable by a $1,000 fine and one year in prison, with disqualification from holding offices; attempt was punishable by up to $500.[32] Legislative bribery was typically described broadly, encompassing far more than simply selling a particular favor. Officials were guilty if they were found to be partial or to treat one side more favorably, and bribers were guilty for trying to influence anything, even judgment. For example, in Michigan, the briber was guilty if he gave something of value "with intent to influence his act, vote, decision, or judgment on any matter."[33] In Colorado it was illegal to give or receive a gift in exchange for intent to treat one side more favorably than the other.[34]

Starting in the middle of the century, the elements of bribery and extortion were increasingly fused, and the bribery statutes become even broader. Kentucky's 1851 statute provided that "if any member of the general assembly, or if any executive or ministerial officer, shall take or agree to take, any bribe to do or omit to do any act in his official capacity," he shall forfeit his office, be disqualified from holding office, forfeit the right to vote for ten years, and be fined.[35] Minnesota's 1859 statute said: "No person shall give, deliver, receive or accept, or offer to give, deliver, receive, or accept, either directly or indirectly, any sum of money or other valuable thing, or from any person or persons, to procure or aid, or for having procured or aided, the passage or defeat of any measure or Legislative enactment acted upon or passed by the Legislature of either House thereof."[36]

As institutional capacity grew, the number of reported cases grew as well, albeit at a snail's pace. There remained a disconnect between an apparent prosecutorial tolerance of bribery and the virulent denunciation of it when a rare case appeared in court. In theory, for instance, treating (giving food or drinks for a vote) was a foundational wrong. The North Carolina Supreme Court in 1850 held that treating is "among the most corrupting practices of candidates for office, is the one we are considering in this case; it is bribery of the most vicious and destructive tendency."[37] But it seems to have happened all the time, and was rarely punished.

As the statutes expanded, so did the common-law understanding. Most state courts recognized some kind of common-law crime of bribery or extortion. Blackstone provided the common-law definition: extortion was a failure of trust by "taking, by colour of his office, from any man, any money or thing of value, that is not due to him, or more than is due, or before it is due."[38] In 1881 the Maine Supreme Court had to decide whether it was against the law to bribe someone to vote. There were no precedents or statutes, but the court concluded that vote buying "strikes at the foundation of republican institutions. Its tendency is to prevent the expression of the will of the people in the choice of rulers, and to weaken the public confidence in elections. When this confidence is once destroyed, the end of popular government is not distant." The practice "shakes the social fabric to its foundations."[39] Therefore, it was implicitly illegal.

Federal statutory law also expanded. The first general federal U.S. bribery law was passed in 1853 after concerns about fraudulent claims related to the Mexican War.[40] It was directed at the misuse of federal funds by any person charged with a public trust, but the terms of the act were broad enough to encompass a broad variety of behaviors. It prescribed punishment for anyone who promised something of value (or accepted it), to officers of the United States, including legislative officers, with the intent to influence "his vote or decision on any question, matter, cause, or proceeding which may then be pending, or may by law, or under the Constitution of the United States, be brought before him in his official capacity, or in his place of trust or profit."[41]

After the Civil War, the states continued the march toward capacious statutes. An 1871 Indiana statute, covering judicial, legislative, and executive offices, forbade anything that would "influence" the "behavior" of a public official in the discharge of official duty.[42] The 1873 Louisiana statute appeared determined to cover all possible kinds of behavior that might plausibly be called bribery. I quote a substantial part of it here, highlighting the most expansive sections, to illustrate the sprawling nature of bribery statutes. A person is guilty of bribery if they

> Shall directly or indirectly promise, offer or give, or cause or procure to be promised, offered or given, any money, goods, rights or valuables, bribe, present or reward, or any other valuable thing whatever . . . [to any officer] . . . whether such officer be legislative, executive, judicial or ministerial, or in the discharge of any official function under or in connection with any department of the government of the State of Louisiana, or under the Senate or House of Representatives of the State of Louisiana, after the passage of this act, with intent to influence such officer or Senator or representative in the decision of any question, matter, cause or proceeding which may then be pending, or may by law or under the constitution of the State of Louisiana be brought before him in his official capacity, or in his place of trust or profit.[43]

Under this statute, any gift of any kind to any legislator with intent to influence official activity is illegal. On its face, it would cover any campaign contribution designed to influence policy (let alone the wheelbarrows of cash that were reportedly in fashion). Law, practice, and culture were disconnected, each from the other.

Perhaps the best example of the the transformation of bribery law from a judicial realm to the legislative realm is a much-cited 1868 case interpreting the common law of corruption. The New Jersey Supreme Court concluded that despite the early association of bribery with the judicial realm, the weight of the

British common-law authority was toward a broader under-standing. Faced with a choice of defining common-law bribery narrowly as a payment to a judge, and more broadly as "the tak-ing or giving of a reward for offices of a public nature," the court chose the latter. "Any attempt to influence an officer in his official conduct, whether in the executive, legislative, or judicial depart-ment of the government, by the offer of a reward or pecuniary consideration, is an indictable common law misdemeanor." The court relied on the eighteenth-century British jurist Lord Mansfield's broad understanding of bribery and on cases that had found that the common-law understanding of bribery in-cluded paying people to vote for members of a corporation. Re-call how the founders reclassified gifts as bribes? The New Jersey court's analysis conclusively reclassified bribery as a tool to fight legislative corruption. Otherwise, "votes of members of council on all questions coming before them, could be bought and sold like merchandise in the market."[44]

Other states, faced with similar questions of whether bribery included all kinds of offices and behaviors, took the same ap-proach, reading a broad background bribery principle for repre-sentative democracy. Illinois had an 1845 statute that did not cover aldermen, but in an 1872 case involving charges of an alder-man being bribed, the court nonetheless concluded that common-law bribery must cover this offense, working from these general principles and the threats to public integrity. Temptation—a watchword for the founding era—grounded the Illinois court's reasoning:

The offer is a sore temptation to the weak or the depraved. It tends to corrupt, and, as the law abhors the least tendency to corruption, it punishes the act which is calculated to debase, and which may affect prejudicially the morals of the community. The attempt to bribe is, then, at common law a misdemeanor; and the person making the offer is liable to indictment and punishment.[45]

The case involved the question of attempts; attempts to bribe were also punishable, for their tendency to corrupt the morals of the community. But it reflects how the ethos of the common law of contracts—which I discuss later—blended into the criminal common law.

Some courts still did not require corrupt intent in extortion cases.[46] Two major commentaries on the criminal law, however, concluded that corrupt intent was an essential element of conviction for bribery or extortion. Bishop's *Commentaries* said: "No act, carefully performed, from motives which the law recognizes as honest and upright, is punishable as a crime. And it has always been held that extortion proceeds only from a corrupt mind."[47] Wharton's widely read treatise on criminal law claimed that "both by statute and at common law, it is necessary that the taking should be willful and corrupt."[48]

Few cases examined the scope of what it meant to bribe a legislator, in part because there were so few convictions. One of the closest examinations of the scope of bribery and its relationship to corruption may appear in a libel case, in which the defendant brought forth extensive evidence of what it considered bribery in its libel defense. The *Detroit Evening News* wrote a damning article about Michigan state legislator James A. Randall, arguing that he inappropriately corrupted other members of the legislature by providing all kinds of inducements and entertainments, in forcing through a bill that would never have passed if the public alone were asked. Randall sued for libel and won, but on appeal the Michigan Supreme Court remanded the case because there was no direct evidence of a contractual exchange. The lower court, it held, appropriately instructed the jury that there was no evidence of bribery because the evidence consisted largely of Randall holding open house and providing liquor and food. "To give entertainments for the purpose of unduly influencing legislation is wholly bad in morals, but does not constitute the crime of bribery."[49] However, the jury could still conclude that the "entertainments were given by plaintiff for the purpose charged, viz. improperly influencing the legislature, the truth of which would be a complete defense to this portion of the article." In other words, the court held, the *Evening News* was well within its rights to call Randall corrupt, even if there was no evidence of criminal bribery. Like the framers of the Constitution, that court saw that corruption and quid pro quo bribery were different things and played different legal roles.

The libel court avoided the trickiest issues that came to dominate twenty-first-century bribery law: to constitute bribery, how specifically must one describe an official action or actions that one intends to influence? Does a gift alone constitute a bribe, if no official act is ever talked about? What if a gift is given to influence a whole suite of actions or an agenda, but neither the gift giver nor the official signals the desired actions or agenda? There were hints of these future debates. A Hawaii indictment failed, for instance, when a defendant gave a deputy sheriff $20, but the indictment did not state the acts the $20 were intended to influence.[50] On the other hand, a Texas court, addressing the bribery of a lawyer, noted that it is easy to define the scope of acts that executives or judicial officers might have before them but much harder in other cases—and therefore a Texas indictment need not allege with specificity the kinds of things a lawyer might do in response to a bribe, so long as it alleges that the bribe is intended to influence.[51]

That Texas court noted the most striking feature of nineteenth-century bribery law: "Prosecutions for bribery have not been frequent in our courts." What was true in Texas was true all over the country, and particularly true with regard to legislative officials.[52] In the rare conviction, when Tammany Hall's Boss William Tweed was convicted on corruption charges (after an initial hung jury), the court did not examine whether his activity was "corrupt" or not—there was ample evidence that he had taken a cut of publicly raised money in his role on the board of supervisors—but a divided court, in a lengthy opinion, held that the attorney general had the right to bring the action.[53] It had few American cases to call upon because similar cases were so rare.[54]

The lack of enforcement in the early years needs to be understood in terms of the much smaller role criminal law played in society.[55] Criminal anticorruption laws were particularly hard to prosecute in the political economy of the time. The wrongdoers—the briber and the bribed—had no incentive to complain. While a victim of a robbery might complain, the defrauded public was dispersed, with no identifiable victim who would drive the charge. Moreover, it likely took great courage to indict local politicians—who might be related to local prosecutors—using political bribery laws.

In his book *Bribes*, Judge Noonan details the dozens of cases of known bribery in which there were no criminal prosecutions, noting that although a handful of council members were prosecuted, major bribery cases were not subject to major bribery prosecution. He writes:

> Legal realists, understanding by "the law" the statutes actually applied, would have to conclude that no criminal law against the bribery of these high officers [Presidents, vice presidents, federal judges, members of the cabinet] was in force in the early years of the Republic, in the entire nineteenth century, or in the first quarter of the twentieth century. Over 140 years of American history elapsed before any one of this rank was criminally convicted as a bribetaker.[56]

Federal bribery laws mattered for a brief moment, largely because of the brave efforts of Kentucky native Benjamin Bristow. Bristow was a Republican reformer dedicated to breaking up the Klu Klux Klan and a strong supporter of African-American rights. He had been a Union Civil War general and was the nation's first solicitor general and the secretary of the Treasury under Ulysses Grant. In his tenure at the Treasury he discovered that the tax revenue from liquor was far below what would be expected. Bristow—without the knowledge of the president—set up sting operations and exposed a "whiskey ring" scheme involving hundreds of government agents, distillers, and shopkeepers who were defrauding the Treasury of millions of dollars. According to reports, over 110 people were convicted, but Grant was worried that Bristow was getting too close to his own administration and forced him to resign.

The Whiskey Ring prosecutions are important for how unusual they were. The country did not lack for bribery scandals, but when one looks at the most notorious corruption cases of the hundred years after the nation's founding—the XYZ affair in 1797–1798, the 1850 Galphin Affair, charges against Lincoln's secretary of war Simon Cameron, Crédit Mobilier in 1872, the dozens of other Ulysses Grant scandals—no one was convicted under criminal bribery laws. They resigned, fled the country, or simply soldiered on, but criminal bribery laws played more of a symbolic role, naming the behavior that was dubious instead of leading to prosecutions.

In 1906, political scientist George Henry Haynes published a popular book called *The Election of Senators*, carefully detailing all the arguments for and against direct election of senators, an issue of intense popular interest. Under the constitutional regime, senators were elected by state legislatures. Reformers advocating for direct election argued that the system then in place corrupted both the senators and the state legislatures, because candidates for Senate office would pledge money and promise offices to state legislators to secure support. Haynes reviewed the substantial evidence of bribery and corruption in the election of senators, including national scandals in seven states between 1890 and 1906 and ten Senate investigations into bribery by senators from California, Pennsylvania, Ohio, Kansas, Arkansas, and Montana. None of the investigations led to censure, although twice the accused senator resigned before action. These ten cases did not include the countless ones that never even made it to investigation. The Senate, according to Haynes, "has shown extreme reluctance to investigate such charges, and has bound itself by precedents which make not only the unseating of a member, but even the pursuit of a thoroughgoing investigation, practically impossible, except where the evidence of guilt is overwhelming and notorious."[57]

Haynes did not even consider or discuss whether there were any criminal investigations of senators. The default expectation appears to have been that, as in England, corrupt senators were a matter for the chamber to deal with, not criminal law. Or, to answer Sir John Eardley-Wilmot's question at the beginning of the chapter, there was a remedy for bribery—sort of. There was a remedy for judicial bribery and bribery of police officers, jurors, and voters. There were remedies for legislative bribery and the corruption of legislative officials, at least on the books. But, at least at the higher levels of government, that remedy rarely led to successful criminal prosecution and more often consisted of public shaming, failure at the polls, or nothing at all.

CHAPTER SIX

Railroad Ties

IN MID-NINETEENTH-CENTURY AMERICA, railroads signified growth, progress, and romance. They made America seem simultaneously bigger and smaller, promising transformation of individuals and each state of the union. They were also the engines, so to speak, of corruption. Railroad moguls sought state and federal support for incorporation, approval of track placement, cheap loans, subsidies, and land grants. Their demands were sometimes legitimate: without governmental backing, few private funders would have invested. But many railway projects were accompanied by allegations, often true, that legislators' favorable treatment of railroads came from conflicts of interest, not conviction.

During Reconstruction, lawmakers and superlatives came cheap. Union Pacific Railroad and Crédit Mobilier were discovered in what, according to the *Sun* newspaper, was "the most damaging exhibition of official and private villainy ever laid bare to the eyes of the world."[1] Congress had given the companies nearly $150 million—over $2 billion in today's dollars—ostensibly to pay for railroad services across the country. However, the appropriation was partly a sophisticated Yazoo scam, where the companies gave lawmakers stock to distribute among their colleagues, assuring that they would continue to subsidize the railroads and not investigate fraudulent accounting for expenses. Massachusetts Republican Oakes Ames was at the center of the scheme. He was deeply invested in Union Pacific and Crédit Mobilier, and sold stock to members of Congress, the vice president, and the Speaker of the House far below the market rate. When the bad books were exposed, Ames's defense was simply that the conflicts of interest he created had no impact. He hadn't needed to bribe anyone in government because they were already completely supportive. His attitude exemplified a Gilded Age split between popular and political meanings of corruption, but it didn't save him from censure. He was also the epitome of growing fear that the "gigantic associations which command great influence" threatened the liberty of the country. Congress investigated his activities, and in February 1873 Ames was formally reprimanded.[2] The offenses, the committee held, "were not violations of private rights, but were against the very life of a constitutional government by poisoning the fountain of legislation."[3] No criminal charges were ever brought.

The Crédit Mobilier scandal is now remembered as a symbol of corruption in the Gilded Age and for threatening the newly united country's faith in itself through a scandal that touched legislators from every party. But it should also be remembered as a monument to the weakness of criminal bribery laws, as explained in the previous chapter.

Instead, some of the most interesting legal discussions came when judges were faced with three choices, echoes of the three options facing Justice Marshall in the Yazoo case. Most courts did nothing, although one overturned a corrupt law, and the Supreme Court pretended to follow *Fletcher v. Peck* while actually creating a surprising new doctrine.

The Longest Case in Tennessee History

Mid-century Tennessee had a bad case of what was sometimes called "railroad fever." The state borrowed heavily in order to finance the building of railroads. The fever came back to haunt it in the early 1880s when Tennessee struggled with how to deal with a crushing state railroad debt held by northern bondholders. The state's political class disagreed on the best way to settle the debt. Republicans were generally in favor of paying it off, but Democrats literally split into two parties, the "low tax" Democratic Party and the "debt paying" Democratic Party, who ran against each other in the gubernatorial election of 1881. The division handed Alvin Hawkins, a Republican, a victory with 100,000 votes because the Democratic vote was so divided.[4] After Hawkins's election, a Republican bill was proposed to repay $27 million by issuing bonds at 3 percent. Given the politics of the Tennessee General Assembly, everyone assumed that the bill would not pass. The first time it was introduced, indeed it did fail as expected.

But then, to everyone's surprise, the debt repayment bill was reintroduced on April 5, 1881, at 11:30 a.m., and passed. The vote was big news, reported in the *New York Times* as "sudden as it was startling." A "scene of disorder ensued in both houses." The debt-paying people across the state rejoiced, and the low tax people denounced it. It was a "red letter day in Tennessee's history."[5] Why was everyone so surprised? Senator Smith had switched votes. He had been no fence-sitter, but was an avowed low tax man whose politics were tied to his pledge to the public to oppose any bonds. He had even told another senator that he would sooner "have his right arm cut off" before voting to pay off the debt. In case a missing arm was not vivid enough, he had sworn he would "live on potatoes and molasses before he'd do it."[6]

According to the low tax opponents, the only possible explanation for the changed vote was that Smith had been bribed. Several taxpayers sued, asking for the law to be declared invalid. As they argued, Smith's vote was suspect because "no new argument or fact addressed to his reason or light shed on his conscience, was presented to him which could have changed his convictions and absolved him from his pledges to his constituents." Smith changed his mind because he was "influenced to do so by the use of considerations other than reasons, or arguments to his judgment or conscience."[7]

They had evidence to support their claim. Smith had allegedly told a colleague he had been offered $15,000 to vote for the bill. Senator Barrett from another low tax district had allegedly asked a colleague about the ins and outs of stocks, long and short sales, and asked whether it would be wrong to engage in betting on legislation. Barrett had suspiciously asked "if he could resign in case an investigation would be made, or if he could avoid an investigation by resignation."[8] The lawsuit charged that Barrett bought the stock, voted for the bill, and also received $10,000. A third senator allegedly was given $5,000, but then he changed his mind, gave the money back, and voted against the bill.[9] The litigants claimed that a "powerful, active and efficient lobby" was charged with "persuading" the legislature to change its position.

The lawsuit led to violence.[10] The *New York Times* reported that in the state Senate after the trial on the facts, Senator Smith stood up and called the lead attorney, John Vertrees, a "liar, and asked for an investigation. . . . Vertrees was within 10 feet of Smith when the latter called him a liar, and immediately all eyes were turned in that direction, but no disturbance was made."[11] People were anxious enough about a fight that they called for "five stalwart policemen" to be present in the Senate chamber. Smith appeared "somewhat excited." He sat down to read a paper—or at least claims he was about to—when Vertrees walked up to him, "spat in his face, drew a revolver, and as Smith rose, fired at him." That was Smith's account. According to friends of Vertrees, Smith was drawing a pistol. The first bullet missed; the second stuck in his shoulder. The shooting was not fatal—the bullet was removed and Smith recovered. In the wake of the shooting, Vertrees's friends followed him around, wanting to be available if any further dispute erupted. The *Louisville Courier-Journal*, which followed the trial closely, said that "affairs look decidedly warlike."[12]

The legal issue that flowed from these wars and cross-allegations was less violent but equally difficult. Putting aside the question of whether anyone was bribed, should evidence of bribery invalidate a law? It was the Yazoo moment for Tennessee. The railway kickbacks were different than the land scams of Yazoo in the evidence presented, and in the fact that there were at least some bribery laws available for willing prosecutors to take on Smith and Bartlett. But in essence this was a state law replay of *Fletcher*, with state judges who did not like the *Fletcher* precedent but were bound by it. As in Yazoo, the public stakes were high. An attorney said in a speech twenty years later to the Tennessee

Bar Association: "Perhaps no case has been before our courts in which the whole people took so lively an interest. The question had been so long in controversy that the position of every public man, including the Judges, as to whether the settlement was a wise one, was well known."[13]

Court watchers likely guessed that the law would be upheld. Three of the judges were "state credit" men, and inclined to support such a bond; two others were "low tax" judges, and inclined against it. Justice Robert McFarland said: "No case of greater importance, I suppose, has ever been presented to this court." They had to decide two issues. First, whether bribery in the process made what appeared to be a law, not a law. Second, whether the law was unconstitutional on its face because the bond measure would tie the hands of the sovereign state of Tennessee for up to ninety-nine years.

Judicial opinions in cases about the law of corruption are notoriously long, overwrought, and anguished. Judges and justices disagree about the basics of what corruption means, who should police it, and whether it is even a constitutionally weighty concept. The longest cases in U.S. Supreme Court history involve corruption. *Buckley v. Valeo*—the longest Supreme Court case, about the right of Congress to fight corruption through limiting campaign expenditures—was 76,000 words, or a little longer than *The Catcher in the Rye*. The second longest—*McConnell v. FEC*, about the right of Congress to pass a suite of laws governing election-related spending—ran to 70,000 words, or a little longer than *The Sun Also Rises*. They are long in part because more justices write separately than in other opinions. And of course, the recent notorious iteration of corruption and democracy discourse, *Citizens United*, ran to 48,000 words, "or about the length of *The Great Gatsby*."[14] The case deciding these issues in Tennessee, *Lynn v. Polk*, was no exception. It became the longest case ever published by the Tennessee Supreme Court, about the length of Faulkner's *As I Lay Dying*.

All five justices wrote separate opinions. Justice Turney found the law unconstitutional on the grounds that it fundamentally violated the legislative sovereignty to bind future iterations of the government. One legislature should not be allowed to "exceed the length of its own life in its appropriations of public moneys." Instead, each legislature should only be allowed to "provide for the contingencies of the two years intervening between stated sessions." To do otherwise would be to force the state into a position where, in "prosperity or adversity, in peace or war, in health or pestilence, in plenty or famine, still nothing can be drawn from the treasury until the creditor has been paid annually eight-tenths of a million dollars." The current legislature was actually taking sovereignty away from the future, because it in effect put sovereignty in the hands of federal jurisdiction, because of the impairments of contracts. The logic, in essence, was that because of the ban on the impairment of contracts between the state and private parties (a ban created by the Yazoo case), a contract between the state and private parties that reached into the future was unconstitutional. He refused to address the question of bribery, finding it unnecessary to the case. However, the argument Turney made was so unusual and novel—and would make it impossible for states to do almost anything involving promises to repay—that it is hard to believe that the bribery charges, or the judge's own politics, did not influence the case. The opinion by Justice Freeman is what really makes this case noteworthy. It is the most thoroughly judicial exploration I have found of the argument that judges should overturn corruptly passed law. Freeman framed the question in contract law terms—much as Justice Marshall had, but with a different result. Could a contract procured by bribery be enforced against the people of the state? In other words, could a corruptly created contract create a "complete and executed contract; and the taxpayer, on whom the liability to pay and bear the burden of the contract thus imposed, has no remedy, and no possible means of legal redress or legal help against the threatened wrong to be inflicted on him"? If such a corrupt contract could be enforced, it would mean the courts could provide no meaningful remedy to an obvious wrong. Such a rule would require "our own people" to "bow the lip of honor in the dust." The public would have to take the seal of the state to a law that came from corruption. Law, he argued, could not be party to that transaction. Citizens had no other meaningful remedy when their representatives had been bribed. Criminal law convictions after the fact would do nothing, because the state would still be bound. The rule in *Fletcher v. Peck* about the impairment of contracts also would forbid the legislature from changing the deal. Finally, elections—kicking out the bribed representatives—would not do much. The result would be the same. He called it "almost farcical" to "talk of inflicting the penalty of non-election on a member who has ten or fifteen thousand dollars corruptly in his pocket, for his vote. He could well afford to stay at home on these terms." The people are left with the burden of corruption. Comparing it to a forged check, he said it is not enough to put the forger in jail—the victim should still be able to get the money back.

Therefore, as he put it, to believe that bribery has no impact on the enforceability of a law would be to say either that bribery is a legitimate way to procure passage of a law or that there is a wrong for which there is no meaningful remedy. Later criminal prosecutions of bribery would do nothing for the people of the state who would still be bound to the contract procured through bribery. Instead, judges should refuse to enforce corrupt legislative acts.

One of the great problems with this kind of judicial review of corruption is that identified by Marshall: how can one determine what "caused" a bill to pass, and what constitutes a corrupt motive behind a law? Is corruption defined by criminal law statutes, civil law statutes, the Constitution, or a general sense of corrupt action? If this is the standard, how is a court to judge between two legislatures, one revoking the other, both claiming the prior body to be corrupt? Moreover, even if there were a standard, wouldn't the argument that a state statute could be overturned on corruption grounds lead to endless litigation? Imagine the discovery process, and the way in which one might have to structure pleading standards, if it were possible to plead corruption to undo legislation. Wouldn't it become endless?

Seventy years later, however, Freeman was living in a different era, in which bribery was more practically criminalized. He directly engaged the question. The problem with motive, which Justice Freeman acknowledged, is that it is an impossible thing to ascertain if understood in an internal, psychological sense. "What is the motive that prompts an act? It may be defined to be, the last and controlling impulse that impels to the act, or all the impulses combined that so prompt. If this be correct, then I say motive is internal, subjective, to use the language of philosophy, a thing we can not ascertain—can only approximate at best, or infer from conduct." This, he concluded—agreeing with

Marshall—is beyond the capacity of the judiciary. However, one can nonetheless determine whether an exchange took place, and whether the exchange satisfied the key elements of bribery.

A bribe, he says, might be taken for all kinds of good and moral reasons—helping an indigent family, loving one's wife and child. It might be taken to pay off a debt that a "brother or a son" had taken on. It might be taken when one is already sure of voting in one direction. But regardless of the reason, it is still a bribe. A bribery indictment would depend upon whether there was motive to exchange and influence, not whether the motive was from a corrupt source. In criminal law, "he is guilty of the entire felony defined by the statute, regardless of all the motives that stirred his heart, and controlled his act, and prompted what he did." The question is not of motive, but of fact.

Freeman portrayed the bribery as a fundamental process failure. A law that is passed because of bribery is like a law passed when votes were miscounted. A law born in bribery is not a law because it was based on an illegal process. Any private contract based on fraud or bribery is always void: it would be strange, wrote Justice Freeman, if that principle applied in every case of public contract but not in this one. That would lead to an exception to the law of contracts for contracts between the state and corrupting agents.

Freeman's approach, though grounded in contract and criminal law, necessarily involved a vision of the nature of legislative power, just as Marshall's did. Representatives, he argued, "are required, by the very character given them in that instrument and the very nature of the thing to be done, to act freely and of choice for the people. They are solemnly sworn 'to vote without fear, favor, affection, partiality or prejudice.'" If a representative sells his vote, he "vote[s] under the compulsion of a contract, corrupt and forbidden, and thus ceases to be the representative of his people, and becomes the agent and tool of his purchaser." Such an action is an essential abandonment of legislative duties in the Constitution. It creates a shelter for corrupt actions.

The fear that bribery could undermine political society itself drives the opinion: "All history is full of the lesson, that Republics fall from this fruitful source of decay, that saps their foundation more surely than by all other means, and I would guard my own State from its fearful power for ruin."

But what about the judiciary usurping the legislative role? Justice Freeman argued that separation of powers (and functions) cannot mean that the legislature has the right to be bribed. Instead, he examined the different roles of the different branches of government and argued that the core function and power of the legislative department is to enact laws. Interference with a coordinate branch would exist if the judiciary were to decree laws. However, reviewing process is the judiciary's job. The examination of corruption and bribery is merely part of the general judicial role of deciding upon the "validity of the act when done, or contracts resulting from it."

According to Freeman, judicial usurpation was limited by the fact that the judiciary can act only when cases are brought before it for its consideration. The legislature might still be able to meet again, sell their votes again, and that "body would be perfectly free to engage in as much corruption as it chose," until a case was brought. But when a case is brought, it is the job of judges to declare a law's legitimacy. If there were a parallel felony case brought against Smith, with an indictment for bribery, then it is clear that the judiciary would hear the proof behind the charge. The prohibition of bribery of the members of the legislature makes no sense without this; therefore, the inquiry into whether there was bribery in this case is no more interfering than an inquiry in a criminal case. A felony charge against a legislator would force the judge to "go close even to the bleeding heart, to prevent the approach of the eating cancer of corruption and bribery to our legislative halls," but it would be the job of the judiciary to follow that charge, as close as it cut to the heart of the coordinate branch.

The case, in the end, was not decided by Freeman. Instead, the swing vote providing the majority came from Justice McFarland: McFarland was allied with the state credit politicians, and people thought he would vote to uphold the law. He also engaged in an anguished, extensive discourse on the relationship of the courts to corruption. However, he concluded that courts simply did not have the power to make difficult determinations of what constituted legislative corruption and what did not. McFarland worried that if the court could conclude that the legislature was corrupt, the legislature could make the same charge about the court. The problem, as he saw it, is that no branch can be free of corruption, but it cannot be the case that one branch can be investigated for corruption (the legislative) while the judicial cannot.[15]

Instead, each institution must be responsible for its own integrity within that department, and the only means of checking integrity are the structural means provided for removal. Members of the General Assembly can be impeached or thrown out through election. But as a matter of constitutional design, no individual branch should be able to "sit in judgment upon the conduct of the other." If courts could set aside laws, they could set aside executive pardons, "upon the ground that they were corruptly granted." That, in turn, might lead to governors refusing to enforce judicial orders because they would deem them "corruptly rendered." From such a state of corruption investigation would result "collision and conflict, confusion and chaos."

This might be different if there were a clear standard of corruption, but, as McFarland saw it, there was no such clarity. The judiciary could just use the civil standard—that corruption was more likely than not—but it would lead to the judiciary overturning all kinds of bills. Moreover, in many instances there was some inappropriate influence on both sides of a piece of legislation. In effect, it would undermine the core democratic conceit—that representatives make policy.

Lynn v. Polk, unlike *Fletcher v. Peck*, had no significant impact, except in the short term in Tennessee. Even in its minor features it was an outlier. It is interesting as an artifact, as it shows a path not taken in corruption law in the nineteenth century. But a century later, the seeds of Freeman's concurrence reappear in the writings of the law and economics scholars in a different form: a suggestion that all governmental acts should be subject to a political process review and should be treated skeptically, as likely products of a corrupt process.

The Table for Corruptibles

The final great railroad corruption case of the nineteenth century came out of Illinois. The Illinois Central, employer of both Stephen Douglas and Abraham Lincoln, dominated railroad politics and was arguably the line that led to Chicago becoming the railroad capital of the world. Illinois Central split the state down the middle, north to south.[16] Its growth was heavily dependent on public aid: in 1850 it received over 2.5 million acres of land from the state, land that had been given for that purpose from President Millard Fillmore. By 1856 it was the longest railroad in the world. A spur into Chicago grew into a hub, and the largest building in Chicago became the Illinois Central's Grand Central Station.

As the railroad grew, so did its needs—and, apparently, its greed. As in Tennessee, railroad projects were particularly prone to corruption of their great promise, the concentrated capital available to them, their innovation in purchasing political power, and confusion around land values. In 1869, Illinois Central hired Alonzo Mack, a former state senator, to represent its efforts to get the state to sell its highly coveted lakefront land and the submerged acreage around it. Mack was a powerful lobbyist with connections in every corner of the statehouse, and he had a reputation for using any mode of persuasion available to him. One newspaper correspondent described Mack holding court at the popular Leland Hotel, center of political and social activities for the statehouse. In the hotel, according to the visitor, there was a table for ladies, a table for strangers, a table for honest men, and a table for corruptibles. Mack presided over the table for corruptibles. "When a person leaves the 'honest men's' table and goes over to that of the 'corruptibles,' it is an intimation that he is ready to listen to proposals," the correspondent wrote.[17]

Whether through bribery or persuasion, Alonzo Mack did his job well for Illinois Central, pushing a bill through the House that would force Chicago to sell over 1,000 acres of submerged property for $800,000. An opponent of the bill immediately cried foul: "Various reports are in circulation concerning supposed corruption of members of the General Assembly."[18] A committee was authorized to determine whether any improper influence had been offered or used, but no committee was ever convened.

The bill passed the Senate the next week, and the governor vetoed it. While the governor did not directly charge that members had been bribed, he gave the reason for his veto as the low cost of the sale and the questions of "policy and good faith" surrounding it. The land, according to the governor's sources, was worth at least $2,600,000, not $800,000. Mack, however, had foreseen the possibility of the veto and had already collected the necessary votes in the state legislature to override it.

The bill's opponents claimed that legislators had been bribed. They claimed that newspapers had been given $75,000 not to oppose the project and that votes were sold for $25 to $20,000. They pointed to the fact that on a particularly tumultuous day before the Senate vote, Mr. Mack was seen "running frantically" between offices, playing such an obvious role that the speaker of the Senate asked the sergeant at arms to enforce the rule that prohibited former legislators from approaching the "bar of the Senate." Mack slunk away from the chamber.

The Chicago papers were full of allegations of swindles, steals, and corruption. There were broad claims of "vast sums of money" that had been used to persuade lawmakers, including alleged payments of legal fees—which might not have been legal fees—to legislators or those affiliated with them. For instance, one senator alleged that another changed his lakefront vote because of a direct payment to his law partner.[19] Every scholar who has studied the case has concluded that at least some payoffs helped explain the vote, if not to the degree the opponents alleged.

While the railroad took steps to exercise ownership over the property—spending over $200,000 developing the outer harbor in the first four years—questions about the act's legitimacy remained. Four years after the act's passage, charges of corruption led to popular demand to overturn it. As one senator argued, "the act should be wiped off the statute books as a rebuke to the corruption by which it was passed." The legislature had been full of lawyers on the railroad's retainer, and the Illinois press was bribed and muzzled. "Inequity presided over the conception of the scheme, fraud was present at its birth, and honesty would rejoice at its death. This was worse than Crédit Mobilier, salary steal, and all the inequities perpetrated by Congress." In 1873 Mack was dead, and repeal of the lakefront bill succeeded with an astounding thirty-one votes to eleven.[20]

While the railroad company failed to stop the repeal, they were confident that the repeal had been illegal, just as it had been in *Fletcher v. Peck*: land, contracted away, could not be taken back again. Illinois Central argued, using this logic, that the repeal act of 1873 was a nullity. Several years of litigation followed. When the case—*Illinois Central RR v. Illinois*—finally got to the Supreme Court in 1892, *Fletcher v. Peck* appeared to give the railroads the better case.[21]

However, the Court managed to refuse the railroad relief while neither overturning *Fletcher* nor distinguishing it on technical grounds. Instead, the Court relied upon an old and (then) rarely invoked doctrine called the public trust doctrine. The case held that the state, as sovereign, owns certain lands that it essentially cannot sell. The lands are held in "trust" for the public so that they enjoy them "freed from the obstruction or interference of private parties." A sale of these lands is prima facie void. They are the public's and cannot be sold unless the sale promotes the public interest or does not impair the public interest in the remaining land.

The deep logic of the case itself is not entirely clear, even in the way in which it applied the public trust doctrine. Was it following the first option rejected by Marshall in *Fletcher* and adopted by Freeman in Tennessee: that the grant of land was void in the first place? Or the second choice: that the repeal of the land grant was an illegal impairment of contracts? On one hand, it suggested that the land grant was void: "A grant of all the lands under the navigable waters of a State has never been adjudged to be within the legislative power." But in a later section Justice Field wrote that the grant "of the kind is necessarily revocable" and the trust "can be resumed at any time."

The muddled logic of the decision likely arose from the problem of adjudicating corruption. The Court mentioned that the "circumstances attending the passage of the act through the legislature were on the hearing the subject of much criticism." But it noted the divergence between the initial stated purpose of the act and the content of the act. It was initially designed to "enable the city of Chicago to enlarge its harbor" but "during the passage of the Act its purport was changed. Instead of providing for the cession of the submerged lands to the city, it provided for a cession of them to the railroad company." But without public trust, the Court seemed stuck in the trap laid by *Fletcher*. You'll recall that according to Marshall in that decision, contracts with the state are like time's arrow and go only in one direction. Political bodies cannot reverse those same acts even if they were corruptly passed.

But the *Illinois Central* Court clearly wanted to reverse those acts, or at least allow for the state to do so. As one commentator argued, it ignored the Marshall logic: "*Fletcher v. Peck* was in effect overruled in *Illinois Central*."[22] In this light, the case represents neither the substantive review suggested by the concurrence in *Lynn v. Polk* nor the agnosticism suggested by Justice Marshall in *Fletcher v. Peck*, but rather a broad grant of authority to the legislature to do what it will—at least when water is concerned. In this view, *Illinois Central* is an endorsement of the "mere power" which Marshall derided in *Fletcher v. Peck*. Legislative sovereignty—the ability to enact the general will—trumps other concerns. At least in a limited way, *Illinois Central* appears as a repudiation of both *Fletcher* and *Lynn v. Polk*, and it places the task of defining and punishing corruption squarely in the legislative branch.

Illinois Central remained an oddity for nearly a century, until it was revived as a centerpiece of modern conservation law. In 1970 Joseph Sax wrote an article called "The Public Trust Doctrine in Natural Resources Law."[23] He called *Illinois Central* the "lodestar" of the doctrine, the embodiment of old Roman and common law ideas about the nature of public waters. Sax argued that the doctrine should enable courts to scrutinize particular kinds of legislative behavior—that around water resources—more rigorously than others. He only lightly mentioned the "egregious" nature of the case, touched upon the Illinois state legislature repenting its earlier actions, but recast it as a natural resources case instead of a corruption case.[24] Sax's article has been very influential. While subject to much criticism, he succesfully used the old language to change the debate about environmental obligations of the state—at least as a rhetorical tool, the public trust is now used as a premise, a theory about public obligations to care for ecological resources.

Thanks to the railroads—their ambition to seize political power—we got a marker of impotence in the Credit Mobilier, a wonderful disquisition on power in *Lynn v. Polk*, and the *Illinois Central RR v. Illinois* decision. Railroad behavior was egregious enough that courts repeatedly had to consider whether the public has something like a quasi-constitutional right to be free from corruption. They never answered yes, but they also never answered no. That same question started quietly reemerging in the late twentieth century in a surprising place: from law and economics scholars suspicious of politics itself, interested in using the Constitution's takings clause as a means of reviewing self-interested legislative behavior.

CHAPTER SEVEN

The Forgotten Law of Lobbying

LOBBYING POSES A CENTRAL CHALLENGE to the liberal political vision. Information and reason are among the highest values in the liberal tradition, and lobbying involves the production and communication of information and reason.[1] When viewed in this light, it should be not only protected but elevated. On the other hand, the social function of lobbying is to take money and turn it into political power. Lobbyists are hired as alchemists, to turn money into power through the production of information and the careful use of influence. That they do it within the rhetoric of reason (instead of through brute force) may be no special comfort. Where it is effective, lobbying means that the full power of government shifts itself to serve the social goals of those who can afford lobbyists. Lobbying, at its worst, enables the extraction of public resources from the public.

Part of the puzzle is in figuring where to place lobbying—as good civic behavior, or corrupt anti-civic behavior—derives from the fact that lobbyists have multiple functions. One is information sharing, enabling the wisdom of the car dealer to flow into the office of the member of Congress. But lobbyists are also information gatherers and spend a great deal of their time assessing opportunities, creating information asymmetries for citizens. Furthermore, they enable nontransactional relationships that bear all the hallmarks of transactional relationships but manage to avoid the legal limits that come along with explicit deals. Good lobbyists figure out what political candidates need (typically campaign contributions, but sometimes jobs, help on loans, or direct payments). They then determine what their clients want: sometimes stopping a law or regulation, sometimes changing tax laws, sometimes receiving a subsidy. They then figure out how to enable a series of actions that do not operate like quid pro quo exchanges but allow for the flow from client to candidate, and from politician to client, while taking a fee for enabling the flow, and obscuring the transaction-like elements by submerging them in other, nontransactional elements.

Many modern scholars argue that lobbying is "vital to representative democracy" because it helps gives elected officials information that they need to be able to develop laws, assess impacts, and understand how different groups will react.[2] Lobbyists make government more informed and effective, and they "illuminate the practical consequences of proposed government conduct by ensuring that the insights and professional expertise of a particular business or industry become part of the deliberative process."[3] These scholars argue that lobbyists fill a gap in the information ecosystem and produce badly needed, valuable, and underproduced public information. The content that lobbyists share is "information [that] is likely not only to be underproduced in the private market, but also to be insufficiently protected by the political system."[4] At any rate, they argue, it is too difficult to police the line between acceptable and unacceptable political behavior. The inevitable overreading in line-drawing might implicate and dissuade protected speech.

But lobbying was not always treated this way. One of the most interesting public debates about lobbying and its role in political society took place in Atlanta in the middle of July at the Georgia Constitutional Convention of 1877. The draft constitution made lobbying a crime. Supporters argued that lobbying was taking over their statehouse and corrupting the government. Lobbyists had been paid to use personal influence to pass private legislation, or "private bills":

> The legacy of the public domain . . . was bartered away to thieves and speculators, who have amassed fortunes in this way. . . . These bills were carried through by men who were employed to work in the galleries, at boarding houses, on the streets, in gambling saloons and other disreputable places—and when one thing failed to secure favor another was used.[5]

The representative body had become a set of auctions for public resources, to be sold to private individuals. "I know my good old state is groaning under a debt of millions put upon her by such methods," the lobbying opponent argued. While good men might from time to time engage in lobbying, that does not mean it is good for society, and the question is a societal one, not just an individual one.

However, the concern went further than private laws. Taxes, one man argued, are, in their last analysis, "dug from the bowels of the earth." The earth itself—all the natural resources—were owned by the public and being stolen by lobbyists using influence to take the natural resources of the state to line their own pockets. Lobbyists cost the state money. Of the $11 million in debt, one proponent estimated that a million was currently in the pockets of lobbyists, who had charged money in order to serve private interests.

> What is our experience? . . . what are the facts? . . . Go to the treasury department, and see for yourselves! . . . Lobbying through the legislature acts injurious to Georgia. . . . It is a matter of disgrace and humiliation to us that Georgians profess to be lobbyists—hang round the halls of legislation—and those who have the money can control even the legislature of Georgia. The people of Georgia have sent us here to put a stop to it and to guard and protect the treasury.[6]

Opponents of the lobbying provision pointed out that all kinds of worthwhile laws were championed by good men who were paid for their services. Lobbyists were necessary intermediaries because most people with an interest or idea were "incompetent" to legislate or advocate for legislation. Members of the public needed to have a right to "send parties here as their agents, or lobbyists, or whatever you may call them, for the purposes of advancing the interests of their community." Without such a procedure, people would be unable to communicate their desires.

Moreover, a lobbying ban was a philosophical impossibility. As the opponent argued, a lot of our good ideas come from people who are interested in the outcome of legislation. Since one could not outlaw self-interest, outlawing lobbying seemed to merely cut out a particular class of self-interest. Finally, many good men were what one might call "lobbyists." What was worse, criminalizing lobbying would cast a pall of suspicion over citizens who wanted to push for legislation or even come to the halls of the Georgia legislature to watch the procedure.

The opposition failed. Georgia's 1877 constitution included this provision: "Lobbying is declared to be a crime, and the General Assembly shall enforce this provision by suitable penalties."[7] The next year Georgia passed legislation that defined lobbying. It included any personal solicitation that was "not addressed solely to the judgment of the legitimacy of the bill," or in which there was misrepresentation of the interest of the party pushing the action, *or* in which someone was employed by a party with an interest in the outcome of the legislation. It did not include those services that were "of a character" to "reach the reason of legislators," such as drafting legislation, drafting bills, taking testimony, collecting facts, preparing arguments, and submitting them orally or in writing. Lobbying was punishable by a prison term of up to five years.[8]

The majority of the Georgia convention represented the mainstream view of a different time in American history. Throughout the country, from the early 1830s through the early 1930s the sale of personal influence was treated as a civic wrong in the eyes of the law. A citizen did not have a personal right to pay someone else to press his or her legislative agenda. Nor did anyone have a right to be paid to use personal influence for legislation. Paid lobbying was looked down upon, criminalized in some cases, and treated as against public policy.

I use the criminal law in Georgia as an example of the ethos, but criminal law played a minor role. Instead, lobbying was policed almost entirely by civil law. Virtually all of the cases dealing with lobbying were contract cases, with courts deciding whether or not to enforce contracts for "lobbying" services. Typically, there was no investigation into whether the underlying activity was illegal (as a criminal law matter) or not: in many states it was not. Courts would simply declare lobbying contracts invalid. As Supreme Court justice Field wrote, "all agreements for pecuniary considerations to control the . . . ordinary course of legislation are void as against public policy."[9] A popular contracts hornbook with repeated publications in the late nineteenth and early twentieth century said:

> What are known as "lobbying contracts" . . . fall within this class of illegal agreements. Any agreement to render services in procuring legislative action, either by congress or by a state legislature or by a municipal council, by personal solicitation of the legislators or other objectionable means, is contrary to the plainest principles of public policy, and is void.[10]

The contract law of lobbying represented something like common law of contract law and political morality, enforced by all courts.

Unscrupulous Agents

The word *lobbyist* was first used in the beginning of the nineteenth century as paid influencers started to hang around the lobbies of legislative buildings and hotels, using indirect and direct means to serve their clients. Lobbyists included "peddlers of personal influence, propagandists, or amateurs promoting causes in which they sincerely believe."[11] Many early influence sellers were lawyers. Some were reporters. They would make money through selling a blend of services related to legislative actions: drafting bills, preparing research, and personally attempting to influence lawmakers. Sometimes lobbyists would bribe lawmakers; other times they would identify and enable legislative trades. The big lobbyists were associated with bondholders and railroads: the railroads were interested in land grants and the bondholders were interested in states and cities issuing bonds to cover enormous postwar debt.

The first case in which a court refused to enforce lobby contracts using the language of "lobbying" was likely *Harris v. Roof* in 1851.[12] The question as the court put it was the right of a "lobbyagent" to enforce a contract. An old man hired Matchin (a young man who later married the man's granddaughter) to go to Albany and get compensation from the government for an interest in land he said that he had gotten over fifty years earlier. Matchin agreed to try to get the claims in return for an agreed-upon amount. The two had a falling out, and the young man asked to be paid for the work he had done. The older man refused. This led to court, and a heated exchange about the value of what had been done. Matchin presented evidence that he had talked to a committee, met and spoken with members, and spent money on traveling to and from Albany. There were several witnesses who testified to the value of his work and his presence at the statehouse. The older man called witnesses to show that he had not really gone to Albany and had been fairly ineffective.

The court, hearing this evidence, decided not to settle the matter on the question presented—whether Matchin had done his job and fulfilled his contract—because the kind of contract itself was outside of public policy. According to the decision, all citizens have a right to petition the legislature and present documents accompanying that petition. Putting those documents together and planning may cost something, and all citizens have the right to pay for those preparations. However, "all petitions go to a committee through the house."

According to the court, every member of every legislative body has a duty to give the "proper and necessary attention to the business before it" and "always have truth and justice before their eyes." It would interfere with this vision of representative duties to hold that "the employment of individuals to visit and importune the members, is necessary to obtain justice. Such practices would have a tendency to prevent free, honorable and correct deliberation and action of this most important branch of sovereignty."

With little American precedent, the court recognized it had to improvise. "Very few cases similar to this, or bearing any analogy thereto, are to be found in our law books; and it is to be hoped ever will be, for the best of reasons." The court drew upon the general rule against champerty for its logic, as well as its sense of political theory. Champerty means that a party to a lawsuit agrees to pay a lawyer a percentage of whatever is won in a lawsuit. In common law this was generally illegal.[13]

Around the same time, the federal government passed its own lobbying law. In 1852 Congress prohibited anyone who worked for a newspaper "who shall be employed as an agent to prosecute any claim pending before Congress" from being on the House floor. Several newspapers were funded in order to support or oppose parties that wealthy individuals found favorable or distasteful. A few years later, a committee was charged with examining whether money was offered to members to make them vote for or against bills.[14]

That same vision grounded the Supreme Court decision in *Marshall v. Baltimore & Ohio Railroad Company* a few years later.[15] Faced with evidence that the plaintiff, Marshall, had been promised a contingent fee if he could secretly secure the votes needed to pass legislation, the Court held that the contract was void as against public policy. It explained itself this way:

> Legislators should act from high considerations of public duty. Public policy and sound morality do therefore imperatively require that courts should put the stamp of their disapprobation on every act, and pronounce void every contract the ultimate or probable tendency of which would be to sully the purity or mislead the judgments of those to whom the high trust of legislation is confided.

On the one hand, the Court held, there is an "undoubted right" of all persons to make their claims and arguments personally, or through a lawyer, in front of legislative committees. But any agents they hired would need to disclose their true incentives. The secrecy surrounding the contract necessarily invalidated it. Moreover, the lure of high profit combined with secrecy otherwise creates a "direct fraud on the public." Legislatures had an obligation to the whole, and a court should not subsidize, through the enforcement of contracts, the opportunity for interested and "unscrupulous agents" to influence policy. Furthermore, the practice corrupts the agents themselves.

The lure of profit undermines the citizen who in turn undermines the country:

> He is soon brought to believe that any means which will produce so beneficial a result to himself are "proper means"; and that a share of these profits may have the same effect of quickening the perceptions and warming the zeal of influential or "careless" members in favor of his bill. The use of such means and such agents will have the effect to subject the State governments to the combined capital of wealthy corporations, and produce universal corruption, commencing with the representative and ending with the elector. Speculators in legislation, public and private, a compact corps of venal solicitors, vending their secret influences, will infest the capital of the Union and of every State, till corruption shall become the normal condition of the body politic, and it will be said of us as of Rome— "*omne Romae venale.*"

Marshall involved a mishmash of reasons for invalidating the contract—the contingency fee and the commitment in the contracting documents to secrecy among them—and this blend of reasons made it unclear whether contracts for influence would be disfavored generally or only when these other features existed.

The 1855 New York case of *Rose v. Truax*,[16] which became one of the most cited authorities for the principle that lobbying contracts should not be enforced, also involved secrecy and a contingency fee. In that case the parties agreed that the lobbyist would "use his influence, efforts and labor in procuring the passage of a law by the said legislature, having for its object relief to the undersigned." In exchange, he was promised 10 percent of the amount of money received. The key holding of *Rose*, which made it particularly powerful, regarded the legal elements of the contract. The court held that it was impossible to sift apart the contract and separate the legal from the illegal elements. While there was evidence that some of what the lawyer did in this case was pure professional preparation, work which could have otherwise been lawfully compensated, the agreement to use influence to pass a law rendered the other parts of the agreement entirely void.

The scope and meaning of these cases was clarified in *Trist v. Child*,[17] which made clear that paid personal influence was against public policy even when a lawyer performed the services, when the person purchasing the services might otherwise be without ability to influence, and even when it was not done secretly.

The Old Man and the Court

In 1866 an old man, too weak to travel to Washington himself, began a journey that would lead to the Supreme Court's most explicit pronouncement on the role of lobbying in political society. Mr. N. P. Trist hired a lawyer to go to Congress and demand payment for an eighteen-year-old debt. He claimed—apparently with good reason—that the United States owed him money for helping to negotiate the Treaty of Guadalupe Hidalgo in 1848. He hired Linus Child, a Boston lawyer, to represent him. Trist agreed to pay Child 25 percent of whatever he secured. In 1871, after Child and his son and partner, L. M.

Child, made visits to Congress and wrote letters and made arguments proving the claim, Congress appropriated the sum of $14,559 to Trist. After the lawyer successfully persuaded Congress of the value of his claim, the old man's son refused to pay the lawyer. Child sued him for the money owed. Trist's defense was based on the logic of *Marshall*—the lobbying contract was void as against public policy. The courts, he argued, had no business in enforcing something so corrupt.

The case was—and remains—so interesting because at stake was lobbying itself, not just underhanded lobbying. Unlike in *Marshall* or *Rose*, there was no allegation of secrecy. Instead, it seemed like a straightforward, aboveboard claim where a lawyer was hired to do something that an old man could not do. If the court was going to invalidate this contract, all contracts to lobby were clearly at risk.

One could hardly imagine a more sympathetic context for enforcing a lobby contract; this was the constitutional test of the logic of *Harris*. Child had been "open, fair, and honorable." There was no evidence of anything suspicious: there was no evidence of secret collusion, or payments or promises to members of Congress. The age and inability to travel of the client made it seem he could not prosecute his claim without terrible hardship. If there was any right to petition the government, ought it not extend to the aged, who might need to hire someone on their behalf? Child argued that Trist had a right to personally petition Congress, and that this right must mean the right to hire an agent to petition on his behalf.

The Court sided with Trist. It concluded that the sale of influence itself, whether or not accompanied by payments or suspicious behavior, was a civic wrong. The Court addressed the contingent nature of the claim—the "pecuniary interest of the agent at stake" made it "contrary to the plainest principles of public policy." The contingency made it more likely to "inflame" the avarice, making it a worse problem, but the core problem was the practice of paying someone else to make one's arguments to people in authority, which threatened to undermine the moral fabric of civic society. The practice would have the tendency to corrode public ethics indirectly and to enable exchanges. The members of Congress, who might be offered something (directly or indirectly) in exchange for political action, might be more likely to forget their obligations.

The Court was concerned about corrupting citizens as well. Citizens' virtue is the "foundation of a republic," the Court explained. Citizens have an important public office to fill, as "they are at once sovereigns and subjects." While public servants are obliged to be "animated in the discharge of their duties solely by considerations of right, justice, and the public good," citizens have a "correlative duty" to "exhibit truth, frankness, and integrity" in their conversations "with those in authority." According to the Court, "Any departure from the line of rectitude in such cases, is not only bad in morals, but involves a public wrong."

The citizens in this case are *both* Child and Trist. The lobbyist's own integrity was threatened by the practice, because he was paid to represent political views he did not hold. This is unlike a lawyer-client relationship, because in general in a lawyer-client relationship, the lawyer has no separate, independent civic relationship to the private matter. In a lobbyist-client relationship, the lobbyist, by virtue of being a citizen, has a distinct relationship to what he himself might believe. He is selling his own citizenship, or one of the obligations of his own citizenship, for a fee. In this sense, agreeing to work for pay on political issues is more akin to selling the personal right to vote than selling legal skills. Lobbyists have a separate and distinct obligation to pursue public ends, and while they may be allowed to express self-interest in the vote, they have, as citizens, an obligation to honor and love the equality of the political system.

As in *Marshall*, the Court treated lobbying in terms of its general effects—what the Court in *Marshall* called the potential for a "compact corps of venal solicitors"—not just its individual ones. A general acceptance of lobbying would lead to a corrupt culture. Lobbying paid by individuals could not be allowed because it would lead to lobbying paid by corporations:

> If any of the great corporations of the country were to hire adventurers who make market of themselves in this way, to procure the passage of a general law with a view to the promotion of their private interests, the moral sense of every right-minded man would instinctively denounce the employer and employed as steeped in corruption, and the employment as infamous.

Why would the "right-minded man" denounce the practice? Is it because of a quasi-religious sense that this kind of market is morally wrong, or because of something else? The Court emphasized public morality, arguing that "if the instances [of lobbying] were numerous, open, and tolerated, they would be regarded as measuring the decay of the public morals and the degeneracy of the times." Since we do not live in the minds of the time, we can only guess what was imagined—that people would start to see government as a place from which resources could be extracted, instead of a source of aggregated interests and beliefs. Lobbying would lead to strategic use of public resources and plunder.

Child unsuccessfully argued that the case should simply be understood as a classic lawyer-client relationship. Civic virtue might be threatened if lobbyists could be hired on bills related to general matters, he argued, but not when it is simply an old man getting what he is due. However, the Court concluded that there was no clear way to regularly distinguish between secret, inappropriate lobbying and appropriate paid lobbying. Furthermore, because small private bills are not known by the public, and the discussions around the bills are often "whispered," advocacy for private bills creates huge opportunities for advocates to induce legislators to support these bills for the wrong reasons and, again, for bribery. Instead of engaging in objective fact-finding, "those whose duty it is to investigate" hear unsupported facts by self-interested parties; without a check on the facts communicated by the self-interested parties, legislators might simply rubber-stamp the bill.

Personal or Professional

Trist was cited for many years for its principles. A few years later, in an 1880 case to enforce a contract for influencing the Turkish government's purchase of arms, the Supreme Court reiterated the broad principle, even though the Turkish government, not the American government, was at stake.[18] The defendant in that case sold over $1 million in arms to the Turkish government in 1870 and 1871. The choice of arms was directly influenced by the plaintiff, a consul for the Turkish government, who then sought a commission, as previously agreed. The consul first "use[d] his influence . . . to condemn the Spencer gun," and then "brought out a Winchester gun, a sample of which he always kept in his office for the very purpose, whenever opportunity offered, of presenting its claims. It appears, however, that the Bey did not, from the first, like that gun." Therefore, "'Oscanyan had to use all his ingenuity and skill and perseverance and patience'" to get the Bey to agree to purchase Winchesters. Such a contract, the Court held, was not valid.

> Personal influence to be exercised over an officer of government in the procurement of contracts, as justly observed by counsel, is not a vendible article in our system of laws and morals, and the courts of the United States will not lend their aid to the vendor to collect the price of the article. . . . This is true when the vendor holds no official relations with the government, though the turpitude of the transaction becomes more glaring when he is also its officer.

The *Oscanyan* Court distinguished between private vendors and professional services, as the *Trist* Court had. The principle does not answer the question, though: the *Oscanyan* Court had to grapple with how to distinguish personal influence from the routine activities of salespeople. In selling goods, contingent fees—fees based in some way on success—were routine, and those cases were cited for evidence that the court should enforce the contract. Therefore contingency could not be the evil. Instead, the civic wrong was based on the sale of private influence in public procurement decisions.

> Where, instead of placing before the officers of the government the information which should properly guide their judgments, personal influence is the means used to secure the sales, and is allowed to prevail, the public good is lost sight of, unnecessary expenditures are incurred, and, generally, defective supplies are obtained, producing inefficiency in the public service.

The sale of the *personal* ability to influence was perceived to lead to poor choices by public officers, as they are influenced to make choices for reasons that are pressed by those who have profit, not the public good, behind them.

This political morality required drawing a line between professional services and personal influence. As the Supreme Court said in a frequently cited passage, "*personal influence . . .* is not a vendible article in our system of laws and morals, and the courts of the United States will not lend their aid to the vendor to collect the price of the article" (emphasis added). The language sometimes drew on property law, where a sellable item was called a "vendible."[19] The question of what was and was not vendible was a matter of public policy, determined by the courts in common law. "Personal influence" was a good that individuals could use on their own but could not sell. It was more akin to the right to have children or to vote or to defend oneself—a powerful personal right but not one that can be sold. Like the modern right to vote, the right to contribute to campaigns, the right to intimate relations, the right to serve on a jury, or the right to have a child, the right to speak one's mind to Congress could not be personally limited, but it was not protected past the personal right. The key difference between lobbying and not lobbying was the sale of influence. Lobbying, as described in these cases, is "the sale of an individual's personal influence to procure the passage of a private law by the legislature."[20]

The key to the doctrine was the ability to distinguish between illegitimate sale of private influence and legitimate, lawyer-like behavior. Courts would generally invalidate any contracts where people were paid in order to use their *personal* influence to shape official action. Contracts for personal influence were "not merely voidable, or capable of rescission, but are mala in se, absolutely void, and without effect."[21] Personal services involved personal visits; nonpersonal services involved presenting to committees or in public forums. For instance, a contract to help pass legislation was upheld because the plaintiff "was not a lobbyist, and he had no acquaintance or influence with any member of the legislature. . . . It [did] not appear that . . . he asked or solicited any member of the legislature to vote for the bills."[22] The popular hornbook that I mentioned above, which stated that lobbying services were generally illegal, added that:

> The rule, however, does not apply to an agreement, for purely professional services, such as the drafting of a petition to set forth a claim for presentment to the legislature, attending the taking of testimony, collecting facts, preparing arguments, and submitting them orally or in writing to a committee or other proper authority, and other services of like character. They rest on the same principle of ethics as professional services rendered in a court of justice, and are no more objectionable.[23]

Many of the more interesting cases involved this line drawing. In California, when an attorney "prepared the bill, which afterward became a law, and made arguments in support of it, and caused it to be introduced in both departments of the legislature, appeared and argued the measure before at least one committee of that body, and also before the governor when the bill reached his hands," the contract was valid. There was no evidence that the attorney used any dishonest, secret, or unfair means.[24]

A critical factor in California, and elsewhere, was *where* the arguments were made, and whether or not they were public. If the arguments were made in a committee setting, the services were likely legal. If the lobbyist was drafting or helping create materials for private or secret meetings, it was more like personal influence lobbying, and therefore illegal, whereas public arguments were presumptively legitimate. An individual had an absolute right to privately meet with a representative but might not pay someone else to do the same. Private persuasion brought a risk of bribery and undermined the system; public persuasion was more akin to arguments in court. In Oregon, for example, lobbying was defined as meeting with individual legislators, using personal influence to "privately importune" them. Presentations to the entire legislature, committees, or any group were permissible.[25] In Nebraska, the line was also between public argument and private solicitation. Writing a petition or making a public argument before the legislature or a committee thereof was permissible, but using personal influence was prohibited. "It is certainly important . . . that the legislature be perfectly free from any extraneous influence which may either corrupt or deceive the members of any of them."[26]

In Wisconsin, by 1896 lobbying was defined as a corrupt action involving personal influence or solicitation around legislation.[27] The "preparation of petitions, taking of testimony, collecting of facts, preparing of arguments, and submitting them, orally or in writing, to committees or other proper authority, and services of like character, which are intended to reach only the reason of those to be influenced, are legitimate." In Vermont, while it was illegal to sell personal influence, a person could hire someone else to "conduct an application to the legislature" and pay for services related to putting together documents, statements, evidence, or arguments related to that application. However, all of the relevant work had to be related to petitions that would go to the legislature itself or a committee of the legislature, not a committee member or individual politician.[28] Relatedly, a representative could not hide his interest in a pending bill's success.[29]

Contracts for influence involving lawyers were difficult because of the blend of services that were offered and provided. The services to draft a bill, for example, might lead to an attempt to personally influence legislators to support a bill. In Wisconsin, two railroad companies agreed not to compete for the same government land grant, and one of the companies offered to help the other procure the grant in exchange for a portion of the land if it were granted. According to the court, a lawyer could contract for compensation for services like drafting bills or presenting evidence and arguing before the legislature or its committees. But a nonlawyer was "incapable of rendering such services." "What efforts could they make, what aid or assistance could they give, what services could they render, except such as are justly characterized as lobbying?"[30]

The Plains States, where the populist political movements were the strongest, were the least forgiving of any hint of personal influence. In one case, a landowner agreed to pay a lobbyist to procure legislation allowing parties who had settled on land to buy it for a low price. The court held that contracts to procure legislation can be enforced when only fair and honorable means are used, and especially when the legislation results in a public benefit. However, this contract was void because "the unavoidable inference [was] that he solicited the personal aid of members of congress in doing all that was necessary or could be done to secure the passage of the law."[31]

Contract making was treated as a privilege that should not be extended to lobbying because lobbying would undermine the rule of law that it was using to enforce. For example, when the Vermont Supreme Court wrote about lobby contracts, it wrote that "the law will not concede to any man however honest he may be, the privilege of making a contract which it would not recognize when made by designing and corrupt men."[32]

The evil of lobbying came not from the corrupt intent in any particular case but rather from the fact that the "contract tends directly to those results."[33] The fact that one can pay another to get legislative results "furnishes a temptation to the plaintiff, to resort to corrupt means or improper devices, to influence legislative action." This, in turn, leads to a broad array of influences with a tendency to "subject the legislature to influences destructive of its character" and can be "fatal to public confidence in its action."[34]

Lobbying threatened to lead people to put private interests before public ones. As the early Kentucky case said in refusing to enforce a contract to get a remission, someone paid to persuade will be induced to use his influence for the money he is to obtain; when, as a patriot and a citizen, he should only act for the good of his country, and under an impartial sense of justice, tempered with mercy. We can readily imagine the dangers likely to result from the corrupt artifices of mercenary managers in procuring pardons and remissions.[35]

If a commitment to civic virtue is the foundation of the republic, as Montesquieu and the drafters of the Constitution believed, lobbying encourages at least one class of citizens to imagine themselves outside of government, bringing neither their own interests nor the public interest to the attention of government. Interests that are private are recast in public terms or in private terms that may not be accurate. Those citizens who sell their service are violating their own individual civic promise to the state by giving up their own responsibility to think of the public good and to use the public privileges they have been given for the public good. A private citizen often plays a public role in political society, as when she casts a vote. She has an obligation in the moment of casting the vote to use it in a way consistent with her own beliefs either about public good, or about her own private good, or about familial or group interest. But if she sells that vote, she violates her own obligations to the public in the moment of sale. Lobbying legitimates a kind of routine sophistry and a casual approach toward public argument. It leads people to mistrust the sincerity of public arguments and weakens their own sense of obligation to the public good. In these lobbying cases courts filled what they saw as an essential gap: protecting political society from the threat of oligarchic pressures, but also from the threat of a cynical political culture.

On a more pedestrian level, lobbying was seen as the gateway to bribery. Bribery does not now and never has had neat lines dividing it from acceptable activity. Bribery at common law was "the offering of any undue reward or remuneration to any public officer or other person intrusted with a public duty, with a view to influence his behavior in the discharge of his duty."[36] In the mid-nineteenth century, many states passed bribery statutes with broad language covering any kind of effort to influence by using things of value, but they were rarely enforced.

The language of lobbying was not always neatly separated from the language of bribery: high contingent fees, for example, were referred to as "bribes."[37] As a matter of association and categorization, lobbying enabled bribery or, in some cases, *was* bribery. This lumping allows for passages like the following one, which skips between ideas that play distinct roles in modern legal grammar—influence, lobbying, and bribery—as if they are presumptively connected: "A contract for lobby services, for personal influence, for mere importunities to members of the legislature, or other official body, for bribery or corruption, or for seducing or influencing them by any other arguments, persuasions, or inducements than such as directly and legitimately bear upon the merits of the pending application, is illegal and against public policy and void."[38]

The California constitution defined lobbying as follows: "Any person who seeks to influence the vote of a member of the Legislature by bribery, promise of reward, intimidation, or any other dishonest means, shall be guilty of lobbying, which is hereby declared a felony."[39]

Even where lobbying was not defined in a way that we might currently define as bribery, paid personal influence was seen as the first step toward bribery. The "law forbids the inchoate step" in bribery.[40] Lobbying leads to bribery through temptation— private meetings with money and no one watching make it hard for enough individuals to resist, even if the majority succeed. "If the tempted agent be corrupt himself, and disposed to corrupt others, the transition requires but a single step."[41] Legal lobbying allows citizens to tell other citizens that they can take money and turn it into political power, and once that traffic is legal, they will figure out ways to skirt the law but in fact engage in offering value in exchange for influence.

Because lobbying leads to bribery, the job of the courts was to protect against the temptation. Courts routinely held that it was not necessary to find that the parties agreed to some "corrupt" or "secret" action. Instead, the question was whether the "contract tends directly to those results."[42] A contract was problematic when it "furnishes a temptation to the plaintiff, to resort to corrupt means or improper devices, to influence legislative action." Such a temptation leads to bribery, which in turn leads to destroying the institution and undermining public confidence.[43] Much as a later Supreme Court in *Buckley v. Valeo*[44] (a case I explore in Chapter 13) would describe "appearance of corruption" as being just as important as corruption itself, the courts in these contract cases were concerned that the public would lose trust in institutions with the growth of lobbying.

The role of temptation in lobbying contracts was treated much like the role of temptation in conflict of interest cases, except that with lobbying, the conflict posed was between the role of citizen or legislator and the role of lobbyist or lobbied. In *McGhee v. Lindsay*, an Alabama case, the court refused to enforce a public contract in which a state-employed supervisor had an interest. The court talked about how no man can serve two masters with conflicting interests.[45] Doing so creates "a temptation, perhaps . . . too strong for resistance by men of flexible morals, or hackneied in the common devices of worldly business, . . . which would betray them into gross misconduct, and even crime." The court focused on creating structures where temptations do not exist for men with "flexible morals" or those who are steeped in the usual run of business behavior. In fact, even though there was no evidence of bribery or an incorrect price, the court adopted the policy of not enforcing these contracts as a "preventive check against such temptations and seductions." The Vermont Supreme Court, for instance, held that "the sale by an individual of his personal influence and solicitations, to procure the passage of a public or private law by the legislature, is void as being prejudicial to sound legislation, manifestly injurious to the interests of the state, and in express and unquestionable contravention of public policy."[46] It is totally irrelevant to look at whether the sale was effective or not, and whether or not anything improper was done. "The principle of these decisions has no respect to the equities between the parties, but is controlled solely by the tendency of the contract."[47] A person cannot "with propriety be employed to exert his personal influence, whether it be great or little, with individual members, or to labor privately in any form with them, out of the legislative halls, in favor of or against any act or subject of legislation."[48] The court should discourage those practices "if it corrupts or tends to corrupt some, or if it deceives or tends to deceive or mislead some."[49]

Many of these cases involved contingency fees. Courts would routinely declare that contracts for contingent fees to obtain legislation were void.[50] The prominent role of contingencies in these cases has led some commentators to see the lobbying cases as a reflection of an attitude toward champerty and contingencies, not toward lobbying. However, *Trist* explicitly held that contingencies were not the source of corruption. On the other hand, in a contract in which "it does not appear that they were employed by reason of any personal or political influence," the fact that it was contingent did not render it void.[51] The language of the decisions emphasized personal influence, not contingencies. Some did not treat contingent fees as a factor at all.[52]

Some would simply void a contract if it sounded at all like lobbying. Lobbying services for one Nebraska court were "corrupt in its nature and against public policy." It was not clear what the service was, exactly, though there was some testimony that it was "to pay somebody to keep still and do as we wanted them to." The court held: "Every consideration of public policy demands that money paid out by a public contractor to induce men to keep still, to make them do as he wants them to, to lobby to secure him contracts, or to secure the allowance of estimates, should be considered as a corrupt and unlawful expenditure."[53]

Lobbying Becomes Legitimate

One might think—reasonably—that a major Supreme Court decision might be required to overturn this massive body of law. But the lobbying cases were never directly overturned; they were gradually shunted aside. When the Supreme Court in *Citizens United* mentioned in passing that "Congress has no power to ban lobbying itself," it could cite no direct reference.

The old law of lobbying changed in three steps. First, state courts started recoding lobby contracts as contracts for professional instead of personal influence as a general matter. Instead of default suspicion, they defaulted toward assuming lobbying contracts were legitimate. Second, judges changed their attitudes toward contracts. While nineteenth-century judges saw themselves as providing public subsidies that ought not be used for activities that were against public policy, twentieth-century courts saw themselves as neutral arbiters, agnostic as to the content of contracts, responsible only for a technical, not moral, review. The third step involved a changing view of the First Amendment, as the Supreme Court gained prominence in the political vision of the mid-twentieth-century justices.

In 1890, Massachusetts enacted a lobbying registration law, followed by Wisconsin and Maryland, and several other states. The registration law created a sense that lobbying was itself professional, instead of personal, and made it harder to argue that nonlawyers could not lobby without offering personal services. Moreover, the growing power of the industry, and legitimization of key players within it, likely made it seem less distasteful to courts. Courts started to classify behaviors like private informational meetings as professional services, behaviors that they might have previously classified as the illegitimate sale of personal influence.[54]

A Supreme Court case exemplifying that transformation came in 1927. In *Steele v. Drummond*, one partner in a business deal agreed with the other to use his personal influence to pass a law enabling the construction of a railroad line in a particular location.[55] After the arrangement fell apart, the lobbyist was sued by his partner. He confidently defended himself on the grounds that a contract to use personal influence for legislative action voided a contract. The Court gave lip service to the long line of cases striking down contracts for personal influence. But it gave far greater weight to the importance of contracts. "It is a matter of great public concern that freedom of contract be not lightly interfered with," the Court held, and public policy is too "vague and variable."

The Court upheld the contract on a technical difference between this and other cases: Drummond had a personal property interest in the charter, so he was not prostituting himself, as it were, but pursuing his own interest. However, practically, the Court erected a significant barrier to the use of contract law as a way to police the use of personal influence in politics. After *Steele*, few cases struck down lobbying contracts for any reason.

In 1941, in a case called *Textile Mills*, the Supreme Court addressed the constitutionality of treasury regulations that stated that "sums of money expended for lobbying purposes" are not tax deductible.[56] It did not consider a First Amendment argument, and inasmuch as a policy argument was raised against the differential treatment of lobbying versus other business expenses, the court shrugged it off, citing *Trist v. Child*. As with the previous century's holdings, lobbying was still treated as "insidious" and lobbying contracts those "to which law gives no sanction."

The next two cases—*United States v. Rumely*[57] and *United States v. Harriss*[58]—signal a more important shift. While they do not directly address the constitutionality of lobbying, they strongly hint at a constitutionally protected right. Both cases deal with the scope of the authority of Congress to mandate disclosure by lobbyists, and both come in the wake of the 1946 Federal Regulation of Lobbying Act. In both cases, the Court reads the power of Congress narrowly, in part to avoid constitutional issues. However, the cases are doctrinally complicated because while they imply that there is some First Amendment right around lobbying, they provide no guidance on the scope of that right, or the logic or reason for that right. Because they don't technically establish a right, they don't have to confront the conflict between the existence of a right and the former cases that clearly treated paid lobbying as outside the scope of constitutional protection.

Rumely suggested that there were fewer constitutional rights for representations made directly to members of Congress than member-to-member or public political activity, because it read the authority of investigation to encompass only the former. It held that Congress had not authorized the investigations of non-lobbying behavior, therefore implicitly creating a First Amendment divide between lobbying behavior and non-lobbying political behavior, with the latter having more protection.

In *Harriss*, the Court held that because of a narrower definition held in the lobbying act, Congress was within its rights to demand disclosure. In response to a challenge that it was unconstitutionally vague and violated the First Amendment, the Court limited its scope to only those paid lobbyists who have direct interaction with members of Congress on pending legislation, and who are principally interested in influence. After *Harriss*, lobbying is presumptively protected in the American legal imagination. In 1959 the Supreme Court addressed whether a treasury regulation denying business expense deductions for political activity was constitutional. It held that it was not unconstitutional, and approvingly cited *Textile Mills*.[59] A few years later, the Court construed the Sherman Act in such a way that it would not cover publicity campaigns. It held that as a matter of statutory construction, private entities are immune from Sherman Act liability for efforts to influence legislation[60] and included language indicating that an alternate construction would violate the First Amendment. However, the Court's guidance was again indirect: the activities challenged were largely public campaigns, so the Court never addressed the scope of a right to sell or buy private influence.

These cases—and the quiet transformation—are so interesting now because despite the central role lobbying plays in our political culture, the Supreme Court has never directly addressed the very difficult questions around the values that lobbying both serves and undermines. They are also important because in the twentieth century, as courts started enforcing criminal bribery statutes more routinely, they borrowed from the language of integrity developed in lobbying law.

CHAPTER EIGHT

The Gilded Age

AFTER A CIVIL WAR fought in the name of abolishing slavery, southern African Americans were almost entirely politically and economically disenfranchised. After a powerful women's suffrage movement, women couldn't vote. After a constitutional commitment to equality, the country was divided between rich and poor. And after a flourishing of political parties and populist ideas, top-down corporate politics triumphed over valiant grassroots movements. The country had changed from a largely agrarian to an increasingly urban society and grew five times greater in population from 1830 to 1880 (from 12 million to 50 million). The number of voters outpaced population growth as the vote expanded to poorer (mostly white) Americans and there was growing cross-class public involvement in politics. Less than half a million voted in the 1824 presidential election: by 1880, there were roughly 9 million voters. The nature of work shifted from a combination of owned farms in the North and slave-dependent farms in the South to industrial labor. Railways, which started to replace waterways as the mode of transportation in the late midcentury, were dominant, and the financial speculators of Wall Street had come to assert political and economic control. Political money had an unclear legal status. Bribery law ostensibly criminalized giving anything of value with intent to influence a lawmaker, but politicians were financed by oil, banking, and railroad barons who fully intended to influence governmental action. Neither courts nor legislatures had provided a way to distinguish between campaign contributions and bribes. The penny press papers, enabled by the steam press, started to cover politics in a vivid and often critical way. As the public got more involved in campaigns, reformers became increasingly anxious about money's ability to influence politics through elections. The changes in the country led to new challenges for corruption law.

Distributed Democracy or Spoils?

One of the most difficult questions facing reformers was how to deal with the relationship between campaign money and government salaries. In the very early years of the country, candidates stood for office instead of campaigning for office. That had changed with Andrew Jackson: his 1828 campaign is categorized by historians as the beginning of the Second Party System, where candidates actively mobilized voters, held rallies, and used pamphlets and newspapers to directly engage potential voters.[1] Jackson and his close ally Martin Van Buren also promoted the idea of "rotation in office." Too long a time in government, the Jacksonians believed, created dependencies and temptations that led to corruption. Therefore, both civil servants and public representatives should come in and out of government service instead of treating either as a long-term job.

The rotation-in-office system worked to fund the increasingly expensive campaigns as well as to get rid of stale civil servants. Throughout the middle of the eighteenth century, successful candidates would provide jobs to supporters, and the government employees paid an "assessment"—a fraction of their income—to political parties. This spoils system—called that because "to the victors go the spoils"—incentivized broad political activity. Political machines developed a culture around the political parties; families would attach themselves to parties in the hope of getting a job for one member of their family, and the social aspects of parties increased the bonds of connections with other partisans.

Early efforts to replace the spoils system with a civil service examination or other methods of employment were criticized as antidemocratic. But the institution had many pathologies, not the least of which included incompetent government workers. Reformers also worried that government was becoming an elaborate mechanism to provide jobs for those who would bribe the right person. The founders' fear that people would go into public office in order to get jobs for their friends turned out to be all too true. President James Garfield was elected as a reformer, and he showed a commitment to his anticorruption creed in the first months in office in 1880.[2] But in July of that year, Garfield was shot in the back by Charles Guiteau, a Garfield supporter who believed he was owed a job for his campaign help. Garfield struggled with infections and complications relating to the wound, dying two months later.

In 1883, in part due to the country's response to Garfield's assassination, Congress passed the Pendleton Act, creating a mechanism for hiring federal employees based on merit rather than party affiliation. It made it illegal to hire, fire, or demote governmental employees for political reasons; criminalized soliciting campaign donations on federal property; and made it difficult to offer a job to a prospective campaign organizer in return for work because such an offer was now illegal. The act was designed to be implemented gradually: each outgoing president had the capacity to turn whatever jobs he identified into nonpatronage jobs, so when the presidency changed hands between political parties, the president had an incentive to transform as many jobs as possible. The Pendleton Act and other efforts at civil service rules gradually impacted political culture. Machine politics, kickbacks, and governmental positions as rewards for political work did not leave politics but started to play a less important role at the federal level. Over the next several decades, civil service reform was adopted in almost every state.

But the Pendleton Act didn't tell politicians how they should raise money, only how they shouldn't. Campaigns were still expensive, and with no government employees to fund the cost, candidates turned elsewhere—to newspaper owners, wealthy individuals, and corporations with an interest in legislation. Many of the big donors were monopolists—or trusts—in railroads, oil, metals, and banking. Industry was rapidly consolidating. They donated their money to parties, which in turn took that money to buy votes at the polls.

The Ballot with the Flaming Pink Border

Referring to the previous century, historian Eldon C. Evans wrote in 1917, "elections in the United States . . . were not a very pleasant spectacle for those who believed in democratic government."[3]

Parties and candidates raised great amounts of "soap," or cash, just for the purpose of buying votes, and the more effective vote buyers were rewarded with positions of power in government. In the late 1880s, influential men in a community could sell their votes for the current cash equivalent of $250 to $500. The "floaters," or men with bad reputations, would get as much as $30 in today's dollars, paid in two dollar bills. The Indiana election of 1888 was said to have been bought for $2.5 million in today's dollars, vote by vote.

Voter intimidation was equally widespread. Landlords and employers gave out ballots for their preferred candidates and punished those who refused to comply with their directives. An 1889 federal investigation into voter intimidation described employers driving employees to the polls, working men staying away from the polls, and mill managers standing at the polls watching their employees as they voted. Vote peddlers would pay for votes and then ensure bribes were successful by standing outside polling stations and watching voters enter. The political parties each printed their own ballots and would refuse to pay the bribe, or even physically intimidate voters, if they failed to walk into the polling place with the correctly colored ballot.

The methods of voting used throughout the country made bribery and intimidation easy. The voice vote, used in many regions, made it very clear who had voted for whom: a voter who sold his vote for $50 could find the party who bribed him waiting outside, ready to demand his money back if he voted for the wrong person. Midcentury reformers believed that written ballots would lead to secrecy, but they rarely succeeded in achieving the desired end. Some jurisdictions required a signature next to a vote, making bribery accountability easy. However, the most common way in which a written ballot became a public ballot was through the use of color.

Parties would print out ballots in different colors, on different kinds of paper, and give them to "ticket peddlers" who would pay people to accept them on the promise they would use them. The peddler charged with enforcing the bribes could simply watch as the bribe taker entered the polling place. The tickets were designed to be seen from a great distance. The 1878 Republican Party in Massachusetts had a "flaming pink border which threw out branches towards the center of the back, and had a Republican [e]ndorsement in letters half an inch high."[4] The Democrats in Orangeburg, South Carolina, used blue tissue paper for its ballot. The broad use of tissue paper throughout the South was presumptively designed to make it harder to change the name on the other side of the piece of paper.

Reformers began by trying to make the ballot color uniform, hoping it would deter vote buying. Fifteen states passed laws about the color of the paper and the kind of ink to be used in order to make bribery more difficult. New York required "plain white printing paper, and without any impression, device, mark, or other peculiarity whatsoever upon or about them to distinguish one ballot from another in appearance, except the names of the several candidates, and they shall be printed with plain black ink."[5] The parties cleverly responded by printing ballots on very different shades of "plain white" paper. Vote buying took slightly better eyesight, but was still easily rewarded.

In 1888, Louisville, Kentucky, was the first U.S. jurisdiction to adopt a new system, borrowed from Australia. This system of voting, called the secret ballot or the Australian ballot, required the state to print on the ballot the names of candidates and parties. A voter would show up at the polls, receive a ballot with the nominees of all the parties on the ballot, and then in private mark his choice. The next year, seven states followed suit. By 1892, thirty-nine states started using preprinted ballots for most offices and general elections. A treatise of the time explained that the secret ballot "checks bribery, and all those corrupt practices which consist in voting according to a bargain or understanding."[6] Instead of criminalizing bribery, the secret ballot laws were passed on this premise: "Take away all interest in committing an offence, and the offence will soon disappear." The treatise argued for the laws on the grounds that "the secret ballot approaches these more or less elusive evils, not merely with the weak instrument of a penal clause for this and that offence, but with the effective methods of modern legislation."[7]

Isolated Elites

The Pendleton Act and the Australian ballot reforms played an important role in rethinking the kind of anticorruption law that was possible. Still, at the end of the nineteenth century, democratic politics was increasingly dominated by wealth and the country had no general theory about how money and politics should interact. Some late-century elites who condemned vote buying and the spoils system thought the use of money to influence official behavior was legitimate and simply part of political practice. Members of the public, on the other hand, condemned the corporate trusts and their corrupt campaign contributions.

In *The Gilded Age*, Mark Twain and Charles Dudley Warner's wry novel about lobbying and land speculation, the protagonist, Laura Hawkins, is transformed from an unsophisticated woman into a savvy Washington lobbyist. Her understanding of what is acceptable and normal mutates: her language shifts, her clothes change, her tone adjusts. Twain and Warner wrote: "When Laura had been in Washington three months, she was still the same person, in one respect, that she was when she first arrived there—that is to say, she still bore the name of Laura Hawkins. Otherwise she was perceptibly changed."[8] As Twain and Warner illustrated, a conceptual gulf existed between political and financial elites' understanding of corruption and that of the general public. The title of the novel became the name of the era, and the gulf only widened after the novel was published.

The 1896 presidential race embodied this dissonance. The "Great Commoner," Democrat William Jennings Bryan, ran for president against Republican Ohio governor William McKinley. Bryan brought four assets: eloquence, complete determination to win, issues that resonated with grassroots organizers, and the backing of many small newspaper owners and a few big ones, including William Randolph Hearst. He made over 500 speeches in his first campaign, an inexhaustible 36-year-old railing against railroads, big banks, the gold standard, and the concentration of economic and political power. Bryan's opponent, McKinley, was supported by the wealthiest men in the country, and he had the additional asset of the creative political entrepreneur Mark Hanna. The Ohioan Hanna maneuvered patronage deals and created a fund-raising system by applying an "assessment" model to centers of concentrated wealth. Banks were assessed .25 percent of their capital to fund McKinley's campaign. (In current terms, that would be about a $5 billion assessment on Bank of America.) Critics called Hanna's method a "corruption fund."[9] On October 13, 1896, the *New York Journal* railed: "Can Mr. Hanna buy the voters of the Midwest? The Standard Oil Company, the great railroad corporations, the big manufacturing trusts, the bond syndicates, Mr. Carnegie, Mr. Pierpont Morgan, Mr. Huntington, and all the rest of the high-minded patriots who are furnishing Mr. Hanna with the means to defend the national honor, think he can."[10] Whether through purchase or persuasion, or a blend of the two, Hanna's tactics worked, and McKinley defeated Bryan in 1896, and again in 1900.

On September 6, 1901, a "medium sized man of ordinary appearance" approached President McKinley in the Temple of Music at the Pan-American Exposition in Buffalo, New York, and shot him in the abdomen. McKinley died a week later. Vice President Teddy Roosevelt became the president of the United States. Roosevelt brought an almost religious, prosecutorial zeal to the office and made fighting corruption, "and above all corruption in public life," a centerpiece of his eight years in office.[11] Roosevelt was a former New York City police commissioner who fancied himself capable of rooting out individual vice, an ambitious politician who dreamed of building his heroic stature through individual indictments. And, like Franklin, his experience led him to be particularly drawn to structural reforms that would change systems. He was in many ways a corrupt old fox like Franklin and knew how to work his way around a room of millionaires.

Whether driven by fear of another Bryan challenge—or something similar—or his own convictions, he came into office proclaiming a vision of ridding the country of the corruption of the prior generations. Roosevelt's approach formed the basis of twentieth-century anticorruption law.

CHAPTER NINE

Two Kinds of Sticks

POLITICAL CORRUPTION LAWS come in two general types, both of which were used by Teddy Roosevelt. First, there are corrupt intent laws, laws that prohibit actions only when they are accompanied by some kind of intent on the part of the giver (or receiver) to influence or reward official behavior. Corrupt intent laws include laws criminalizing gifts given with intent to influence government action. Because many interactions with government involve a wish to influence, and value is a deeply subjective idea, these laws can theoretically encompass a great deal of democratic activity, and certainly all offers of mobilization and support by political groups. Corrupt intent laws require a jury or court to make a determination about what counts as corrupt. To be clear, not all corrupt intent laws use the words *corrupt* or *corruptly*, but all of them use language that requires some kind of judgment about the appropriateness of the particular action.

The second kind of law is prophylactic or structural, a law that makes corruption less likely by outlawing behavior that might lead to corruption. This second type of corruption law is

designed to change overall incentive structures rather than punish bad actors. These corruption rules don't require a court to
make determinations about individual cases.

Most of the structural laws that we'll discuss in this book are
what lawyers call "bright-line" rules: clearly defined rules made
up of objective elements, with little room for different interpretation. A classic bright-line rule from another area is a numer-
ical speed limit: anyone going over sixty-five miles per hour
violates the law. Just as the speeding law reflects a societal determination that the risks attending driving over sixty-five are
too great to allow, even if the law punishes innocent and safe
driving, the bright-line residency requirements in the Constitution reflected a societal decision that the risks attending newcom-
ers were too great, even if the law keeps out potentially brilliant
and important candidates. Structural rules have always governed
financial gifts to judges: such actions create such a risk of corruption that they become treated as inherently corrupt. A
bright-line rule can become so widely adopted and accepted that
it takes on moral weight, even though it is prophylactic. To use
the legal Latin phrases often associated with these words, that
which was at first *malum prohibitum* becomes *malum in se*—that
which was just a necessary administrative structural law becomes
a broad cultural expectation. Any violation of it is also one of
the social fabric. Both the Australian ballot and the Pendleton
Act represent bright-line rules that have become embedded in
our moral political fabric. Public balloting now sounds wrong:
the attachment to private ballots has grown beyond its utilitar-
ian foundations. Likewise, partisan civil service sounds not just
inefficient, but somehow inherently corrupt.

The First Stick: Prosecuting Corrupt Officials

The first part of Teddy Roosevelt's anticorruption crusade involved prosecutors digging up dusty, unused laws to indict and convict two federal elected officials on corruption charges for the first time. Roosevelt's 1903 address to Congress condemned bribery and named corruption the central sin against democracy. Corruption, he said, "strikes at the foundation of all law." He directed his ire at private corporations doing the bribing and at public officials alike. The "bribe giver" is "worse than the thief, for the thief robs the individual, while the corrupt official plunders an entire city or State." He is worse than a murderer because a murderer takes one life while "the corrupt official and the man who corrupts the official alike aim at the assassination of the commonwealth itself." If governmental bribery is allowed, "government of the people, by the people, for the people will perish from the face of the earth."[1] (Notably, he gave this speech in a discussion headlined "Trusts.") When he spoke, the federal bribery laws were strong on paper but rarely used and they had never been used to successfully convict a senator, congressman, or high-level federal official.

Roosevelt's administration changed the long-standing practice toward "the weak instruments" of bribery law with two major prosecutions in Oregon and in Kansas. Public officials in Oregon helped facilitate illegal sale of public land, which came out of a federal plan designed to encourage settlement. The United States offered land for the very low price of $2.50 an acre for homesteaders, a price unattractive to settlers but very attractive to timber companies. Seeing an opportunity, speculators rounded up men, paid them cheaply to swear they were homesteaders to "buy" the land, and then repackaged the land and sold it for huge profits to a timber company. Government officials were then paid to certify the validity of the claims.

The federal government launched an aggressive prosecutorial campaign against hundreds of the coconspirators in the land frauds scheme and indicted Senator John Mitchell of Oregon, a twenty-year veteran of the Senate. Mitchell allegedly accepted $2,000 to recommend that the commissioner of the General Land Office certify homesteads as valid that Mitchell knew were invalid, and another $1,750 to use his influence to get another set of land claims certified. He was convicted in July 1905. He died the same year from tooth complications before he could appeal. Should Mitchell have even been convicted? As one historian noted, a "free and easy attitude" toward the lands had been the norm for years, and "whatever the laws might have said in letter, in spirit they intended that all the lands should be in private ownership."[2] The prosecution of Mitchell as part of Roosevelt's crusade against "interests" struck many Oregonians (and some historians) as an unfair political bait and switch. Mitchell was caught in the gears of changing norms.

At about the same time, in Kansas, Senator Joseph Burton was prosecuted for fraud and did live to appeal it. His appeal laid the groundwork for a new generation of federal prosecutions. He was convicted in 1905 of accepting money to influence a post office decision, in violation of an 1863 law that prohibited receiving compensation for services related to proceedings in which the United States is "interested." He appealed on several grounds, arguing that the word *interested* was interpreted too broadly; that although Congress had passed the statute, it over-reached its power to reshape the relationship between governmental branches. The statute, according to him, could not reach federal elected officials. If it could, it would lead to executive branch meddling in legislative branch affairs.

The Court concluded that the efforts to influence were unprotected nonlegislative conduct and that the executive branch had the authority to prosecute bribery.[3] The statute was a legitimate mechanism to protect administrators from being corrupted by members of Congress:

> The evils attending such a situation are apparent and are increased when those seeking to influence executive officers are spurred to action by hopes of pecuniary reward. There can be no reason why the government may not, by legislation, protect each department against such evils, indeed, against everything from whatever source it proceeds, that tends or may tend to corruption or inefficiency in the management of public affairs.[4]

Prosecutors indicted hundreds of people, and dozens were convicted. A new era of criminal enforcement had begun, one of intermittent, and often politically charged, targeted prosecutions.

It took another twenty-three years before another prosecution of a federal official took place. Secretary of the Interior Albert Fall was convicted for his involvement in giving oil leases in the Teapot Dome scandal. And it was years later, when federal prosecutors started to reach into the states, that the modern criminal federal law of bribery truly took flight.

The Second Stick: Campaign Finance Law

Roosevelt's second approach was exemplified by the Tillman Act. Roosevelt's first presidential campaign was based on a theme of "Clean Government," and in 1905 he introduced the first campaign finance reform legislation. He advocated for public funding of elections, bans on corporate contributions, and full disclosure of campaign sources.[5] He pushed through the passage of the Tillman Act of 1907, barring corporations from contributing to political campaigns.[6] The Tillman Act was a bright-line rule; it did not require prosecutors to prove corrupt intent or the absence of corrupt intent. All it asked was whether a contribution was made or not. A few years later, the Tillman Act was followed by the Federal Corrupt Practices Act (FCPA) and its amendments, limiting political party and candidate spending in U.S. Senate races and primaries. It also required full disclosure of all federal campaign expenditures. Neither of these acts defined corruption, but they both used the word *corruption*, pointedly. The "corrupt practices" in the titles of these acts referred to businesses corrupting government through campaign donations and to politicians extorting contributions from businesses.[7]

These laws had a substantial impact on limiting the overall spending in political campaigns. While they were notoriously weakly enforced, they caused a shift in the amount—and source—of money spent in campaigns after they passed. Campaign spending might be expected to rise after the successes of *McKinley* but not after the Tillman Act. Republicans spent around $70 million on the 1900 presidential campaign, and the amount went down to something closer to $20 million in 1912.[8]

Roosevelt's anticorruption vision also led to the direct election of senators and antitrust law. In 1913, bolstered by Roosevelt's public support, the Seventeenth Amendment to the U.S. Constitution passed, establishing direct election of U.S. senators by popular vote and joining the dozens of other anticorruption provisions of the Constitution. And Roosevelt is known for his trust busting and his use of the bully pulpit to connect economic power to corruption. Although historians have questioned his seriousness and his commitment to decentralized power, he laid out a promise of antimonopolization. Franklin Delano Roosevelt later fulfilled it. It was the premise that private concentrated power—like the foreign powers of the founding era—could systemically corrupt politics.

Still, there were judicial stumbling blocks to the legal rejection of gilded age corruption.

Free Speech or Free Elections?

For nearly seventy years after Roosevelt left office, courts upheld his general approach toward campaign finance rules against an array of constitutional challenges. But it wasn't easy. There were many technical hurdles and central philosophical questions about how to allocate power in a democracy. The biggest difficulty—then as now—was how to reconcile the need to use bright-line rules to limit corruption without allowing legislators to write self-serving or propagandistic laws under the pretense of being motivated by an "anticorruption" zeal. Politicians in power are likely to write laws that benefit themselves, including laws that make their own campaigns easier to fund and their opponents' more difficult.

The first time that the Supreme Court invalidated an anti-corruption statute was in 1921. In *Newberry v. United States* the Court reviewed a restriction on how much money congressional candidates could spend in primaries.[9] *Newberry* challenged the law on the grounds that regulating primaries was not within Congress's enumerated powers.[10] The Court basically agreed, holding that a primary was not an "election," and the federal government had no authority over private political behavior. Notably—considering the central role it has come to play in the last forty years—the First Amendment was not mentioned. Nonetheless, a similar question arose—whether Congress could use this power to "attempt to control the educational campaign."

> Upon what ground can it be said that Congress can provide how many meetings shall be held, where meetings shall be held, how many speakers shall be allowed to speak for a candidate, how many circulars may be distributed, how many committees may act in behalf of a candidate, how they shall be organized and what shall be the limit of their honest activity?[11]

Ultimately, Justice McReynolds concluded that Congress had no inherent or textual constitutional power to regulate the amount of money spent in congressional primary campaigns. The opinion of the court does not outright reject a strong deference to concerns about corruption; it simply does not discuss it. The concurrence, written by Justice Pitney and substantively joined by two other justices, rejected not only McReynolds's constitutional conclusions but also his framework. Pitney concurred with the conclusion that the judgment at issue should be reversed, but only because of faulty jury instructions.

What is most interesting is how McReynolds and Pitney respectively treat corruption. Pitney's concurrence harps on the central fragility of the state, insisting that Congress cannot be left without power to legislate in this area: Pitney defers to Congress in questions of preventing against corruption, noting that Congress might conclude representative government was threatened by a primary "subject to the more insidious but (in the opinion of Congress) nevertheless harmful influences resulting from an unlimited expenditure of money in paid propaganda and other purchased campaign activities." Congress must be able to protect, he argues, "the very foundation of the citadel" from "sinister influences."

But what is the foundation of the citadel? Twenty years later, as the First Amendment gained prominence in the Court, Justice William Douglas was torn between two different ideas of what is at the center of the Constitution—the First Amendment or the integrity of the electoral process. He first confronted this tension in *United States v. Classic* in 1941, another case on whether Congress should have the power to regulate primary elections at all.[12] The Court's majority in *Classic* concluded that it is part of the inherent power of Congress to regulate these primaries, despite the fact that this puts the tentacles of Congress fairly deep inside private associational political organizations. Justice Douglas dissented, but he did so "with diffidence," only after spending a page discussing the following threat:

> Free and honest elections are the very foundation of our republican form of government. . . . The fact that a particular

form of pollution has only an indirect effect on the final election is immaterial . . . the Constitution should be read as to give Congress an expansive implied power to place beyond the pale acts which, in their direct or indirect effect, impair the integrity of Congressional elections. For when corruption enters, the election is no longer free, the choice of the people is affected.

Ten years after this opinion, Justice Frankfurter, in his concurrence in *United States v. Congress of Industrial Organizations*, was just as absolute about free speech as Douglas had been about corruption.[13] That case involved the construction of a section of a statute that prohibited expenditures for elections. The question was whether the statute unconstitutionally limited union members' capacity to send out pamphlets. The plurality opinion, by Justice Reed, ducked the question. Reed concluded that the constitutional issue need not be resolved; the statute was not intended to apply to membership newsletters. Reed mentions that the legislation was motivated by the "necessity for destroying the influence over elections" exercised by corporations but goes little further in discussing the corruption interest.

Frankfurter's concurrence went much deeper into the problem posed by the case than Reed's opinion. He tacked back and forth between discussions of corruption and free speech but ultimately settled on a treatise about the virtues of free speech, arguing that the right to speak—and to hear speech—is too deeply important to be trammeled by the interest in preventing corruption. "The most complete exercise of those rights is essential to the full, fair, and untrammeled operation of the electoral process."

He equated corruption with undue influence. "Undue influence," he argued, "may represent no more than convincing weight of argument fully presented." This syllogism where corruption equaled undue influence, and undue influence equaled rhetorical persuasiveness, therefore corruption equaled rhetorical persuasiveness, did not completely satisfy him. But he explored the dangerous possibilities in the connections between corruption and expenditures only to dismiss them. We do not need to discuss them, he wrote, "except to say that any asserted beneficial tendency of restrictions upon expenditures for publicizing political views, whether of a group or of an individual, is certainly counterbalanced to some extent by the loss for democratic processes resulting from the restrictions upon free and full public discussion." His refusal to engage is all the more striking because he acknowledged that the legislative reason behind the bill was to root out the conditions for breeding corruption and the political culture in which corruption could possibly occur—not just the most obvious instances. "In the claimed interest of free and honest elections, [this statute] curtails the very freedoms that make possible exercise of the franchise by an informed and thinking electorate."

The foundational question did not disappear. Frankfurter returned in 1957 to the same difficult issues with a far greater respect for the importance of anticorruption interests. In *United States v. UAW-CIO*, Frankfurter painstakingly summarized the history of public-financing debates, pumping up the dangers of corruption by referring to historians, debates on the House floor, and his own commitment to the integrity of the democratic process.[14] He affirmed the job of Congress in framing-era philosophy, the job to create and support the "active, alert responsibility of the individual citizen."

Frankfurter acknowledged the "popular feeling that aggregated capital unduly influenced politics, an influence not stopping short of corruption." He did not expound directly on the difference between undue influence and corruption, but the sequence following the word corruption is telling: "The matter is not exaggerated by two leading historians," he reported, quoting them as saying that the nation's wealth "was gravitating rapidly into the hands of a small portion of the population, and the power of wealth threatened to undermine the political integrity of the Republic." Frankfurter in effect adopted the framers' view of corruption. The view is wide (not limited to public actors, but including the role of private citizens) and deep (not limited to bribery, but including the moral crimes of failing to be an active, alert citizen). Undue influence is not merely persuasive power. Moreover, corruption is intensely important. "Speaking broadly," he wrote, "what is involved here is the integrity of our electoral process, and, not less, the responsibility of the individual citizen for the successful functioning of that process. This case thus raises issues not less than basic to a democratic society." Douglas dissented with an absolutist vision of the First Amendment. "When the exercise of First Amendment rights is tangled with conduct which government may regulate, we refuse to allow the First Amendment rights to be sacrificed merely because some evil may result."

His dissent finds voice, as we will see, more than fifty years later in *Citizens United* and *McCutcheon v. FEC*.

CHAPTER TEN

The Jury Decides

IT WAS THE MID-1930S in New Orleans. Huey Long had just died, and one of Long's closest associates, Abraham Shushan, was using political connections to make money. The political economy of prosecution was changing in the early twentieth century, with the press eager to cover corruption scandals. Elected prosecutors, keenly aware of how they were portrayed in the media, knew they could gain political acclaim—which could lead to political power—for prosecuting elected officials under corruption statutes. As these public prosecutors flexed their newfound abilities to take on those in power, courts affirmed their convictions with references to the principles that were used to disavow lobbying in the previous generations. For most of the twentieth century, that meant that juries were given broad authority to determine whether something was corrupt or merely friendly. The courts were permissive, rarely describing exactly what constituted "corrupt" behavior or a failure to provide honest services but allowing prosecutors to bring cases and allowing juries to choose between innocent and "corrupt" gifts and actions. The use of the mail fraud statute exemplified this permissiveness.

The use of influence by Shushan, the former head of the New Orleans Levee Board, and Herbert Waguespack, a member of the finance committee of the same board, was at the heart of the case. They had successfully persuaded the board to authorize a New Orleans bond repayment at a lucrative percentage when they both had a major financial interest in the authorization. They stood to earn hundreds of thousands of dollars in fees, to be split between them and their coconspirators.

Shushan's job had been to persuade the Louisiana governor, who had influence but lacked formal authority. Waguespack had argued for the bonds in his official role. An employee of the board was paid to spy on what competitors in the bond business were doing. None of the people involved had direct decision-making authority except Waguespack, and he did not have a deciding vote. All of these agreements were concealed from the other decision makers.

The story stank when it came out, but prosecutors had two problems. First, there was no evidence that the city of New Orleans was actually hurt by the decision. Second, the general federal bribery law did not reach state officials. To solve both of these problems they turned to a federal law that had been passed sixty years earlier, the federal mail fraud statute. The mail fraud provision, enacted in 1872, was designed to combat abuse of the post office. It criminalized using the mail to advance "any scheme or artifice to defraud." In 1909 Congress amended it to prohibit "any scheme or artifice to defraud, or for obtaining money or property by means of false or fraudulent pretenses, representations, or promises." It was written in a broad way, and the prosecutors took a chance by trying to convict using this archaic tool.

Shushan and Waguespack argued that they had done nothing wrong: Shushan had merely used personal influence, well within the right of any citizen. Waguespack argued he had a right to obtain personal income outside of his professional role. Neither Shushan nor Waguespack had the final authority to make a decision, they argued: Shushan was not an elected official any longer, and Waguespack was an elected official, but he didn't have the power to make a decision on his own. The Levee Board would have voted the same way without him.

The philosophical question was similar to that faced by the framers in categorizing foreign gifts: Is being paid to whisper in someone's ear corrupt or not? The prosecutor wanted to take personal influence and put it in the category of bribery and corruption, whereas Shushan and Waguespack wanted to put it in the category of essentially protected personal political rights.

The jury agreed with the prosecutor. They found Shushan and his gang guilty of a "scheme . . . to defraud" the public. The court of appeals upheld the conviction. It concluded that there was sufficient evidence that a jury could conclude they had attempted to deprive the public of the honest services owed the public by public officials. In effect, corruption was a question for the jury. "A scheme to get money unfairly by obtaining and then betraying the confidence of another, or by corrupting one who acts for another or advises him, would be a scheme to defraud though no lies were told." Fraud, in other words, included cheating the public. The court was driven by the same kind of logic that had led earlier courts to refuse to enforce lobbying contracts. It pointed to the "essential immorality" of any deal with a public official where there was "use of undue personal influence." It held that "no trustee has more sacred duties than a public official and any scheme to obtain an advantage by corrupting such an one must in the federal law be considered a scheme to defraud." According to the court, the intent to influence the governor and cheat the public of the attention of public servants was the essence of the crime. Even if the city had not been hurt by the sale, the harm lay in this kind of faithlessness, whether or not there was material harm in the form of public monetary loss. Was there corrupt intent? What was corruptness? The *Shushan* court concluded that the requisite intent was that "there must be a purpose to do wrong which is inconsistent with moral uprightness."

Over the next forty years, the theory accepted by the court of appeals in *Shushan v. United States* was adopted by every federal court of appeals, making mail fraud *the* statute of choice for prosecuting bribery of state officials. In a series of cases, district after district expanded the mail fraud statute to include a criminal prohibition against efforts to induce public officials (and others) to use their public roles for private gain and self-dealing by public officials for their own good. As one explained in 1980, "When a public official is bribed, he is paid for making a decision while purporting to be exercising his independent discretion."[1] The same logic applied to the failure of a public official to disclose his ownership interest in a corporation when he recommended that the city use the corporation's services.[2]

The conduct covered was not merely successfully completed exchanges, where one thing was changed for another, but bribe attempts, where gifts were given and the public action was *not* modified. It also covered situations where the public officials privately gave themselves preferential treatment. Prosecutors in every federal jurisdiction were allowed to bring mail fraud cases to the jury when there was evidence of intent to defraud the public.[3] Courts varied slightly about the precise need for proof of harm. For many courts, "material misrepresentations and active concealment," along with a personal benefit, were enough to bring a case in front of a jury.[4]

Defendants repeatedly objected to the uncertainty at the margins of this kind of charge. If there was no actual impact on the public, how could there be a crime? They objected to the idea that there was something lost when the loyalty of a public servant was lost. But most courts held that the mail fraud statute was violated if a person defrauded the State out of the loyal and faithful services of an employee.[5] In case after case, the courts reinforced the classic American view of corruption and political obligation of public servants. The public had a right to "honest and faithful services," because democratic society depended upon such an obligation. As the Ninth Circuit explained in 1975, "When a public official is bribed, he is paid for making a decision while purporting to be exercising his independent discretion."[6] The public, in this view, has a right to know whether a public official has ownership interests in a corporation that he is recommending.

The effect of these honest services cases was to give juries enormous power to determine what constituted corruption. The same general tendency exhibited itself across a wide variety of statutes. Along with the mail fraud act, the Hobbs Act became the tool of choice for extortion prosecutions. Passed in 1934 as an antiracketeering act and amended in 1942, the Hobbs Act was enacted to protect against organized crime. The Hobbs

Act defined extortion as "the obtaining of property from another, with his consent, induced by wrongful use of actual or threatened force, violence, or fear, or under color of official right." Prosecutors argued—eventually successfully—that obtaining property of another "under color of official right" included obtaining bribes or kickbacks by state or local public officials. With this new interpretation, federal officials could go after public officials in the states for being involved in any bribery scheme so long as there was any connection to interstate commerce, which was not hard to find. The use of the Hobbs Act became widespread in the 1970s, and most appellate courts adopted the "official right" extortion, relying on common law principles to interpret what was required for extortion.

Permissiveness

State courts allowed prosecutions for bribes that were offered but not accepted and bribes that did not clarify the precise official action that the briber wanted done.[7] A public official could be guilty of accepting a bribe even if he had no intent to change his behavior. She could be guilty of bribery for being influenced on actions over which she had no authority.[8] The criminal law, like the lobbying law before it, was designed to protect citizens from situations in which they might be tempted.

The language that surrounded these cases emphasized the democratic harm that bribery posed. As one court said, "the gist of the crime of bribery is the wrong done to the people by corruption in the public service."[9] In a 1940 case, an Oklahoma court explained why bribery had to be interpreted broadly.

While "in ancient times and later among the Romans"—the predemocratic past—"the giving of rewards and gifts to public officers was tolerated and even encouraged," the advancement of civilization led to a public recognition of the "danger of any such custom." In a modern society, the offense is heinous, all the more so because of greater personal wealth increasing the threat:

> The spirit of any democratic government is utterly abhorrent to anything which tends to debasement in the representatives of the people, or threatens the purity of the administration of government. The influence of money has become a powerful force in this dangerous direction; the protection of the rights of the people demands that a severe penalty be imposed upon any person who gives or offers to give anything of value to any public officer as an inducement to official action. The gist of the crime is the danger and injury to the community at large. The rights of the citizens of this state cannot thus be corruptly tampered with and bargained away.[10]

Statutory elements varied broadly. Some courts required that a bribe be given for an identified official action in order to trigger criminal liability.[11] An extortion case from 1975 said that in order to be convicted for extortion, something more than a payment "in connection" with services was required—it needed to be clear that the payment was intended as part of a quid pro quo.[12] In other jurisdictions, a general intent to influence sufficed: the prosecutor did not need to argue that the gift was directed toward causing a specified official action. Criminal liability existed when there was proof of intent to influence any matter "that could conceivably come before [an] official."[13] As a California court noted, there was testimony regarding a huge range of official actions that were before the board of supervisors, including zoning approvals, gas tax allocations, use of space, and ongoing supervision about how to allocate some land, which could also impact the developer. There was no need to name a particular deal or agreement. A different court described it this way: "It is sufficient that the evidence reflect that there existed subjects of potential action by the recipient, and that the bribe was given or received with the intent that some such action be influenced."[14]

What Is "Corruptly"?

As the Hobbs Act and other motive-based criminal laws started being used by prosecutors with increasing frequency, courts had to confront jury instructions for decidedly political terms. Did juries need to be told that an act had been done "corruptly"? If so, what constituted "corrupt"? If "corrupt" was an element of the crime, courts largely left the definition of corrupt up to the jury or described it in equally moral and imprecise language. Nor was it always entirely clear whether "corruptly" was a separate element of an offense that needed to be found, a superfluous adjective, or an essential adjective. Corruption could mean "improper motive."[15] It could mean "intent to influence" governmental action.[16] One court held that New Jersey law required a "corruptly" instruction to accompany an extortion charge, concluding that "corruptly" meant knowing the payment was unlawful.[17] It could mean "committed for a personal benefit."[18]

Michigan has a crime of misconduct in office, which includes a "corruptly" requirement. The court tried to follow the meaning of corruption to its logical end, tracing the dictionary meanings of corruption and ending up with nothing more clear than that the jury could determine corrupt intent. Corruption was defined as "depravity, perversion, and taint." Depravity was defined as morally corrupt. Perversion was "misguided; distorted; misinterpreted"; and "taint" was something with a "bad or offensive" trace. The definitions fold in on each other; therefore corruption, it held, exists when there is "intentional or purposeful misbehavior or wrongful conduct pertaining to the requirements and duties of office by an officer." No simple silver bullet exists to define it.[19] In Alabama, corrupt intent was the key, and measured by the jury.[20]

On its face, "corruptly" appeared to be redundant—it added no additional finding of fact. Instead, "the element of corrupt intent requires that the facts described by the other elements be subject to characterization as wrongful, and thus requires the application, implicitly or explicitly, of normative political standards."[21] Those normative standards were supplied, for most of the twentieth century, by the jury.

That meant for most of the twentieth century that the country lived inside Teddy Roosevelt's vision of bright lines and broad enforcement. The job of figuring out how to resolve difficult questions of what kinds of laws would decrease corruption, and how to manage new challenges, was left up to state and federal legislators. The job of policing political morality in close cases was a jury matter. If Roosevelt could have passed every one of his reforms, the courts would have let him, if he stayed within the scope of federal power. If state and federal courts got involved, it was to increase disincentives for corruption, not to limit legislative reforms. But starting in the 1970s, the Supreme Court started curbing legislative power, in part by narrowing the definition of corruption and giving the word *corruption* a peculiar role in constitutional jurisprudence.

CHAPTER ELEVEN

Operation Gemstone

IT WAS CALLED Operation Gemstone—a name that King Louis might have approved. The plan was to disrupt the Democratic National Convention (DNC) and to protect the Republican National Convention from agitators. Instead, in June 1972, police caught five burglars in the DNC offices with cameras, cash, and electronics. They were there to bug the phone of the Democratic chairman.

H. R. "Bob" Haldeman, Nixon's White House chief of staff, played a key role in the cover-up of the burglary, now known as Watergate. He directed and approved efforts to hide connections to the president. Haldeman was convicted of conspiracy and obstruction of justice. In his defense, Haldeman brought two complaints about the word *corruptly* in law. Before trial, he argued that the obstruction of justice statute was unconstitutionally vague because it included the word *corruptly*, which did not sufficiently designate what was covered. Afterward, in his appeal he complained that the way the judge used the word *corruptly*—"evil or improper purpose or intent"—had misled the jurors into thinking that no criminal intent was required.

In essence, Haldeman argued that the word *corrupt* had no coherent content.

The Watergate scandal led to a redefinition of corruption of the same type he requested, but on a far greater scale than Haldeman imagined. In campaign finance criminal law, courts gradually came to find the term *corruptly* (and its ilk) too vague to be left to the jury, while in campaign finance law, the concept of corruption became too empty to signify much of anything except explicit exchanges. Both of those changes can be traced back to *Buckley v. Valeo*, a Supreme Court case that struck down a centerpiece of the post-Watergate reforms.

By the time Haldeman was on trial, the cost of campaigns had been growing for over two decades. More money flowed into expensive federal races, television advertising costs exploded, and people and corporations seeking ways to influence the exercise of power gradually learned how to use campaign contributions effectively. By the early 1970s, someone willing to invest a lot of money could use campaign contributions to influence policy outcomes directly. As the Gemstone story unfolded, the country learned about enormous individual donations, private slush funds, private contacts with donors, and a network of trades of money for influence. The Federal Election Campaign Act (FECA) had been passed initially in 1971, before the Watergate scandal, but momentum for reform after Watergate led to strict new rules, passed in 1974. The reforms grew both from public disgust and from politicians who wanted to spend less time fund-raising to keep up with the growing costs of campaigns.

FECA's goal was to create new norms of fund-raising and influence. The law included mandated comprehensive disclosure, criminalized campaign contributions over a certain amount, and criminalized campaign spending over set amounts. It also created the Federal Election Commission to oversee and enforce the campaign finance restrictions. And it created a mechanism for publicly funding presidential campaigns. Republicans and Democrats alike supported the basic provisions: the major debate in Congress was about the scope of the public funding mechanisms, not about the contribution or expenditure limits. The most outspoken opponents of FECA were opposed to it because they worried that it could become a corrupt tool that entrenched politicians wanted to use to protect their own power. They worried that if government could punish candidates for spending money on political communication, those in power would limit the amount spent so much that insurgents, who needed more than incumbents to get attention, would be unable to reach the public.

Buckley v. Valeo

The law was immediately challenged in court. In 1976, in *Buckley v. Valeo*, the Supreme Court upheld most of the law but struck down the spending limits on First Amendment grounds. It upheld the contribution limits, disclosure, and the presidential system for publicly funding elections. The unsigned opinion, 138 pages long, held that legislatively passed spending limits were unconstitutional because they infringed upon the First Amendment and were not sufficiently related to solving the problem of corruption. The primary interest of the Federal Election Campaign Act, the Court concluded, is "the prevention of corruption and the appearance of corruption spawned by the real or imagined coercive influence of large financial contributions on candidates' positions and on their actions if elected to office."[1]

The key to understanding the meaning of *Buckley* in our legal history is how it created a limited framework with which courts should process campaign finance restrictions. Litigators, judges, and academics have been operating within this architecture ever since, many under protest. The four premises of that framework are the following:

1. Spending money on elections is a protected First Amendment right.
2. Combatting corruption, and the appearance of corruption, are interests that might justify incursions on the First Amendment right to spend money on elections.
3. Campaign contribution limits are presumptively valid, and courts will defer to legislative judgment.
4. Campaign expenditure limits are presumptively invalid, and courts will look skeptically on them.

The Court treated spending and contribution limits differently for two reasons. First, the speech interest is different in the contribution and expenditure context. It held that the expressive content of a contribution is largely in the fact of a contribution, not the amount, because the political speech of the candidate will control how the money is used. An expenditure, by contrast, is completely controlled by the spender, and therefore the expressive interest is greater. Second, it held that the corruption justification differed for spending and contribution limits. It upheld the limits on campaign *contributions* because the justices concluded that unlimited campaign contributions were likely to corrupt the democratic/political/electoral process. Candidates would become beholden to large contributors. Bribery laws would not be enough to stop that corruption, because they punish only "the most blatant and specific attempts of those with money to influence governmental action." On the other hand, it struck down the limits on candidate and individual campaign *expenditures* because there was less danger that expenditures would be "given as a *quid pro quo* for improper commitments from the candidate."

Buckley gave birth to a new jurisprudence, in part because of the charter-like status it achieved. Justice Scalia calls it a "seminal case."[2] Political theorist Thomas Burke analyzes the concept of corruption in case law "beginning with *Buckley*," and Dennis Thompson calls it the "original campaign finance decision."[3] One of the leading textbooks in the field states that *Buckley* is the "one inevitable starting point" of the Supreme Court's jurisprudence on money and politics.[4] However, even as it achieved canonical status, few jurists were persuaded by the *Buckley* logic. Some— more likely to be on the left—objected to the characterization of political election spending as speech, instead of speech-facilitating. Others—both liberals and conservatives—found the line between spending and contributions difficult to defend, in practice and theory. Liberals wanted to uphold the spending limits, and conservatives wanted to strike down the contribution limits. The jurisprudence has survived forty years largely because the Supreme Court has never cobbled together a majority to strike down the spending rule, nor to strike down the contributions rule.

The unlimited spending led to even more candidate time fund-raising. And, as Robert Kaiser details brilliantly in his book *So Damn Much Money*, "the more important money became to the politicians, the more important donors became to them."[5]

Lobbyists grew in importance as they helped candidates with fund-raisers; candidates came to depend upon the lobbyists and listen to the needs of their clients. We cannot know what would have happened if all of FECA had been upheld, but we know what happened when it was not.

On its face, it might seem to be an important moment for the concept of corruption. It settled Frankfurter's questions in the earlier cases, choosing to value the integrity of the elections even when First Amendment interests were implicated. The opinion elevated corruption and gave it a designated place in our constitutional framework. However, the elevation was accompanied by a simultaneous lack of guidance on how to understand the concept. The Court used the word *corruption* but didn't explain where we should look to define it, or how we should understand it. As a result, as I'll show, many people have turned to white-collar bribery law for support without explaining why modern criminal bribery law should define a constitutional concept.

Second, because *Buckley* legitimated a focus on corruption, and not equality or other concerns, as a reason for restriction, litigators have had to try to claim that all the myriad purposes that one might want campaign finance to serve are corruption interests. Several justices on the Court have interpreted the second part of the framework described above to mean that combatting corruption, and the appearance of corruption, are the *only* interests that might justify campaign finance laws. These justices have read language in the opinion that rejected equalizing speech in the public sphere as a rejection of the legitimacy of political equality altogether.

The corruption-only rationale has in turn led to disingenuity in scholarship and litigation. Litigators and articles renamed the interests they think of as important as *corruption* interests, which had the effect of confusing the term. It was and is considered foolish for a litigator to mention that campaign finance limits might be designed to increase participation: a participation argument must be recast as a corruption argument. Not without reason: in a recent case, the Supreme Court held that a provision in an Arizona law that provided additional public funds to candidates who were seriously outspent was illegitimate because the Court concluded that equality was the motivating reason for the law. According to the Court, "It is not legitimate for the government to attempt to equalize electoral opportunities in this manner."[6] Similarly, opponents of campaign finance reform who argue for a narrow meaning of *corruption*, the word, do so regardless of their other prior beliefs about corruption, the concept.

In short, *Buckley* took a difficult but important concept and turned it into a centrally contested concept without any guidance on where or how the contestation might take place. *Buckley* quasi-constitutionalized corruption, making it as contested as the right to bear arms or any other constitutional concept, but it did so in an entirely ahistorical way. After *Buckley*, respect for the precedent meant that the Court was rhetorically committed to the belief that corruption was a significant government interest, without any guidelines that could referee debates about the meaning of corruption.

Justice Byron White's dissent displayed more continuity and connection to history and democratic theory. Unlike the other justices, he doesn't try to separate the corruption interest from general foundational interests in self-government. The majority, according to White, gets the whole idea of corruption wrong and treats it too lightly, and understands it too thinly. He quotes extensively from the nineteenth-century case *Ex parte Yarbrough*, arguing that Congress clearly has the authority to "protect the elective process against the 'two natural and historical enemies of all republics, open violence and insidious corruption.'" Corruption is "the consequence of 'the free use of money in elections, arising from the vast growth of recent wealth.'" Throughout his dissent, the strength of his concern about corruption reveals itself in language—it is "a mortal danger against which effective preventative and curative steps must be taken" . . . "expenditure ceilings reinforce the contribution limits and help eradicate the hazard of corruption" . . . "the danger to the public interest in such situations is self-evident."[7]

Buckley opened the door to generations of litigation. Before the case came down, both campaign expenditure limits and contribution limits were presumptively valid, the First Amendment status of political spending was unclear, and corruption was one of many possible reasons that campaign finance laws might be passed. Afterward, every state or federal law involving a regulation of money and politics became suspect and open to challenge.

Corruption in the Wake of Buckley

After *Buckley*, a series of previously uncontroversial laws became controversial. The Court divided on whether any kind of expenditure limit was acceptable. Two important decisions for understanding the current corruption jurisprudence involved corporate spending. In a 1978 case, *First National Bank of Boston v. Bellotti*, the Court struck down a Massachusetts law that prohibited corporations from spending money in a referendum.[8]

The opinion relied on a novel First Amendment approach, one that protected speech instead of the speaker, and found that the state could not ban particular kinds of corporate speech. It then considered whether there was a countervailing interest to justify the First Amendment incursion, and concluded no. Unlike in an election where donations are tied to candidate success, corporate spending in a referendum doesn't lead to corruption or the appearance of corruption. *Bellotti* held that the "creation of political debts" was the essence of corruption, but it spent very little time discussing definitional questions.

Then in 1990, in *Austin v. Michigan State Chamber of Commerce*, the Court upheld limits on corporate spending around election campaigns.[9] It again found a First Amendment interest but justified upholding limits for anticorruption reasons. *Austin* described corruption in terms of "the corrosive and distorting effects of immense aggregations of wealth that are accumulated with the help of the corporate form and that have little or no correlation to the public's support for the corporation's political ideas." *Austin's* definition of corruption reflected the ways in which equality concerns were being recast as corruption concerns. But it also harked back to older conceptions of corruption, where corruption and equality are related. In *Austin* Justice Scalia dissented, arguing that this kind of understanding of corruption was so essentially unmanageable: "When the vessel labeled 'corruption' begins to founder under weight too great to be logically sustained, the argumentation jumps to the good ship 'special privilege'; and when that in turn begins to go down, it returns to 'corruption.' Thus hopping back and forth between the two, the argumentation may survive but makes no headway toward port, where its conclusion waits in vain."

In 2003, in the longest case in constitutional history—*McConnell v. FEC*—a majority of the Court upheld campaign finance reforms, including limits on when certain kinds of ads could be broadcast, relying on *Austin* but developing the concept more fully.[10] Corruption, *McConnell* held, is far more than "simple cash-for-votes corruption" but includes "undue influence on an officeholder's judgment, and the appearance of such influence." The problem, according to the Court, included evidence of access and the use of influence. It explicitly rejected a more transactional "straight cash-for-votes" understanding of corruption, and concluded that "the best means of prevention is to identify and to remove the temptation." This language, as Rick Hasen has argued, is "suggestive of the nineteenth and early twentieth century courts' concern about the threat to self-government posed by 'personal influence' and private solicitations."[11] The language was heavily critiqued in the dissents, which argued that corruption was nothing more than quid pro quo. Those dissents became majority opinions in 2006.

CHAPTER TWELVE

A West Virginia State of Mind

WHEN, IF EVER, is a campaign donation corrupt? Is a $15 contribution designed to influence a state senator on fracking policy corrupt? What about a $15 million contribution? Outside of lobbying and independent spending, these are among the hardest questions in modern corruption law, modern campaign finance law, modern First Amendment law, and arguably modern democratic theory.[1]

The questions are so difficult because electoral democratic practice poses problems for defining corrupt or corruption that do not exist to the same degree when defining corruption in judicial or executive branch interactions. It doesn't seem hard to say that a judge is corrupt if he demands a gift or campaign contribution from someone appearing before him, or that a police officer is corrupt if she accepts payment to ignore a traffic ticket. But what about a candidate at a fund-raiser?

Legislative corruption—particularly that tied to election campaigns—is complicated to regulate for several reasons that do not apply to these other areas. There are several minor differences. When a judge is given a campaign contribution by a litigant while the litigant is appearing in front of him, the judge faces a binary choice, and the payment seems designed to illegitimately influence him in that official act. But if a political figure is paid, it will not be clear *what* she is paid for, both because a politician typically faces an array of possible political actions, and because doing or not doing them will have an impact on every member of the society. Unlike the judge and the litigant, there is no limited time frame in which a politician has power over the donor, or a limited number of people whose lives she can influence. Second, it takes multiple representatives to pass any given law, unlike the typical police officer or judge, so if *one* is influenced by a bribe, it will not be clear whether the bribery caused the law to pass or not. Relatedly, a gift to a legislator with no formal power over an issue—but with connections to executive agencies—may be designed to influence, even though the technical power to influence does not reside in the legislator. Representatives, unlike judges or police officers, frequently hold other jobs, so people seeking favors might interact with the representatives in their commercial capacity, creating the opportunity for an exchange of favors. A member of Congress, unlike a judge, is often also a lawyer, and a mayor also runs a construction company. Separating legitimate outside employment from the illegitimate payments depends upon difficult factual determinations: Was the state representative hired as a lawyer for a gas company in order to sway her, and if so, is that illegitimate if she is not overpaid?

But the biggest difference is this: a legislator must regularly appeal to members of the public for help—votes and gifts—to get elected. Democracy is premised on that plea. He promises policies and actions, and people help him get elected by telling their neighbors, campaigning for him, perhaps throwing an event for him. A constant flow between public and candidate is supposed to exist in a representative democracy, because that ensures that the representative will be thinking of the best interests of her constituency. This responsiveness is different from the barrier of nonresponsiveness that ideally exists between judges and the people who appear before them. The candidate, by definition, has to get the public to help him, so bans on public aid do not work—he is permitted to ask someone to spend twenty Saturdays canvassing but not permitted to pay for a vote.

Creating laws that deter bribery of legislators, but do not deter democratic organizing, has been among the most vexing problems of the American political experiment. To put it another way: democracy's internal threat (responsiveness to donors) is deeply intertwined with democracy's greatest promise (responsiveness to citizens). The decision on which activities fall into the category of threat and which ones fall into the category of promise is a vital job in democratic design. Is a $5,000 anti-fracking campaign contribution corruptly offering a price for official action or virtuously engaging in activism? Daniel Lowenstein pointed out these difficulties in a 1985 essay that included this provocation: "Under most bribery statutes as they have been interpreted by most courts, most special interest campaign contributions are bribes."[2]

Bribery statutes typically require five elements: (1) giving a thing of value or a benefit (2) to a public official or candidate (3) corruptly (4) with intent to influence (5) an official action. Extortion laws are similar, with the defendant reversed: a thing of value is corruptly requested by a public official with the understanding that it will influence her official actions. Gratuities statutes (gifts statutes) are also severe, creating liability for giving gifts after the fact for an official act already done. Lowenstein argued how these five elements, applied, neutrally would cover a member of Congress agreeing to introduce a bill in order to get a union endorsement, as well as a member of Congress voting against a bill in order to receive a campaign contribution. They would also likely apply to a public statement by a well-funded independent organization that it would spend millions of dollars on an independent expenditure if a candidate would change her vote. Lowenstein argued, therefore, that the idea of neutral application was impossible: the requirement that the offer or demand be done "corruptly" meant that a normative political element was part of the statute, and either courts or juries had to make some determination based on ideas outside the statute—political theory— about whether campaign contributions should fit within the ambit of "bribes."[3]

A Question of Fact

The earliest cases confronting the prosecution of campaign contributions as bribes treated them the same as other bribery charges. A 1927 case put it simply: "If it was accepted as a campaign contribution it was, nevertheless, bribery. It is not the use to which the money was put, but the purpose for which it was paid."[4] A 1938 appeal upheld a jury conviction for bribery based on campaign contributions. There was conflicting evidence about a series of interactions between a de facto public officer and the owner of a pipe company. The jury heard statements like "If we would get together, we might do both ourselves some good," that led the owner of the pipe company to believe that he was being asked to give campaign contributions in exchange for a government contract. On appeal, the Washington Supreme Court concluded: "The question was not what was done with the money after appellant secured it, but the reason and purpose of receiving it."[5]

A 1956 New Jersey court dismissed the argument that campaign contributions are somehow different by reference to the core logic of bribery laws:

> The aim of the statute is to punish those who betray public office. In our opinion the gist of the offense charged here was the solicitation of Money by defendants bargaining for their votes with a corrupt mind; and it mattered not whether the money was to go to them personally or for campaign funds or to some recipient designated by them. As has been said in cases where money has been handed a public official for campaign purposes as a price for his official action, it makes no difference to what use the money is to be put; it still is bribery.[6]

When prosecutors charged campaign contributors with bribery, courts had to choose between elite norms of political behavior in which such contributions should be treated as gifts—much like the *boîtes a portrait* were in France—and the norms of political behavior announced by the bribery statutes.

Prosecutions for campaign contributions were relatively rare, and the federal prosecutorial guidelines limited prosecutions to only those cases where a contribution request was explicitly conditioned upon an identifiable government action. Nonetheless, convictions for campaign contributions were upheld under the federal gratuities statute, the federal bribery statute, and the Hobbs Act.

In a 1974 case examining whether the gratuities statute could apply to campaign contributions, the D.C. Circuit concluded unequivocally that it could. The defendant in that case argued that the gratuities statute was overly broad because its terms covered campaign contributions, "which arguably can be characterized as the sort of political, associational activity protected by the First Amendment." The court summarily rejected the argument, holding that Congress had passed a law against gifts given for official acts, not for lawful campaign contributions. The illegality under the law was in the "knowing and purposeful receipt by a public official of a payment, made in consideration of an official act." Congress, said the court, has "an indisputable interest in proscribing such conduct as a means for preserving the integrity of governmental operations. This interest supersedes any conceivable First Amendment value related to such conduct."[7]

A $10,000 campaign contribution from the president of a medical college to a congressman while a grant was pending for funding of a building was the alleged bribe in a 1979 federal case. The defendant argued that the donation was part of normal business practice to promote a good business climate by donating. The district court said that this argument infringed upon the jury's role:

> Defendant's first claim, that the money given to Congressman Flood was part of a traditional business practice of tendering political contributions to promote a favorable business climate for federal funds which Hahnemann needed, is essentially a challenge to the truth of the allegation that defendant "*corruptly*" gave the Congressman

money to influence his official action on Hahnemann's application for federal funding. Whether defendant paid this money to the Congressman with "corrupt" intent or merely as a "traditional" political gift is a question for the jury to decide at trial.[8]

The question of corruption "require[d] a determination of defendant's intent, which is a question of fact." A few years later, a court upheld a jury conviction for bribery when a woman gave a state representative a handwritten note saying, "Mr. Swanstrom the offer for help in your election & $1000 for your campaign for Pro ERA vote."[9]

The elements of a federal Hobbs Act violation were similar to the general bribery elements. Under the logic of most courts, an official violated the Hobbs Act when he obtained a payment with knowledge that the payment was in return for specific official acts.[10] There, as well, courts held that "appellants' conduct here constituted extortion regardless of whether the payments went into appellants' pockets or their party's coffers."[11] At least three circuits had sanctioned prosecution for extortion where public officials had asked for campaign contributions.[12] The courts explicitly recognized the argument that the scope of the act could lead to expansive prosecution, but "our need to avoid hampering honest candidates who must solicit funds from prospective supporters does not require that the courts abandon this necessary, if troublesome, realm of political maneuver to those who would abuse its opportunities. A moment's reflection should enable one to distinguish, at least in the abstract, a legitimate solicitation from the exaction of a fee for a benefit conferred or an injury withheld."[13]

To summarize, on the state and federal level, courts maintained the general trend toward permissiveness: the bribery statute had no special exception for campaign contributions, and the jury should decide which contributions were corrupt and which were not. These cases assume that while campaigns are privately financed, campaign funders cannot give with the goal of influencing behavior. They may give out of allegiance, expression, or personal affection, but not in order to shape the exercise of power. Likewise, candidates can raise money on issues that they care about, but they cannot allow fund-raising to shape their actions. To do otherwise would be corrupt.

The McCormick *Moment*

"It's hard to tell whether West Virginia is a state of mind, a state of chaos or just a good soap opera," said the local president of Common Cause, interviewed about the state's problems in 1989.[14] The treasurer, the attorney general, the president of the state Senate, and dozens of other public officials were caught up in scandals. Many were convicted of extortion or other improper uses of office.

West Virginia had a program to allow foreign medical school graduates to practice in the state while studying for the state licensing exams. In the face of threats of ending the program, a number of temporarily licensed doctors formed a group and in 1994 hired a lobbyist to push for legislation extending the program. The lobbyist, Vandergrift, got in touch with Robert L. McCormick, a delegate. In 1984 McCormick sponsored legislation extending the program and agreed to sponsor legislation that would grant permanent licenses.

McCormick had a phone call with the lobbyist where he "expressed to me that his campaign was rather expensive, the election was coming up, and that he had put out a couple of thousand dollars out of his pocket and he hadn't heard anything from the foreign physicians and he wanted to know what I was going to do about it."[15] The lobbyist then called one of the doctors and "stressed to him I thought it was very important that we get some money to help Bob in his campaign." The lobbyist was very straightforward about the reason: "We were facing a very important legislative session, and I wanted to be in a position to *help Bob with his campaign* and to strengthen the ties of influence that this would generate." According to the lobbyist, the "tone of his voice was that he wanted a campaign contribution, that he needed it." He was as direct as one could be in terms of his own needs. "He had mentioned that he had just put 2,000 dollars out for campaign expenses in cash, and I thought it would be appropriate at least to replace that and some more if we could." The lobbyist learns how much needs to be given and knows why. There is an implicit threat, but not an explicit one.

The lobbyist told him he would "see what he could do." The foreign doctors gave five cash payments, some in envelopes. Neither McCormick nor the doctors' organizations recorded the gifts. In 1985 McCormick sponsored the promised legislation. The law passed. Two weeks later he received another campaign contribution.

When federal prosecutors learned of the relationship, McCormick was tried and convicted of violating the Hobbs Act by extorting payments under color of official right. In the charge to the jury, the trial court instructed the jury that they could find him guilty if he knew payment was made on the expectation that it would influence his official conduct.

The Supreme Court overturned McCormick's conviction and held that to be convicted under the Hobbs Act, the payments must have been made in return for an "explicit promise" to do (or not do) an official act. A broader reading, according to the majority opinion, would violate contemporary norms of political behavior. Therefore, proof of quid pro quo is required for a Hobbs Act violation.

The key reasoning in *McCormick v. United States* is a description of how the Court understands politics to work. According to the majority, the job of a legislator is to work for constituents; constituents support campaigns, therefore supporting legislation that furthers the interest of some constituents who have given campaign contributions is inevitable. It is unrealistic to call official actions "extortion" simply because they benefit certain people and are taken shortly before or after campaign contributions are solicited and received from those beneficiaries. That can't be what Congress meant, the Court held, when it made it a crime to obtain property from another, with his consent, "under color of official right." To hold otherwise would open up conduct "that has long been thought to be well within the law" to prosecution. Most important, private campaign contributions made with intent to influence elections are "unavoidable so long as election campaigns are financed by private contributions or expenditures, as they have been from the beginning of the nation." The Court doesn't reject the possibility that Congress might mean to criminalize private campaign contributions intended to influence government but "it would require statutory language more explicit than the Hobbs Act contains to justify a contrary conclusion."

The holding in *McCormick* has been bedeviled by problems and confusion. Subsequent decisions are unclear about the meaning of "explicit" and how the quid pro quo requirement is defined.[16] The confusion was amplified by a Supreme Court case a year later, *Evans v. United States*, that seemed to hold that a jury could find a Hobbs Act violation with an implicit deal that was not openly stated.[17] Providing a critical concurrence in that case, Justice Kennedy added that "the official and the payor need not state the *quid pro quo* in express terms, for otherwise the law's effect could be frustrated by knowing winks and nods."[18] The meaning of the case was particularly confusing because the bribes included a blend of campaign contributions and private payments.

Nearly twenty-five years later it is still not clear exactly what kind of campaign exchange constitutes a violation of the Hobbs Act.[19] It is not clear exactly how explicit the deal must be, and whether a specific government act needs to be identified. It is not entirely clear whether the logic of *McCormick* applies to all federal bribery statutes or just the Hobbs Act. And it is not clear how much of it is statutory interpretation and how much of it is political theory.

There are three ways to read *McCormick*, each of which has substantial implications for law. The first is that it is an expression of the justices' beliefs about how politics is supposed to work and a description that describes the outer bounds of corruption in a campaign context. This interpretation is the way the Roberts Supreme Court has understood *McCormick*. Under this reading, the case provides good authority for definitions of corruption, extortion, and bribery.

The second is that *McCormick* is not about a fundamental definition of corruption or extortion, but simply about judicial unwillingness to read a potentially powerful statute broadly without direct guidance from Congress. If this is your view, Congress could pass a law next year that criminalizes campaign contributions given with the intent to influence policy.

The third is that *McCormick* is driven by the mismatch between criminal bribery laws and our political system because criminal corruption laws with a corrupt intent requirement are traditionally very vague at the margins. Due process lurks in the background of *McCormick*, and the statutory interpretation allowed the Court to avoid striking down the law more generally. In this view, the decision has nothing to say about foundational meanings of corruption but simply about the legitimate scope of a particular kind of law.

McCormick was startlingly silent about the republican ills that the bribery statute might be designed to dissuade, particularly in the political sphere. It did not discount corruption, but it did not take the potential impact on self-government particularly seriously. But this silence corresponds with all three theories, suggesting that all three were at play. Whatever the deep motivation, the prosecution of *McCormick* redefined the relationship between campaign finance law and bribery in twentieth-century bribery law. The Court took an activity that had traditionally been coded as potentially corrupt—a question for the jury to decide—and recategorized it as normal political activity.

CHAPTER THIRTEEN

Citizens United

THE GIFT OF A FRAMED PRINT was at the heart of a little-noticed case that foreshadowed the Supreme Court's political theory in *Citizens United*. The case came to court after a trade association, Sun Diamond Growers, gave Secretary of Agriculture Mike Espy tickets to the 1993 U.S. Open Tennis Tournament worth $2,295, luggage worth $2,427, and $665 in meals, as well as the print and a crystal bowl worth $524.[1]

When the gifts came to light, the government prosecuted Sun Diamond for violating the federal gratuities statute, a section of the 1962 bribery law that forbids gifts "for or because of any official act performed or to be performed."[2] They argued that Sun Diamond gave the gifts to curry favor. There were two reasons that Sun Diamond members might have cared whether they had the affection of Secretary Espy. He was considering a plan that would provide federal aid for foreign marketing to "small sized entities," which wasn't an obvious designation for companies such as Sun-Maid Growers of California, Sunsweet Growers, Valley Fig Growers, and Hazelnut Growers of Oregon. Espy's department was also considering a new pesticide regulation.

The jury convicted and Sun Diamond appealed, arguing that the jury instructions were too broad. It pointed out there was no evidence connecting the bowl, luggage, tickets, meals, or print to either of Espy's two potentially powerful actions. As far as the trade group was concerned, the statute only covered situations where the government could prove that a gift was given to influence a particular government action.

The Supreme Court sided with Sun Diamond, against every court of appeals decision before 1999. It held that the government had to prove that the gift was given for a particular official act. As white-collar crime specialist Peter Henning argued in his review of the case, it was a plausible reading of the statute, but only barely. It was "difficult to see" how it made sense of all the language of the statute, which clearly contemplates before-the-fact gifts. *Sun Diamond* makes it nearly impossible to prove a violation of the gratuities statute for *any* gift given before an official action. *Sun Diamond* effectively turned the bright-line gratuities statute into a more demanding bribery statute.

The case was technically a matter of statutory interpretation, and Senator Patrick Leahy has introduced a law to overturn it. It can be made moot tomorrow through legislative action, but it is important for the deep logic of politics that it reflects. *Sun Diamond* revealed just how far the Court had come from the framing era, where gracious presents were understood as swords of power. The gifts clause of the Constitution was never discussed. The opinion shows a lack of understanding of the corrosive power of gifts and subtle influence, and no appreciation for the need for clear rules, because of the difficulty of proving connections between gifts and acts. Instead, the Court concluded that a clear rule would lead to "absurdities." Justice Scalia, writing for the Court, found it incomprehensible that the statute could criminalize "a complimentary lunch for the Secretary of Agriculture" given by Sun Diamond, if he had matters before him that affected their work. He apparently never heard the adage, "There ain't no such thing as a free lunch."

Scalia outright rejected the argument that the statute criminalized the "buy[ing of] favor or generalized goodwill from an official who either has been, is, or may at some unknown, unspecified later time, be in a position to act favorably to the giver's interests." He rejected the claim that it criminalized presents "motivated, at least in part, by the recipient's capacity to exercise governmental power or influence in the donor's favor." If you read the case as political theory, instead of statutory interpretation, the Court suggests that using money to influence power through gifts is both inevitable and not troubling. In so doing, it set the table for the Court's major corruption decision in *Citizens United*.

Justice Scalia began the *Sun Diamond* opinion with this sentence: "Talmudic sages believed that judges who accepted bribes would be punished by eventually losing all knowledge of the divine law." Eleven years later, Scalia and the other justices in *Citizens United* seemed to forget all knowledge of what in America is the closest we get to divine law—the laws of human nature and democratic politics.

Democratic Responsiveness

Nine years after *Sun Diamond*, a small, conservative nonprofit corporation named Citizens United wanted to air a ninety-minute movie about Hillary Clinton on DirecTV. It was right before the 2008 Democratic presidential primaries. Citizens United also wanted to air thirty-second advertisements for the movie on broadcast television. The transcript of one of the ads went like this, with different lines spoken by different people:

"Questions"

Who is Hillary Clinton?

She's continually trying to redefine herself and figure out who she is . . .

At least with Bill Clinton he was just good-time Charlie. Hillary's got an agenda . . .

Hillary is the closest thing we have in America to a European socialist . . .

If you thought you knew everything about Hillary Clinton . . . wait 'til you see the movie.

The Federal Election Commission moved to block the movie and the advertisements for violating the Bipartisan Campaign Reform Act (BCRA), a 2002 campaign-finance law that prohibited corporate-funded campaign commercials within thirty days of a presidential primary. Citizens United challenged the decision. According to its lawyers, it was a documentary, it was not offered over broadcast, and BCRA did not apply. According to the government, it was a ninety-minute ad designed to hurt Mrs. Clinton in the primaries, the distribution counted as broadcast, and BCRA did apply.

During the initial oral argument of the case in 2008, Justices Scalia, Kennedy, and Roberts asked questions that implied something far more expansive, and declaratory, than statutory interpretation. They wanted to hear arguments about whether the law banning corporate election spending could be justified at all. With the nature of the case changing, the Court requested that the parties write new briefs and reargue the case, explaining the constitutional legitimacy of independent corporate spending limits. However, there was no chance to research the underlying factual issues. No record was created to address these new foundational constitutional questions.

The case came back to the Supreme Court in 2009. Ted Olson, the lawyer for Citizens United, argued that there was no justification for the law because there is "no quid pro quo there [when corporations spend money in campaigns], and if there is it would be punishable as a crime." In essence, his claim was that Congress's power to protect elections from corruption was limited to the power to punish and deter explicit bribes. Anything else is not corruption.

In January 2010 Justice Anthony Kennedy, writing for a majority of the Court, adopted Olson's argument and struck down all limits on corporate expenditures.[3] The decision was within the *Buckley* framework and assumed that political spending is protected speech, and that nothing except corruption or the appearance of corruption could justify restrictions on that speech.

Citizens United is a complicated opinion, with many moving parts. But to my mind, the radicalism of the opinion, even beyond the flawed framework of *Buckley*, rests on two connected determinations. First, the Court found that the First Amendment protects political speech regardless of the identity of the speaker. Second, the Court found that no sufficiently important countervailing governmental or constitutional goal was served by limiting corporate political advertising. It conclusively held that corruption was the only possible government interest that might permit First Amendment restrictions and that anticorruption interests were not served by the law. Political equality concerns are not constitutionally legitimate reasons to pass such a law.

The opinion comprehensively redefined corruption, and in so doing, redefined the rules governing political life in the United States. As a matter of federal constitutional law, corruption now means only "quid pro quo corruption." And quid pro quo exists only when there are "direct examples of votes being exchanged for . . . expenditures."[4] Corruption does not include undue influence and cannot flow from donors trying to influence policy through campaign contributions, unless these donors are utterly crass. "Ingratiation and access" are not corruption. Corruption does not include "the corrosive and distorting effects of immense aggregations of wealth that are accumulated with the help of the corporate form and that have little or no correlation to the public's support for the corporation's political ideas." And perhaps as surprisingly, Kennedy held that as a matter of law—regardless of the facts that are presented—"independent expenditures, including those made by corporations, do not give rise to corruption or the appearance of corruption."

But *Citizens United* did not merely exclude alternate definitions of corruption. It actually took that which had been named corrupt for over two hundred years and renamed it legitimate and the essence of responsiveness. Using ideas that were originally espoused in a dissenting opinion in *McConnell*, Kennedy equated "favoritism and influence" with "democratic responsiveness." The jump from unavoidable influence to the legitimacy of influence, by equating it with positive values of responsiveness, happens in five short sentences. Even more than the adoption of quid pro quo, this passage represents a fundamental assault on traditional ideas of corruption:

> The fact that speakers may have influence over or access to elected officials does not mean that these officials are corrupt: Favoritism and influence are not . . . avoidable in representative politics. It is in the nature of an elected representative to favor certain policies, and, by necessary corollary, to favor the voters and contributors who support those policies. It is well understood that a substantial and legitimate reason, if not the only reason, to cast a vote for, or to make a contribution to, one candidate over another is that the candidate will respond by producing those political outcomes the supporter favors. Democracy is premised on responsiveness.

The framers might agree with almost every sentence in this passage, but not with the logical leaps it contains. Madison would agree that access is not equated with corruption, but he would disagree that access does not lead to corruption. He would agree that favoritism is unavoidable—and donor favoritism is unavoidable—but he would disagree that we should therefore stop trying to limit it. He would agree that the donors will likely want to produce responses, but he would disagree that we should call that desire legitimate. And he would agree that democracy is premised on responsiveness, but he would disagree that responsiveness to the wealthy is the same as responsiveness to constituents. In this string of thoughts, connected by a weak logic, Kennedy gives up on the project of separating moral and dangerous forms of responsiveness. In Kennedy's vision, all that is left of corruption is a particular kind of quasi-contract.

Justice Stevens, citing from the majority opinion in *McConnell*, called the majority definition of corruption "crabbed." But it was not just narrow; it represents an inversion of traditional American political language. Kennedy did not merely reject certain arguments, but rather laid out an affirmative vision of political life. The affirmative positive vision is Benjamin Franklin's dystopia. Citizens, in Kennedy's view, are supposed to use money to achieve personal benefits in the public sphere.

Between quid pro quo corruption and democratic responsiveness, Kennedy identified a third sphere of political activity, one that is troubling but not sufficiently troubling that Congress could do anything about it. There is "cause for concern," he wrote, when "elected officials succumb to improper influences from independent expenditures; if they surrender their best judgment; and if they put expediency before principle." However, he did not equate those with corruption, nor did he suggest how Congress could address these ills except through laws banning quid pro quo exchanges. If Jefferson were around to read the opinion, he would doubtless complain of its Yazooism. Like Justice Marshall, Justice Kennedy identifies a fundamental democratic threat for which he says nothing can be done.

The Polity

Kennedy's opinion paints an apolitical vision of democracy, far removed from the founding vision. We are a nation of consumers of information, which corporations supply. Without corporate speech, "the electorate [has been] deprived of information, knowledge and opinion vital to its function." The government has prevented corporations' "voices and viewpoints from reaching the public and advising voters on which persons or entities are hostile to their interests." Corporations must not be prevented "from presenting both facts and opinions to the public." According to Kennedy (again quoting his dissent in *McConnell*) the extensive "censorship" of campaign restrictions has "muffle[d] the voices that best represent the most significant segments of the economy."

In this worldview, associational life happens through the corporate form. Corporations are "association[s] of individuals in a business corporation"; corporations are "disfavored associations of citizens." The political life of citizens in his vision exists through and because of corporations. He counted 5.8 million for-profit corporations in 2006, worrying that all of their speech could be banned. PACs, the method through which corporations could raise and spend political money under Congress's regime, were too demanding to satisfy the corporate associational need to speak. The reporting and administration of PACs led to "onerous restrictions," such that "a corporation may not be able to establish a PAC in time to make its views known regarding candidates and issues in a current campaign." Corporate electoral speech is endowed with positive traits: "On certain topics corporations may possess valuable expertise, leaving them the best equipped to point out errors or fallacies in speech of all sorts, including the speech of candidates and elected officials."

Ironically, citizens qua citizens, instead of citizens qua Citizens United, are hard to find in *Citizens United*. There are "associations of citizens" (corporations) and "citizens and shareholders," a phrase equating citizens with investors. Citizens as civic participants are passive. They are twice mentioned (once in a quote from previous cases) to support Kennedy's argument that "speech is an essential mechanism of democracy," a paragraph that transforms the First Amendment from a personal right lodged in an individual speaker to a disembodied right that is located in speech itself, instead of the speaker. The law "prohibits Congress from fining or jailing citizens, or associations of citizens, for simply engaging in political speech." The clear goal of the sentence is to equate individuals (citizens) with corporations (associations of citizens). And at the end of the opinion, the Court uses this quote, "Citizens must be free to use new forms, and new forums, for the expression of ideas," as an explanation for why corporations must have unlimited rights to spend money.

Citizen was a hotly debated word in early America. Historian John Murrin points out that the idea of ruler and ruled was so deeply entrenched in the thinking of political elites that after the Constitutional Convention it was hard to shake. Some Americans still used the word *subjects* instead of *citizens* for decades.[5] George Washington was affronted when he was criticized between elections because he thought of elections as mechanisms for creating rulers who governed subjects, as opposed to periodic affairs in which representatives rose to positions of power but stayed in constant, dialectical relationship with the sovereign public.[6]

The word *citizen* suggests, in its very invocation, a public role for the person. It implies that a person can take responsibility for a larger political community. In the theory that animated the founding era, the citizen is the essential unit of a political society. In classic liberal theory that dominated the late nineteenth and early twentieth centuries, the citizen was also central in political life.[7] The obligations of public-dealing *at least in public affairs* remained. As the lobbying cases show, various obligations attended entering the public sphere. Throughout our history, a citizen may not, ethically, use government to better her own position if she knows it harms others. She might support laws that help her, but only if she also believes they will help the public as a whole.

In *Citizens United*, that kind of citizen is gone. If Kennedy took a traditional understanding of corruption, he might be concerned for the corruption of the citizens who were using the corporate form to influence politics, and the way in which unlimited corporate speech might exacerbate lobbying culture. Instead, the citizen becomes a consumer of information, the corporation becomes an "association of individuals," and corruption becomes democratic responsiveness. It is a remarkable conceptual triple Lutz.

To be fair, there are serious and difficult issues that *Citizens United* raised, particularly in an Internet era where it is difficult to distinguish between corporations that own "the press" and corporations that make independent expenditures. I do not agree with Justice Kennedy's resolution of those issues, but his misreading was at least partly provoked by living in a time where the fundamental distinction between the corporation and the press, for instance, is being erased. However, the replacement of corruption with a quid pro quo formulation is simply untenable as a matter of legal history. *Citizens United* was a revolution in political theory, disguised as a definitional disagreement.

The balance of this chapter discusses two parents of the decision—the narrowing of corruption to be quid pro quo and the tendency to view all political questions solely through the lens of the First Amendment.

The Quid Pro Quo Mistake

According to Justice Kennedy, corruption isn't corruption if there isn't a quid pro quo. In *Citizens United* he used the phrase *quid pro quo* fourteen times. Inasmuch as the government had an interest in protecting against corruption, it was an interest in protecting against quid pro quo corruption. He relied on other justices who have said similar things. Justice Clarence Thomas long argued in dissents that corruption meant "financial *quid pro quo*: dollars for political favors."[8] In 2000 Scalia scolded others for trying to separate "'corruption' from its *quid pro quo* roots."[9] In dissent in 2002, Justice Kennedy had argued that "the corruption interest only justifies regulating candidates' and officeholders' receipt of what we can call the 'quids' in the *quid pro quo* formulation."[10] The phrase *quid pro quo* shows up in *Buckley* but does not define corruption. Then in 2007 the Court started referring to quid pro quo as the meaning of corruption. Chief Justice John Roberts's opinion for the Supreme Court in *Wisconsin Right to Life* announced that "issue ads like WRTL's are not equivalent to contributions and the *quid-pro-quo* corruption interest cannot justify regulating them." Inveighing against the argument that corruption means anything but quid pro quo, he became exasperated: "Enough is enough."

Such impatience is surprising if one looks either at history, or criminal bribery law, or constitutional corruption law. While some corruption-related statutes have been determined to require quid pro quo and a handful of states in a handful of cases have required that a prosecutor prove a connection with an identifiable act to satisfy a bribery statute, over most of American history there is no deep association between corruption and either the phrase *quid pro quo* or the importance of a specific, identifiable act. Neither bribery nor conflict-of-interest crimes require specificity or explicitness for conviction. Particularized exchange may be part of some of the law but it is far from the essence of the law.

Quid pro quo comes from the Latin, indicating "this for that." Its historical usage is in contracts. It refers, in that context, to the idea of relatively equal exchange between parties. In the absence of relative equality—quid pro quo—a court might question whether there was an actual contract. It was casually and colloquially used in relationship to corruption since the nineteenth century at least, where writers would sometimes refer to the quid pro quo received by bribed voters or elected officials. In those situations, quid pro quo stood in for some kind of exchange, as opposed to a gift. The use of quid pro quo as a legal term in relation to corruption does not appear until the 1970s in relationship to bribery or corruption law.

Prior to *Buckley*, quid pro quo was not part of any definition of corruption. The phrase appeared less than one hundred times in all bribery and extortion cases, anywhere, before 1976, and less than ten times before 1950. Most of those cases were about witness immunity deals (was there a quid pro quo?) or the meaning of quid pro quo in the classic "equality of exchange" sense. In the 1970s there were a handful of cases in which the language of quid pro quo showed up in bribery discussions, but not as one of the elements or an essential feature of bribery.

Buckley mentions quid pro quo, and then courts started associating it with criminal law definitions. Even since *Buckley*, its use is inconsistent, and most states have not adopted a quid pro quo requirement for any of their bribery laws. In New York, the first mention of quid quo pro in the bribery context was in 1972,[11] and it has been mentioned only seven times after that. When the elements of bribery are listed, quid pro quo is not one of them. Florida recently concluded that its statute includes no quid pro quo requirement.[12] The Arizona bribery statute does not incorporate an explicit quid pro quo requirement.[13] Ohio does not use quid pro quo, but measures by "improper influence."[14] In Alabama, corrupt intent is the key and is measured by the jury.[15] Michigan's statutes that use "corrupt" do not have a quid pro quo requirement.[16] Of course, some state courts—like Indiana, Texas, and Massachusetts—have found that the bribery statute does require quid pro quo.[17]

In the minority of jurisdictions that use quid pro quo there is no agreement about what it means. As the Sixth Circuit quipped, just before citing *The Godfather*: "Not all *quid pro quo*s are made of the same stuff."[18] Quid pro quo sometimes means the solicitation or offer of something specific in exchange for some specific governmental action. It sometimes means an agreement without a particular governmental action identified. It sometimes requires a spoken or written request, sometimes something less, when the potential bribe is a campaign contribution. Sometimes quid pro quo means intent to influence unspecified governmental activity "as opportunities arise."[19] As we have seen, quid pro quo also means something different in campaign finance situations, because of the Supreme Court's own jurisprudence limiting the application of general bribery and extortion laws to campaign activity.

The phrase *quid pro quo*, in short, *seems* related to ideas about specificity and explicitness but does not actually stand for a completely coherent concept. It certainly does not refer to a historical one. But quid pro quo is a new phrase, both in relation to corruption laws and in relation to bribery laws. When Justice Scalia refers to the "quid pro quo roots" of corruption, he means, in fact, a rootless phrase, or a phrase rooted in another area of law.

This uprooting has real consequences. It is now legal to spend as much money as possible to influence politics except in two ways: First, you cannot directly offer an exchange of money for official action. Second, you must abide by direct campaign contribution limits. These remaining limits are arbitrary. There is not a deep logic to them.

A Free Speech (Only) Constitution

While corruption has narrowed to quid pro quo, free speech has expanded to encompass all money spent on communication. A full discussion of the First Amendment is beyond the scope of this book, but a brief discussion of the enlargement of the First Amendment doctrine is necessary to understand *Citizens United*. In *Citizens United*, Kennedy's version of the First Amendment is that the Court "must give the benefit of any doubt to protecting rather than stifling speech." The absolute language of "any doubt" confers a veto-providing authority to First Amendment concerns. While the opinion talks a good deal about political speech, it barely mentions politics and only once discusses the integrity of the political process. Despite the fact that the case in front of the Court concerned a bill passed by a majority of Congress after a huge national public debate about the nature of money and politics and their relationship in our country, the opinion treats the question as if it involves only the First Amendment, not politics more broadly.

Political speech appears disembodied in the opinion, without a deep discussion of the political structures within which that speech occurs. Justice Kennedy describes a world in which political rights lie in "they who speak," instead of rights and responsibilities lying in they who are citizens. Corporations gain rights not because they are corporations but because they generate speech. Speech generation is *the* constitutional value, leaving little room for other values like equality or anticorruption concerns. How did this happen? The First Amendment, designed to protect dissent, has become the tiny choke point through which all questions of political philosophy must pass.

The modern First Amendment had its seeds in the convictions of anarchists and activists around World War I. Justices Brandeis and Holmes dissented in several of these cases, arguing for a dissent-based vision for the First Amendment.[20] Their vision was gradually adopted in what Stewart Jay calls the "creation" of the First Amendment.[21] In 1941, in *Bridges v. California*, Justice Black both explicitly Americanized the First Amendment (drawing a clear line between American and British notions of freedom) and placed the First Amendment at the center of political theory: "These are not academic debating points or technical niceties. Those who have gone before us have admonished us 'that in a free representative government nothing is more fundamental than the right of the people through their appointed servants to govern themselves in accordance with their own will.'"[22] While another thirty years passed before the First Amendment was "coronat[ed]" in *Brandenberg v. Ohio*, the groundwork of the new understanding lies in the rhetoric of this period.[23] The First Amendment came to be a point of consensus: liberals turned to it during McCarthyism and Vietnam, and conservatives used it to differentiate America from the communist countries during the Cold War.

The First Amendment represents vitally important values. But in the modern free speech era, questions of politics and self-government are all referred *first* to the First Amendment, and larger questions of what constitutes a republican form of government, the explicit political philosophy clause in the Constitution, come second. As Jack Balkin wrote in 1990, "freedom of speech is the paradigmatic liberty through which one participates in democracy in the pluralist conception. Its constitutional instantiation, the First Amendment, becomes identified with democratic pluralism itself."[24] Owen Fiss wrote in 1991: "There was a sense in the body politic that the First Amendment is . . . rather an organizing principle of society, central to our self-understanding as a nation."[25] While the Court has never technically held that the First Amendment is the first among equals, its valorization has led scholars and judges to engage questions of political theory on the battlefield of the free speech clause even when the core concerns are equality or corruption.

This broad consensus has led to reframing debates about democracy *inside* debates about the meaning of the First Amendment. All constitutional debates about money and politics are played out within the arena conscribed by the First Amendment, suggesting that all central questions of political theory can be resolved there. Justice Cardozo came to call the First

Amendment "the matrix, the indispensable condition, of nearly every other form of freedom," in a phrase that exemplifies modern thinking on the First Amendment.[26] As we have seen, in the nineteenth century the freedom that might have played this vital role would be freedom from corruption. But perhaps, more importantly, there should be no matrix. There are simply important values, each to be weighed against the other.

✦ ✦ ✦

Citizens United changed the culture at the same time that it changed the law. It reframed that which was unpatriotic and named it patriotic. Before *Citizens United*, corporate or individual money could be spent with a good enough lawyer. But after *Citizens United v. FEC*, unlimited corporate money spent with intent to influence was named, by the U.S. Supreme Court, indispensable to the American political conversation.

The question "What does corruption mean?" can, at times, sound as amusing and pleasantly philosophical—and perhaps as arcane—as "Whether a Million of Angels may not fit upon a needle's point?"[27] After *Citizens United*, the difference that one definition of one word makes became clear. Kennedy's definition of corruption leads to unlimited corporate spending; the traditional understanding of corruption allows Congress to ban it. John Adams, in correspondence to a friend about the snuff boxes that everyone was receiving from the French government, wrote that "when I was young and addicted to reading I had heard about dancing upon the points of metaphysical needles; but by mixing in the world I had found the points of political needles finer and sharper than the metaphysical ones."[28]

Citizens United's metaphysical needles have led, as I discuss later on, to sharp real-world swords. After Citizens United, there is only one kind of thing that is clearly corrupt: openly asking for a deal in exchange for a specific government action. The vast range of inappropriate dependencies and self-serving behavior that made up the web of the world of corruption for the founders is gone. It is not merely that the anticorruption value is outweighed by other values—the due process clause, the First Amendment, and statutory interpretation—it is that it no longer exists. The corruption against which the framers said they must provide, lest "our government will soon be at an end"—that is not a value anymore.[29]

CHAPTER FOURTEEN

The New Snuff Boxes

PRIVATE INTERESTS spent about $12.5 million on lobbying in 2012 for every member of Congress.[1] Most of that came from a few hundred companies and individuals. That money, like the king's money of the pre-Revolutionary era, is well spent in realigning the moral obligations of our representatives.

The New Placemen

Recall how the king and his promises of well-paid places, dangled in front of parliamentarians, corrupted government as representatives served the king instead of the public. Conventional framing-era wisdom held that the "principal source of corruption in representatives, is the hopes and expectations of offices and emoluments."[2] What is often called the revolving door plays a similar role in the obligations of staffers and members of Congress. In 1970 only 3 percent of senators and congresspeople leaving office became lobbyists; now over 50 percent do, and the numbers are growing. The *likely* career path of a congressperson is to become a lobbyist. According to former lobbyist Jack

Abramoff, a job offer is one of the most effective ways to influence legislation. He has explained how when they were working with a critical decision maker—perhaps a staffer—in Congress,

> I would say or my staff would say to him or her at some point, "You know, when you're done working on the Hill, we'd very much like you to consider coming to work for us." Now the moment I said that to them or any of our staff said that to 'em, that was it. We owned them.[3]

Lobbyists' use of places in their own future firms has ballooned in recent years, making the imagined future self one of the most venal and obvious forms of non–quid pro quo corruption in our current politics. Jefferson said, "Whenever a man has cast a longing eye on offices, a rottenness begins in his conduct."[4] Congress is now dominated by people who are casting a longing eye on highly paid lobbying jobs. The revolving door corrupts the congressperson before leaving office, and it corrupts the government after the member leaves. A principal source of corruption in representatives and staffers is the hope and expectation of lobbying firm jobs and other benefits. "A man takes a seat in parliament to get an office for himself or friends, or both; and this is the great source from which flows its great venality and corruption," Pierce Butler said.[5] To paraphrase Butler, a man runs for office to get a lobbyist job for himself—and this is the great source from which flows corruption.

Lobbying also undermines political culture and civic virtues in more subtle ways. In the past, as I explored earlier in the book, people assumed that lobbying would always be illegal, or at least looked skeptically upon by courts. Senator Hugo Black said in

1935, "Contrary to tradition, against the public morals, and hostile to good government, the lobby has reached such a position of power that it threatens government itself. . . . You, the people of the United States, will not permit it to destroy you. You will destroy it."[6] Black's outburst—coming just at the moment that lobbying law was vanishing—represents the traditional American theory of the dangers of lobbying. Taking a job as a lobbyist in most cases requires one to separate personal political reasoning—one of the jobs that a citizen has by virtue of public sovereignty—into something that can be bought and sold. There are many instances in which a lobbyist actually shares the ideology of her client. But the growth of mass lobbying depends upon citizens commoditizing their ideology, selling their civic privileges to someone else. It takes intimate friendships and deep bonds of trust and turns them into marketable items. You are worth more, on the lobbying market, if the people you drink and read poetry with are powerful. By separating these two essential human features—reason and friendship—from a basic presumption of integrity, a broad culture of lobbying doesn't just change politics, it changes who we are.

To be fair, it is impossible to imagine a world where this kind of commodification of love and reason never happens. There will always be hucksters, and each of us is a huckster at times. But institutional choices make the commodification of the political person more or less likely. When lobbying becomes a celebrated and widespread job, instead of an odd job, we—like the framers—have reason for concern.

Even those lawmakers and staffers who do not end up taking a lobby firm's place are surrounded by private instead of public interest rhetoric and language. In the social community dominated by lobbyists, citizens' interests are private either to themselves or their clients—the grammar of that world (private interest maximization) bleeds into and becomes the grammar of the political universe. At times, lobbying legitimates a kind of routine sophistry and a casual approach toward public argument. It leads people to mistrust the sincerity of public arguments and weakens their own sense of obligation to the public good.

The New Foreign Gifts

The placemen are not the only ghosts of England that have returned to haunt us. Lobbyists—and donors—are part of creating what Lawrence Lessig calls—wryly—a "gift economy," an economy where gifts, given without particular legislative goals, become the vessels through which power is traded. The gifts are traded in a pattern that takes many forms but follows the basic contours of the West Virginia case, *McCormick*.

There may be many supporting players, but the basic comedy has three actors. The first is an elected official like McCormick, who might have a natural affinity for an issue. In that case, it was health care. The second is a lobbyist, eager for work. And third, there is a group of people with a financial interest in either passing or blocking a law. In the West Virginia instance, it was the "Coalfield Health Care Association." The association pays the lobbyist, and the lobbyist tells everyone involved what gifts to give one another. The foreign doctors could not take $5,000 to McCormick and say, "if we give you this money, will you push through the legislation?" But, using the lobbyist as an intermediary, they can do essentially the same thing—if they call it a gift. They can give far more than a few thousand dollars. And

McCormick cannot say to the doctors, "I will give you legislation if you pay me." But using the lobbyist as a source of information about what gifts the association wants, he can do essentially the same thing.

This tableau would not be so troubling if the forces behind the lobbyists were truly diverse and broadly based. It would represent corruption in the traditional sense, but at least public goods would be somewhat widely shared. But the founders' insight is that corruption and inequality are related because wealth begets more wealth. They might not be surprised that the modern gift economy looks something like the limited number of royalty of the founding era. The number of truly influential people in America is small. Tens of thousands of lobbyists work for a relatively small number of companies, and while trade associations sometimes purport to represent small and medium business owners, most powerful trade associations are themselves representative of just a few companies. This is because most companies don't lobby; usually only big companies do.[7] These gift givers are not the king of France but they are foreign gift-givers nonetheless, the kind of gift givers that the framers of the Constitution worried about.

The framers did not ban "explicit bribes" between kings and officials, just gifts. Even then, it wasn't easy; it ran up against international political culture. But they understood that gifts can be as bad as bribes—sometimes worse than bribes—in creating obligations. Legal theorist Dennis Thompson explains that there is

> no good reason to believe that connections that are proximate and explicit are any more corrupt than connections

that are indirect and implicit. The former may be only the more detectable, not necessarily the more deliberate or damaging, form of corruption. Corruption that works through patterns of conduct, institutional routines, and informal norms may leave fewer footprints but more wreckage in its path.[8]

The current U.S. political economy is an economy that values patterns of conduct involving freely given gifts and has left this kind of wreckage. If we go back to the case of McCormick and the lobbyist, a central facet of its corruption is the way in which the gift embeds itself in something that resembles a real relationship. There is a reason for that. The more these sorts of interactions resemble relationships, the easier communication becomes. Everyone in the dynamic has an interest in making it feel more like an authentic connection and less like a transaction. Or, to use the language of the forgotten lobbying cases, everyone has an interest in making it feel more like personal influence. At the same time, no one questions, or has to question, that the exchange of gifts creates interpersonal dependencies.

Public officials must not tell lobbyists that they need campaign contributions because everyone knows they do. The smallest bit of spadework would illuminate how much money a politician needs. This two-step interaction is called by many people, including former president Jimmy Carter, "legal bribery."[9] Whether or not it ought to be punished as bribery, it is undoubtedly corruption as understood by our founders. The lobbyist in the McCormick trial testified that he did not find the interactions troubling because "it's not an uncommon thing when candidates are raising money."[10] "When" candidates are raising money was once an incidental part of the job. Since the 1990s, however, raising money is the primary job of federal officials: they spend between 30 and 70 percent of their time every week raising money.[11]

If the CEO of a corporation came to a senator and said, "I will give you $1 million to reverse the role of two priorities on your agenda," that would be an illegal bribe. Instead, the corporation pays a lobbyist $1 million to figure out the set of gifts and relationships that will lead to something it wants (or in this case doesn't want—getting taken off the senator's agenda). The interplay presents the same issues as the moral temptations posed by foreign gifts that the framers imagined. From the perspective of each of the parties, a changed agenda seems simply like a genuine need getting met and a genuine appreciation being expressed. To return to West Virginia, McCormick already cared about the lack of medical services, and he met someone who had an idea that related to it. The lobbyist was happy to get paid and to communicate ideas and relevant information about the doctors to McCormick. And the doctors were genuinely supportive of McCormick and wanted him to get reelected. They wanted him to know that they supported him because they knew he was more likely to work on their bill, instead of another, if they gave him money. But they also felt good about him and felt personal warmth and generosity toward him after he passed the bill.

After each positive interaction, everyone involved will look for more ways to connect. McCormick—or his campaign manager—knew the foreign doctors had money, and he needed money to get reelected. The doctors felt their money made a big difference. And the lobbyist was happy to facilitate and get paid, so he would be looking for more ways to connect the two parties.

The key takeaway here—and of this book—is that the play of gifts is *not* the dynamic the framers wanted. Had McCormick been out in his district, talking to voters, he would have heard many things that people were concerned about: credit card interest rates, gas prices, schools, violence, dental services, doctor shortages, and twenty other things. Without the interaction with the lobbyist and the potential source of campaign funds, McCormick would have to figure out what, in general, the people in his district most wanted. Instead, the possibility of campaign money put the foreign doctors on top of his agenda.

The gift economy enables a sophisticated masking of the quid pro quo economy, so sophisticated that even the people inside it may sometimes feel it is a culture of goodwill and not the auctioning off of the public welfare. Quids and quos are not named, but the general obligations are broadly understood, and failure to conform to the expectations of the gift economy leads to gifts drying up.

The New Rotten Boroughs

When these "gifts" are powerful enough, they can lead to representatives working on issues that are not, under *any* theory of representation, in the interests of the constituents. The sole reason for granting some earmarks is that the candidate or elected official needs campaign money. For instance, let us imagine that McCormick has risen to be a U.S. senator and adds $400,000 to a Senate bill for the building of a medical facility where none was needed. He might do this because he expects that such benevolence will lead to between $25,000 and $100,000 in campaign contributions, and this expectation might flow from the fact that the lobbyist for Coalfield told him that they would like a medical facility built. In this exchange, all three actors are happy: McCormick gets $25,000 in campaign contributions, the lobbyist gets a $10,000 fee, and the Coalition gets $400,000. So long as no one explicitly conditions the official actions on the contributions—so long as there is another plausible explanation for all the behavior—no one will be threatened with criminal sanctions. The earmark may sound good and be aligned with McCormick's core ideals—a medical facility—but it is not the result of any kind of representative decision-making process.

The check against this kind of corruption is supposed to be elections. As Madison said, "The security intended to the general liberty in the confederation consists in the frequent election, and in the rotation of the members of Congress."[12] Regular elections, in districts with regular censuses taken, would ensure that members of Congress would be "dependent upon the people alone." In the notes of the Constitutional Convention, the most significant structural protection against corruption was the simplest: regular elections of representatives living in the district in which they live. The census, elections, and residency requirements were the structural protections against wealthy outsiders coming into a district and buying political power. A rotten borough was, as I've mentioned earlier, a district where there were just a few people, but they had the same representation as a borough with fifty times as many people.

If the election system were designed to make representatives work for the people, then we would not have to worry about the gift system described above. People would vote out politicians whose agenda was corrupted and they would vote in politicians whose agenda reflected their own. But the way the Supreme Court has structured politics, the gift economy is not optional. Ever since the Supreme Court struck down expenditure limits in *Buckley*, it has become mandatory. With unlimited spending, federal candidates need to spend 30 to 70 percent of their time raising money in gift increments of $1,000 to $2,600. To secure these gifts, the candidate needs to find the gifts that the gift givers want so that she can tell them, when she calls, that she supports free trade, or strong copyright, and can have a better chance of getting a contribution. The set of people who have $1,000 to $2,000 in disposable income for any individual campaign is tiny. So, in effect, the Court has created the country as one large modern set of rotten boroughs. A few people represent a district, but the rest are all gravestones—at least as far as the candidate is concerned. And money buys the outcome. The private interests, like the agents of the English king, corrupt one of the finest fabrics ever built. At a formal level, everyone gets a vote. But at a formal level, everyone got a vote for Parliament, too. At the level of power, fewer than 1 percent of people get to choose whom everyone else can vote for.

People who want to be ethical still get caught up in a mandatory gift economy like the one I just described. There is simply no alternative way to compete. If contribution limits were allowed, or if the federal government passed public funding of elections, candidates for office would be responsive to a broader public and would have more freedom to be uncorrupted.

The New Yazooism

As the framers understood, there is no natural state of politics and no natural level to which political spending will rise: structures, institutions, and laws either enable or disable the purchase of influence. Political spending rose after *Citizens United*. In 2012, for instance, outside spending topped $1 billion. In some political races, outside spending was greater than candidate and party spending. Within the decade in which I write this, unlimited outside spending by individuals and groups will likely become greater than political party and candidate spending. As of 2012, one ten-thousandth of the U.S. population was responsible for 25 percent of all campaign funding. And after *Citizens United*, one of the available "gifts" that companies can give is an independent expenditure.[13]

Congress has tried many different ways to limit the corrupting power of these interactions, and this Supreme Court has banned all of them. Federal bribery laws once could deter this behavior, but we know from *McCormick* that he cannot be charged with federal bribery, because of the absence of any explicit agreement. Candidate spending limits once could have prevented this behavior because McCormick would not need the money if the amount he needed to raise was limited, but that was struck down as unconstitutional in *Buckley*. Outside spending bans at least limited the amount of pressure that the foreign doctors could bring to bear on McCormick. After *Citizens United*, there is no limit on how much money groups like the Coalfield Health Care Association can wield, so long as it is not technically spent in coordination with a candidate.

John Adams wrote to Thomas Jefferson, wondering about the problem of money and politics: "Will you tell me how to

prevent riches from becoming the effects of temperance and industry? Will you tell me how to prevent luxury from producing
effeminacy, intoxication, extravagance, vice and folly? . . . I believe no effort in favor is lost." Adams did not claim to have any
particular answer. Instead, the commitment he made is that "no
effort in favor is lost."[14] It is always worth trying, experimenting,
working to stave off corruption. In the past forty years, however,
the Court has cut off those efforts in favor. It is not that it is easy
to stop corruption, but that it is impossible without the possibility of constant, structural experiment.

In 2006 a divided Court struck down contribution limits for
the first time, after decades of deference to democratic judgment.[15] Vermont had passed contribution limits of $400 for
statewide offices, $300 for state senators, and $200 for state representatives. Vermont wanted to limit the corruption that arises
when candidates spend all their time fund-raising from the people
who can give more than $200 or $400 in campaign contributions. The corruption justification for the popular law was not
honored. Justice Stephen Breyer, writing for the majority, made
this extraordinary statement: "We see no alternative to the exercise of independent judicial judgment" in determining the appropriateness of contribution limits. There is something deeply
antidemocratic about his claim. What deep intellectual currents
explain how the Court came to feel boxed into a bizarre and
ahistorical theory? Does the narrowing of corruption reflect a
contempt for democratic politics itself?

CHAPTER FIFTEEN

Facts in Exile, Complacency, and Disdain

FACTS, JUSTICE SCALIA suggested in a 2013 oral argument, do not matter in determining whether or not a law might dissuade corruption.[1] At issue was whether the lawyers had been given a full chance to bring evidence of how a law limiting aggregate contributions might work, and what would happen were it struck down. While some of his colleagues asked for evidence and wondered how they could decide the case without it, Scalia rejected the need to develop the record:

> JUSTICE SCALIA: Ms. Murphy, do—do we need a record to figure out issues of law?
> MS. MURPHY: And that's my second point. Really, this is—
> JUSTICE SCALIA: No, no, I agree. I agree—I agree that—that this campaign finance law is so intricate that I can't figure it out. It might have been nice to have the, you know, the lower court tell me what the law is. But we don't normally require a record to decide questions of law.

One might dismiss this as an offhand comment, but it reflects a broader attitude toward the job of the Supreme Court. A majority of the Supreme Court repeatedly chooses to review political law cases without developing a factually grounded understanding of how influence works. The relevance of facts is hotly contested. Dissenting justices—including Breyer, Stevens, Souter, and Sotomayor—have argued that context, history, and evidence are important in assessing the constitutional viability of anti-corruption laws. Corruption, in the dissenters' fact-based approach, is arguably like the most famous of difficult constitutional concepts, obscenity: you know it when you see it. But unlike obscenity, in order to see it, you need more than a snapshot of a centerfold: you need an understanding of politics.

This chapter explores features of the modern Supreme Court that may explain the recent change in the treatment of corruption. I am interested in the judicial habits and deeper belief systems that might lead justices to understand corruption in a particular way. I suggest several possible causes: a conflict between law and economics theory of the person and the historical meaning of corruption, a complacency about democratic collapse, and an unspoken disdain for democratic politics. Finally, facts in exile, a disconnect from the experience of politics, may provide a partial explanation. The less one understands how politics works, the less troubling campaign expenditures and contributions may seem.

Citizens United was decided in the context of a "gaping empirical hole" (Justice Stevens's term). In that case, the majority decided that independent corporate spending was not corrupting *as a matter of law*, with no evidence or apparent curiosity about political facts. The entire opinion was done, as Justice Stevens wrote in dissent, "on the basis of pure speculation":

> In this case, the record is not simply incomplete or unsatisfactory; it is nonexistent. Congress crafted BCRA in response to a virtual mountain of research on the corruption that previous legislation had failed to avert. The Court now negates Congress' efforts without a shred of evidence on how §203 or its state-law counterparts have been affecting any entity other than Citizens United.

The majority's lack of interest in developing a large record may find its roots in the highly formal, abstract intellectual tradition that is often called the law and economics movement. Law and economics scholars prefer models, instead of experience, to understand institutions. The legal impact of this movement, which began in the late 1950s and gained force throughout the 1960s and 1970s, is well documented. Five members of the 2014 Supreme Court—Antonin Scalia, John Roberts, Clarence Thomas, Anthony Kennedy, and Samuel Alito—have had ties to the Federalist Society, a legal association that advocates law and economics principles. Some of the orthodoxies of the law and economics ideology include that people are highly mechanical and selfish rational maximizers of their own welfare, and that the public good is served by efficiency.

Law and economics may also have influenced current corruption thinking another way. One model that law and economics scholars regularly use is the selfish man. They don't claim that people are always self-interested, and can't care for others, but they default to a presumption of egoism. Citizens are modeled as self-interest maximizing, and people are primarily conceived of as consumers instead of citizens. This part of the law and economics model undermines the concept of corruption; excessive self-interest is an idea that sounds incoherent if people are always self-interested. To use the language of corruption is either to accept the possibility of good or bad "intent" in influence seeking, to have a vision of good politics that is corrupted, or to think that corruption has no inherent meaning separate from criminal law statutes.

Scholars who accept the self-interest assumption have not been successful at explaining what political corruption means. For instance, Susan Rose-Ackerman has been one of the most influential scholars of corruption in the last several decades. Her concern about corruption has led her to carefully examine strategies for limiting it, and her contributions to the field are enormous. Her book *Corruption and Government: Causes, Consequences, and Reform*, and a series of articles that have followed, bring what she calls an "economic" approach to the study of corruption. She represents and embodies the recent scholarly effort to strip corruption of ideals of civic virtue and transform corruption to make it compatible with law and economics views about human nature.

Rose-Ackerman begins her major book on corruption with this claim about human nature: "There is one human motivator that is both universal and central to explaining the divergent experiences of different countries. That motivator is self-interest, including an interest in the well-being of one's family and peer group."[2] She then hints at a definition of corruption that indicates limited productivity. Corruption indicates the failure to leverage self-interest for productive purposes. In other words, "we can go a good way toward understanding development failures by understanding how self-interest is managed or mismanaged."

Rose-Ackerman goes to great lengths to try not to use moral language or to examine the intent of the individuals involved, but she then argues that the problem with bribes is that they encourage "unfair" allocation of resources, begging the question of the meaning of unfair. She also argues that organized crime is "unscrupulous." She also tries not to examine intent but then argues that "payments are corrupt if they are illegally made to public agents *with the goal of* obtaining a benefit or avoiding a cost." Elsewhere she defines corruption as the "misuse of public office for private gain," referring to local norms for what constitutes misuse.[3] One can see in Rose-Ackerman the conflict with the language itself. While attempting to stay distant, positivistic, and cool, she cannot help but use either moral language or language that looks at intent, or collapse back into pure positivism. Her third option, defining corruption in terms of social costs and inefficiencies, gives no way to distinguish corruption from any other inefficient or socially harmful activity.

The reason Rose-Ackerman struggles, I believe, is that the starting point is fundamentally flawed. The project is conceptually impossible, because it attempts to combine two opposing ideologies. The ambition is understandable: Rose-Ackerman is less interested in developing a theory of corruption than explaining when it happens. But she wants to work using the concept of corruption (a central concept in political grammar) in terms of a particular strand of economics (a central concept in the academic world in which she lives). To deny corruption as a concept, openly and baldly, would be to deny the grammar of her political community. Yet to deny the positive law structure, and the premise of the self-interested man or woman, would be to deny the grammar of her academic community. The failure of the law and economics movement to provide a theory of corruption that makes sense in modern democracy is a fatal failure, a failure that shows the limits of the theory itself.

Her ambition reflects a widespread effort to replace corruption's historical association with private interest with law and economics' deep association with efficiency, while still using the superficial language of corruption. The problem is that it becomes very hard to talk about corruption without talking about virtue or becoming circular. This view about what constitutes a person—and what constitutes corruption—has deep roots in an older ideological fight, as I discussed earlier, the fight between Montesquieu and Hobbes.

As you will recall, according to Hobbes's theory of language, the word *corruption* refers to nothing. He had little patience for words like *good*, *bad*, or *covetous*, which, to him, just meant "what I like," and "what I don't like." He believed that whoever governs also governs language, so the idea of "injustice" does not make sense, because the lawgiver would not ever accuse himself, and the lawgiver would not create a word for others to accuse him with. The political theorist J. Peter Euben contrasted Hobbes's and Aristotle's ideas about corruption in a lovely essay about the history of the term.[4] He argued that Hobbes's view

> is less a direct refutation of Aristotle than part of a theory
> in which Aristotle's categories and arguments make no
> sense. Once men are seen as irremediably egoistic subjects
> rather than potentially activist citizens, as sharing a nature

which fragments them rather than a history which unites them, as requiring an absolutely sovereign ruler rather than a sharing of power, we confront a political and conceptual universe in which republican political theory is irrelevant.[5]

The same may be true for some of the modern justices' views of corruption. It may not be so much that they disagree with the historical meaning but that it simply does not make sense to them.

Complacency

Given the selfish man model that undergirds much of modern thinking, you might expect the majority of the Supreme Court to have a dismal view of society. But instead, the 2014 Court is striking for its lack of concern about the threat of political collapse. Instead of a Hobbesian battle for food and shelter and power, the government is described as largely, if not entirely, static in the corruption cases. One gets the sense that no theory of government is needed because the democratic state is like air—necessary, a part of life itself, unavoidable in the best sense, invisible because so central. Their thin descriptions of government make sense if problems of political organization are not serious ones. Democracy may be, in their minds, fundamentally solved and stable. While we can quibble at the margins about the scope of government, the basic shape of government is stable and not likely to change.

This feature suggests that the Court's indifference toward corruption might reflect an end of history ideology that has been part of our culture for the last quarter century, an ideology that also has its roots in law and economics. In 1989 the Berlin Wall came down, and the Soviet Union began to splinter. Ron Brown became chair of the DNC, the first African American to head a major political party. Francis Fukuyama wrote an essay (later expanded into a book) arguing that liberal democracy is an equilibrium state and there is no postliberal democracy system. He argued: "What we may be witnessing is not just the end of the Cold War, or the passing of a particular period of post-war history, but the end of history as such: that is, the end point of mankind's ideological evolution and the universalization of Western liberal democracy as the final form of human government."

Fukuyama's article was largely about the nature of thinking, not the nature of events. His argument was essentially that the ideal form of government had been discovered, not that it would stop history. In this, it was not so different from the prior 200 years of argument: that liberal representative democracy was a superior form of government. However, its powerful impact on the popular culture, the thing that turned him into an object of constant discussion, was not the theory of the history of thought but the theory of the history of world events. The key feature of this view—as interpreted, not as written—was its political optimism. Fukuyama came to be a stand-in for the view that liberal democracy is an end of history in a different sense: liberal democracy is unlikely to turn into a totalitarian regime, and it is just a matter of time before other countries catch up to the United States and Western Europe.[6]

Fukuyama caught fire because he said (or was perceived to have said) what so many at the time believed, and continue to believe: that having once achieved representative democracy, America was unlikely to ever become anything else. If one believes or feels that we are at the end of history, self-government is *not* a central problem or puzzle. Little will change. Tyranny and oligarchy have been solved by the modern democratic form. A feature of the end-of-history attitude is also the end of facts, and the end of the role of history and facts. If history is fundamentally over, only analytical questions remain.

A more sinister understanding of the same idea is that history is over because democracy is not required anymore. In his honest essay on "Public Choice v. Democracy," Russell Hardin explains how economic modeling of self-interested behavior has shown us some "grievous foundational flaws—in democratic thought and practice," including that it leads to neither majoritarian rule (because of the aggregation flaws) nor good policy decisions.[7] The conclusion of Hardin and law and economics scholars is that many problems of distribution will be better made by "the market" than by representative systems in a mass democracy. If one part of politics is made up of the question "How should we distribute goods and things?" then the social choice theorist/market fundamentalist answer is "through assigning property rights." The answer voids the need for a central role for other mechanisms—monarchy, representative democracy, direct democracy, lottery—to make decisions about distributions. It gives a political answer, and in so doing narrows the realm of collective decision making via deliberation and decision backed by force.

There is relatively little in the Supreme Court opinions that openly embraces the anti-political stance of Hardin and others. However, the complacency toward corruption that shows up in the opinions suggests that something else might be occurring, something more than a disagreement about a term. It might be that democratic politics itself is suspect. It may be that the real underlying normative idea of the five justices who use a narrow meaning of corruption is that there is a little too much democracy, and it would be better if people had less power.

Disdain

Perhaps, like Russell Hardin, some justices have abandoned faith in democratic politics. There is some evidence that the justices still believe in a broad theory of corruption but think of politics as essentially corrupt, and not worth saving. For instance, the same justices who concluded that no facts were necessary in *Citizens United* argued that there should be close judicial inspection of facts in takings clause cases, to determine whether private interest played too large a role in legislative choices. In the case of *Kelo v. City of New London*, New London used eminent domain to take Suzette Kelo's home and give the land to a private developer with ties to the drug company Pfizer.

The Supreme Court had to decide whether this action violated the Fifth Amendment. The Constitution states that private property cannot be taken for "public use" without "just compensation." The implication of the clause is that taking for public use—the exercise of eminent domain—is legitimate, whereas taking for private purposes is not. It is difficult to draw a clear line between what constitutes a public use and what constitutes a private use. In early law, "public use," was interpreted as "use by the public." Any taking from one private party to give to another private party was outside the governmental power. A "law that takes property from A and gives it to B: It is against all reason and justice, for a people to entrust a Legislature with SUCH powers."[8] Starting in the early twentieth century, courts expanded the scope of legitimate uses for which property could be taken and allowed for the government to take land for a variety of public ends, including urban renewal projects. In other words, "public use" could include taking land to give to a third party if the giving created a public benefit. In *Kelo*, the Supreme Court had to confront whether taking land from one person and giving it to developers constituted "public use." The City of New London argued that the city needed the revitalization that would come along with the new private developments. Kelo and the other plaintiffs argued that the taking was cronyism and outside the bounds of governmental power.

The Court sided with New London. It held that going through a legislative process is itself presumptive evidence of its public purpose-ness. The New London taking was part of a "'carefully considered' development plan" that the city believed would be good for the overall welfare of the public. In dissent, Justice O'Connor argued that the Court eviscerated the "public use" language of the Fifth Amendment and that such transfers should not be allowed unless the land being taken was entirely blighted.

The takings case was, like the corruption cases, in part a review of private versus public interest-motivated laws. One of the subterranean arguments in *Kelo* was about the degree to which the judicial branch should engage in a corruption review of takings. The plaintiff in *Kelo* later put it plainly: she believed that a "high corruption level in New London was the primary factor driving the abuse of eminent domain for private benefit in her case."[9] The Court was less direct but it addressed her concern and rejected it. The majority held that the city would not be allowed to "take property under the mere pretext of a public purpose, when its actual purpose was to bestow a private benefit." This language advocates for a review that *Fletcher v. Peck* arguably precluded: a close examination of the reasons that a legislative body passed something, an examination of motive. Justice O'Connor, in dissent, essentially argued that the "public use" provision of the takings clause was an anticorruption provision: "The beneficiaries are likely to be those citizens with disproportionate influence and power in the political process, including large corporations and development firms."

Justice Kennedy, in concurrence, pointedly argued for greater scrutiny of the process by which takings happen. In *Kelo*, he said that the equal protection clause protects against "a government classification that is clearly intended to injure a particular class of private parties, with only incidental or pretextual public justifications."

Because the different working parts of modern corruption law exist in isolation, each from the other, the dissonance between Kennedy's approach here and in political cases was not addressed. In *Citizens United*, he argued that it was the essence of politics to seek out influence for private reasons. In *Kelo*, he argued against partiality. Scalia reveals a similar schizophrenia. In another case, outside the field of election law, he argues that there is a "fundamental constraint" that democratic decisions "be taken in order to further a public purpose rather than a purely private interest."[10] But in the campaign finance cases, he derides the idea that any public purpose can be understood. To put it another way: anything but quid pro quo corruption seems too vague for Justices Kennedy and Scalia when they are reviewing campaign finance cases, but a broader conception of corruption, with its attending difficulties, is well within their constitutional appetite in the takings arena.

We can't know why, but the dissonance likely speaks to a view about politics itself. The different treatment in these different arenas may come from a fundamental democratic disdain, a suspicion of democratic politics itself, and a desire to relocate power in the judiciary, something very much like what Thomas Jefferson called the "twistifications" that led Justice Marshall in *Fletcher v. Peck* to refuse the power of the people of Georgia to overturn a flagrantly corrupt law. Scalia seems to prefer allocative decisions that are made outside of the collective political sphere.

The takings cases are not alone. Another case that hints that the real driving force behind a narrowing of corruption is disdain for politics, and not a lack of understanding of corruption, is *Caperton v. A. T. Massey*. That case went to the Supreme Court right before *Citizens United*. Just as a $50 million verdict was being heard by the West Virginia Supreme Court, one of the parties to the case spent $3 million in efforts to elect one of the judges. The party never coordinated with the judge, but he clearly knew that the money was designed to help him get reelected. The judge did not recuse himself from hearing the appeal and voted in favor of overturning the verdict.

The other party complained that the election expenditure violated due process, and the Supreme Court agreed. It held that the Constitution required a judge to recuse himself from a case when there is a "probability of bias" created by a past massive campaign expenditure by one of the parties in the case. It was, according to the majority opinion by Justice Kennedy, an extreme case where there was no need for direct evidence of actual bias. Objective facts, he held, raised the probability of bias.

In *Caperton*, Kennedy's language was psychological and referred to temptation and human nature and the dangers that come from actions that are not criminal bribes. He recognized that "the fact that the inquiry is often a private one, simply underscore[s] the need for objective rules." Otherwise, he held, judges could be influenced and there would be no recourse.[11] The same argument about the need for objective rules applies to spending around nonjudicial elections. However, there are two different standards. The best explanation for the different standards may lie in the fact that Kennedy has greater respect for judicial processes than democratic ones.

Biography

The disconnection from political facts, and apparent distaste for politics, may also be exacerbated by the rarified biographies of the modern Supreme Court justices. Personal history may have particular force when it comes to judicial understanding of, and respect for, democratic politics. Our current Court is entirely made up of elite academics and appellate judges. It was not always so.

When Justice Noah Haynes Swayne wrote the opinion of the Court in *Trist v. Child*—the opinion that refused to enforce a contract to lobby as against the public policy of the United States—it was not as a naive academic or utopian but as someone who had lived inside the logic of politics for over fifty years, as a candidate, organizer, appointee, councilman, and state representative. Swayne wrote that lobbying is "contrary to the plainest principles of public policy. No one has a right, in such circumstances, to put himself in a position of temptation to do what is regarded as so pernicious in its character." He went on to argue: "If any of the great corporations of the country were to hire adventurers who make market of themselves in this way, to procure the passage of a general law with a view to the promotion of their private interests, the moral sense of every right-minded man would instinctively denounce the employer and employed as steeped in corruption, and the employment as infamous." Swayne had been Ohio's U.S. Attorney under Andrew Jackson, a council member, state legislator, abolitionist, and political leader and part of the Republican Party's formation in the 1850s.

Or consider the way Justice Samuel Miller, who had also been extremely active in politics, treated corruption.[12] Miller was an abolitionist who moved from Kentucky to Iowa in order to free his slaves and raise his children outside of slavery. He became a leader in Republican Party politics in Iowa and was nominated for (but not ultimately elected to) the state Senate. His passion for politics is revealed in the case *Ex parte Yarbrough*, affirming Congress's authority to pass a law against violence and intimidation designed to keep African Americans from voting. The entire opinion reads as a passionate defense of self-government. Throughout the opinion he references what he sees as the two primary tools for undoing democracy, violence and corruption, which he sometimes refers to as force and fraud:

> That a government whose essential character is republican, whose executive head and legislative body are both elective, whose numerous and powerful branch of the legislature is elected by the people directly, has no power by

appropriate laws to secure this election from the influence of violence, of corruption, and of fraud, is a proposition so startling as to arrest attention and demand the gravest consideration. If this government is anything more than a mere aggregation of delegated agents of other States and governments, each of which is superior to the general government, it must have the power to protect the elections on which its existence depends from violence and corruption.[13]

In fact, when *Yarbrough* was decided in 1884, over half of the justices had successfully run for office. Justice Field had been in the California State Assembly and ran and lost a campaign for state Senate. Justice John Marshall Harlan was actively involved in at least six political parties—the Whigs, the Know Nothings, the Kentucky Opposition Party, the Union Party, the Democratic Party, and the Republican Party. Justice Woods was mayor of Newark, Ohio, and a representative in the state assembly. Justice Matthews was elected to the Ohio State Senate and the U.S. Senate.

Less than a century later, in 1976, when *Buckley v. Valeo* was decided, no justices brought direct electoral political experience to the Court except Justice Powell, who had been the chair of the Richmond School Board. The Court that decided *Citizens United* has an even more cramped pedigree. No members of that Court have ever been elected to any office or run for office.

The transformation from a Court filled with politicians to a Court with no politicians may help to explain how economic models gained more traction, and why judges were drawn to abstract arguments instead of fact-based arguments. The experience of politics is profoundly invigorating, and while people who have lived a political life will undoubtedly admit there are dingy deals and terrible pressures, they may be more likely to believe in the human capacity for civic attention and love. Those involved in politics will bring a more subtle understanding of the psychological ways in which gifts and money change politics. The visceral experience of politics—like the visceral experiences of art, theater, and love, perhaps—is fundamentally different than the imagined, or theorized, life of politics.

At their worst, the lack of experience of politics may lead to the apparent contempt for politics itself.[14] They may perceive corruption as a minor threat, or perhaps they perceive it as part and parcel of politics, which is essentially rabble: not responsive, not efficient. Political theorist Hannah Arendt describes the antipolitical strain in modern society as coming from both the platonic philosophical tradition and the Christian tradition that encourages people to remove themselves from the contaminating political society. A rejection of politics may represent both fear and hope—fear of politics taking over everything and hope for a future without politics. This imagined a-political politics involves a wise bureaucratic state managing policy issues; the citizen is free to pursue his or her own ends without having to engage in self-government. Rationality controls, and the parceling power, is not a primary puzzle. In Arendt's characterization, academics sometimes see politics as a refuge of those who have lesser virtues; it is associated with the antiphilosophical. Politics contaminates thinking. She rejects this view, but her description resonates with some of the academics on the Court.

The antipolitical strain aligns with the way that some justices treat corruption, fully imagined, as an incoherent and outdated idea, or as a synonym for bribery. The virile language of *Trist* and *Yarbrough*—and also that of Hamilton, Montesquieu, Mason, Gerry, and Madison—may simply fail to connect with the modern jurist, more likely to be trained in analyzing policy proposals than in counting votes in a district.

CHAPTER SIXTEEN

The Anticorruption Principle

I AM TRYING to bring corruption back. Not as a societal ill. As you have read, we have enough of that already. But as an idea, something we fight and worry about. My hope is that courts and citizens will recognize that the anticorruption principle is a foundational American principle and will incorporate it into jurisprudence and public debate.

A revival of the anticorruption principle will depend upon engaging difficult concepts of public interest and private interest, excessiveness and greed. Corruption describes a range of self-serving behaviors. Corruption is "abuse of public power for private benefit"[1] or "those acts whereby private gain is made at public expense,"[2] or when private interest excessively overrides public or group interest in a significant or meaningful exercise of political power.[3] An act or system is corrupting when it leads to excessive private interest in the exercise of public power. People are corrupt when their private interest systematically overrides public good in public roles, when they put their self-love ahead of group love. This is true if they are lobbyists or politicians, citizens or senators.[4]

I sometimes imagine that the relationship between citizen or official and the country is like that between a parent and a child, where the parent can distinguish between what is best for the child and what is best for the parent but tries not to understand them in opposition. The parent who thinks about his child, plans for his child's health, protects his child, and comforts his child is a good parent, whereas the parent who does none of these things and ignores his child is not. However, the good parent, in relation to the child, does not ignore his own interests but is capable of being other-interested in his internal thinking. Society recognizes that perfection is illusory. There are many ways to be a good parent, and good parenting doesn't rely on fulfilling technical requirements. Good parenting relies on an attitude and attentiveness to another person. In some ways the parental identity becomes fused with the personal identity, so the parent's personal ambitions include the ambition to serve the child. Similarly, the ambitious public official who constantly looks for ways to improve his constituents' well-being is different from the one who only thinks about his own ambitions or who puts his own need to secure a job when he leaves office before the present needs of his community. The father gets substantial pride from being a father; the noncorrupt official gets pride from his role as well. Some self-interest may be present, and few throughout history would deny the benefits of pride, power, ambition, attention, love, and adulation that can come with public office. But the anticorruption principle depends on the fact that despite these other concerns, it is valuable and possible to aspire to a society where those in government are concerned on a daily basis with the well-being of the public.

The reason I am more drawn to the anticorruption principle than a potential alternate—which one might call the virtue principle—is that it focuses on structures that discourage the worst kinds of systematic self-interest. We should not maintain an impossibly high ideal of public virtue but think of the anticorruption principle as a support for laws that protect citizens and officials from excessive temptation.

I am not alone in pursuing a revival of the anticorruption principle. Laura Underkuffler's recent book on corruption, *Captured by Evil*, focuses on corruption as a moral concept.[5] To her, corruption represents the "capture by evil" of an individual's soul. It is more than a breach of trust or a denial of equality or lawbreaking—it is a powerful personal failing. Lawrence Lessig's book *Republic, Lost* focuses not on individuals but on systems and argues that corruption encompasses far more than direct exchanges but also dependencies, grounding his argument in founding-era understandings of corruption and dependence.[6] Samuel Issacharoff argues that corruption should be understood in terms of the clientelism that arises between private interests and state agents.[7] Deborah Hellman argues that the Court should stay out of the business of defining corruption because such a definition is fundamentally better assigned to the legislative branch.[8]

This is a welcome change from the previous generation of leading legal lights. Many of the major twentieth-century philosophers were unwittingly too sanguine about the nature of politics and thus not greatly concerned in their thought and writing with the threat of corruption. The last century's most prominent English-language political theorist, John Rawls, may have shared Montesquieu's love of equality, but Rousseau's concern is related to concerns about corruption whereas Rawls never really explored corruption. As one scholar put it, "Philosophical literature on justice has shunned the topic of corruption."[9] Legal theorist Ronald Dworkin rarely used the language of corruption to describe either individuals or collectives.[10] And libertarian Robert Nozick's mid-twentieth-century defense of liberty, unlike John Locke's, did not use corruption as a way of thinking about government or human nature. Instead, corruption had been relegated to an increasingly technical role—even Rawls treats it like bribery, and does not explore the meaning of bribery[11]—that is not part of political theory.

To be clear, today's political corruption scholars are in sharp contrast to Rawls et al. but also to one another. Lessig's corrupt world is populated by "decent people, people working extremely hard to do what they believe is right, yet decent people working with a system that has evolved the most elaborate and costly ending of democratic government in our history."[12]

Underkuffler's corrupt world is different still. She argues that the language of corruption requires a conception of evil and the workings of the individual psychologies. Issacharoff's understanding focuses on "how the electoral process drives the discharge of public duties." Hellman ends up agnostic on the meaning of corruption, arguing that defining it is a legislative task. All four, however, are significant, prominent academics pushing a revival of interest in the centrality of corruption in the American political-legal tradition. They all examine it as a concept worthy of its own meaning and not bound by a function of equality or efficiency or limited by the language of quid pro quo: they all explicitly reject either efficiency or equality as the starting point. They all embrace the grammar of corruption instead of trying to erase it or replace it: in so doing they celebrate its power instead of denigrating it.

All of these scholars understand that corruption should not simply live in a criminal law ghetto. It is not just what quids count, and which quos. As most people know, explicit deals and blatant self-dealing are both instances of corruption, but they are not the thing itself. Corruption should not be limited to exchanges or centrally defined by exchanges. It should not be defined by statute; no one should expect a statute to define "corruption" any more than one would expect a statute to define "equality" or "love" or "security."

Part of the revival of corruption would be a renewal of a stronger sense of the relationship of the citizen to the country. An intimate, faithful relationship to a country is psychologically challenging when related to a large bureaucratic state in which most citizens have no intimate interactions with government. All the more reason to encourage it. Corruption, in this sense, would be related to the principle that governs a general fiduciary relationship that all citizens have toward the American public.[13]

Equality and Corruption

Many liberal scholars argue that corruption is not a meaningful idea. They view corruption as a subset of equality concerns. They argue that if it were not for the Supreme Court's use of corruption as a governmental concern in *Buckley v. Valeo*, no one would be concerned about corruption. The principle of equality suggests that each person ought to be considered equally by a governmental representative. When a large campaign contributor can change the view of a representative because of the access and influence that flows from that donation, not all voices are heard equally. Governments should be free to pursue relative political equality in their campaign financing systems. This, equality theorists say, is the real problem, not corruption. Bruce Cain argues that "by littering the intellectual landscape with irrelevant issues, moral idealists obstruct the path to a full, open discussion of the public's views about the proper distribution of power and influence."[14] According to Cain, the language of corruption serves to disrupt a serious discussion of equality concerns.

David Strauss similarly argues that corruption is a "derivative problem." He argues that those who claim they are worried about corruption are "actually concerned" about inequality. He argues that if there were actual political equality, "much of the reason to be concerned about corruption would no longer exist."[15] Any remaining worries would themselves be functions of other inequality concerns that arise when interest group politics takes over the democratic process to give unequal power to voters. Kathleen Sullivan argues that corruption "is really a variant on the problem of political equality: unequal outlays of political money create inequality in political representation."[16]

Rick Hasen has been a prominent proponent of the equality argument as both a normative and descriptive matter. He argues that the non–quid pro quo arguments from the justices after *Buckley* are described in terms of corruption but are actually, and rightly, grounded in equality concerns.[17] As he describes it, "A political equality argument is one which seeks to justify a law on grounds that it distributes political power fairly or seeks to attack a law in court on grounds that it distributes political power in an unequal way."[18] When the Court describes nonexchange corruption, it is often simply describing some of the problems that flow from unequal political power. According to Hasen, "political equality arguments come in three varieties: political input, political output, and political opportunity."

Like these theorists, I think political equality is a foundational American principle to which courts should be attentive, and that *Buckley* was interpreted to exclude equality and inequality from the review of campaign finance laws. Unlike these theorists, I think the anticorruption principle has a different meaning, and is not derivative of equality. The liberal scholars who would have equality stand not alongside but *instead of* corruption believe we can talk about politics and self-government and develop a full political theory of America without ever using the language of corruption. My own view is that there are real equality concerns and real corruption concerns, and while these two troubles overlap they are not identical. Unlike Bruce Cain, I see public morality as the ballast of our country, not its litter.

The Aristotelian roots of our modern conception, as you'll recall, distinguished monarchy from tyranny on the grounds that one was self-interested and the other was not, although both ruled societies with no principle of political equality. The central difference between the equality principle and the traditional American meaning of corruption has to do with the role of emotion and affection and self-interest. Equality theorists look at inputs and outputs—how equally is each person's interest weighted?—whereas corruption requires one to consider whether public figures maintain a genuine attention to their constituency alongside their more egoistic needs. The formal consideration of valuing each person's interest equally is emotionally different from faithfulness and identification with the public good. The goal of the equality theorists and the traditional corruption theorists is substantially similar. But equality theorists are not as focused on public orientation. The grammar of politics, its emotional and intimate role, is less important for them. Political actors (citizens and officials) play a fairly mechanical role in this worldview. They process information (gained by access) fairly directly—the more of one kind of input, the more of that kind of output. The elected officials play a processing role and do not operate as independent moral agents. They are influenced directly: the more pressure from campaign contributions, the more likely their decisions will be shaped. There are stronger and weaker versions of this—radical equality or rough equality, or simply the absence of radical inequality.

One way to understand the difference is to imagine the mind of a senator. The equality theorist would want that senator to consider each member of his constituency equally and would be satisfied if the senator did so because each citizen gave him $100, an equal amount. The framers, on the other hand, wanted that, but *also* a fundamental, emotional identification with the public. A senator who considers each constituent equally only because of the campaign money, but whose core obsession is getting reelected so he can get a great job as a lobbyist afterward, could serve equality goals but still be corrupt. Whereas the equality theorists focus on the equal treatment of multiple private interests, the framers believed that one could imagine "the public interest" and that people, at their best, would put others' interests on equal footing with their own in a nonmechanical way.

Montesquieu treated corruption and equality as related concepts when he described virtue in a republic as the "love of equality."[19] Montesquieu believed citizens should love equality not just as an abstract concept; they should love it in practice, in how they choose to be part of the polity, in how they choose to be not alone, not godlike, not separated but joined in the decision-making venture with those who are not the same but are political equals. Love, for him, is central. As he illustrates, one can tie equality and corruption together at the motivational level—*love* of equality enables democracy. I find Montesquieu too demanding. He demands that the only ambition of a citizen in a democracy should be to love society more than its component parts, and that we should embrace mediocrity and love frugality as well. Even the framers who used him as their fountainhead and also were skeptical of luxury did not imagine a world where people's ambition was submerged in civic patriotism. However, he presents a clear (if stark) picture of how one might think about the relationship between equality and corruption.

The concept of corruption requires one to consider motivations, and I see a real political danger in removing the grammar of corruption from political discourse. The language of corruption helps create cultures and laws that in turn reinforce a culture of laws. One scholarly article from the 1970s claimed that we use definitions that avoid the "emotionalism" usually associated with corruption.[20] My goal would be the opposite: to recognize and structurally channel the emotionalism that necessarily arises in public affairs, following the instinct of the framers, that love and equality are both necessary features of vibrant public life.

Structural Rules

At the Constitutional Convention the anticorruption principle led to many bright-line rules, which have fared pretty well, and a few unclear rules (the terms of impeachment, the takings clause), which have led to confusion. Part of reviving the principle will be an emphasis on bright-line rules, even those that infringe on genuinely innocent behavior. Once corruption is understood as a description of emotional orientation, rather than a description of a contract-like exchange, the idea of criminalizing it seems either comical or fascist. Instead, bright-line rules that discourage temptation and encourage civic virtue are fundamental, essential American goals. Bright-line rules, in other words, are part of the best of our country's past and not merely a squirrelly, annoyed response to contemporary scandals. Strict aggregate limits on spending and contributions are the descendants of strict residency rules, strict veto laws, strict gifts rules, the Pendleton Act, and the secret ballot, as well as the Tillman Act. Rules that limit the age of a senator, for instance, may have been written *because* of corruption, but they do not define it.

In a recent law review article, Steve Sachs succinctly summarized the objection to anticorruption laws: "When politicians put private interests before the public good, they act wrongly—even 'corruptly.' But whether a politician is 'corrupt' in this subjective sense is impossible for the law to police."[21] Sachs is correct, which is why bright-line rules are so important. Criminal law is poorly designed to capture corrupt acts. It is, however, well designed to deter them. If one sees corruption as a motivating concept instead of a statutory term, then the law can successfully police—or at least shape—the likelihood of politicians putting private interests before the public good. The difficulty of connecting corruption to intent-based criminal laws ought to make us wary of using intent-based laws as the best strategy to deter corruption. Because intention, orientation, love, and faithlessness are so difficult to describe in criminal laws, they are very weak vessels for enforcing or encouraging noncorruption. The emotional nature of corruption makes it better suited for bright-line rules that are unconcerned with intent—rules that provide absolute donation limits, for example, or absolute status bans—than for laws that try to separate those acts that are in fact corrupt from those that are in fact not corrupt.

Modern corrupt intent laws, as I've shown, came from bright-line rules that generally didn't have an intent requirement and didn't apply to elected politicians. The old bribery statutes criminalized gifts to judges, and the old extortion statutes criminalized officials taking more than they were owed. As the laws expanded to cover interactions with legislators, the relationship between corrupt intent and private campaign contributions has always been troubled. Moreover, corrupt intent laws are sometimes used to reinforce racial and anti-immigrant stereotypes and associate difference with corruption.[22] These laws give prosecutors—who might be politically motivated—enormous power to decide who is corrupt and who is not in the public eye, as the mere prosecution for public corruption can taint a public figure.

Legislatures regularly pass laws designed to structure the flow of money to limit temptation and corruption. However, if a serious First Amendment or due process claim is raised, most of those laws are struck down, unless they fall within the category called "bribes," with bribes being defined explicitly and about fairly explicit pieces of legislation. Outside of this tiny cluster, money can be used in almost any way to influence and block policy, sway candidates, and pick candidates. The current Court's disfavor for bright-line rules has greatly limited the capacity to protect against corruption. We have seen this with illegal gratuities in *Sun Diamond* and with campaign spending limits from *Buckley* to *Citizens United*.

The reasons for overturning the bright-line rules in those cases are not trivial, of course. Courts should look skeptically upon laws that claim to be grounded in the anticorruption principle but are primarily designed to help incumbents maintain power. They should presumptively strike down laws that discriminate between different political viewpoints. But ideally they would also incorporate into their decision making a deep deference for the difficulty democratic organs face as they try to protect themselves.

Plurality

As Deborah Hellman argued many years ago, a commitment to understanding corruption requires public engagement in defining what does and does not constitute legitimate private interest.[23] One cannot shy away from fundamental determinations about the scope of public and private morality, many of which I cannot fully engage here, but one seems important: the relationship of concepts of corruption to group interest. Is someone who serves their own group interests—like the interests of a church, a union, or a trade association—corrupt, or virtuous? What if they do so knowing it hurts the public good? The classic conception of corruption might seem incompatible with modern "plural" democracies. Modern pluralists note that people tend to be most politically engaged when they work with associations, and these associations work to further their own interests. Democracy is at its best when people form into groups, then wage peaceful battle between groups through electoral pressure. Without fully exploring this fascinating area, I would note two things: first, the invention of pluralism is itself an ideological framework, not a factual one. Second, America was founded on both pluralism and anticorruption, so the apparent conflict is not a new one, and the framers thought it possible to be public interested even while they perceived group interests.

To the first point, all groups, including the group of the "self," have multiple conflicting desires, changing interests over time, and internal "factions." The nature of public interest as a category is often challenged because it is deemed to be incoherent—who is to say what the public interest is? The same kind of challenge can apply to a person, as well—who is to say what self-interest is? As Hannah Arendt writes about the impossibility of escaping pluralism:

> Because I am already two-in-one, at least when I try to think, I can experience a friend, to use Aristotle's definition, as an "other self" . . . the faculty of speech and the fact of human plurality . . . in the . . . sense that speaking with myself I live together with myself. . . . This is also the reason why the plurality of men can never be abolished and why the escape of the philosopher from the realm of plurality always remains an illusion: even if I were to live entirely by myself I would, as long as I am alive, live in the condition of plurality. I have to put up with myself. . . . The philosopher who, trying to escape the human condition of plurality, takes his flight into absolute solitude, is more radically delivered to this plurality inherent in every human being than anyone else, since it is companionship

with others that, calling me out of the dialogue of thought, makes me one again.[24]

To the second point, the framers certainly saw themselves as living in and also creating a plural society: wealthy, poor, farmers, and regional interests existed, yet they did not see the existence of plurality as a threat to the conception of corruption. That said, at the time of the founding, anything that was not public interest was coded as private interest. Cabal, faction, and corruption were deeply connected in the founders' language. They saw group interest as corrupting as individual or familial interest. Unlike other features of corruption law, which were relatively constant until the 1970s, this aspect of corruption law mutated quickly after the founding era. Serving the group interest of a political party was not considered corrupt for most of our history. Instead, the epithet of corruption was reserved for those instances where purely private interests dominated, not collective ones.

While the older, constitutional American view of corruption encompasses those situations where a group interest overrides a public interest in the meaningful exercise of power, it quickly modified to allow for group interest as noncorrupt. I think that is the correct lesson to take from the founding era—one can serve the interests of one's community church or one's Elks Club and vigilantly advocate for it. However, it ought not be *at the expense* of the public interest. A legislator may be a lifelong ally of labor groups, but she only becomes corrupt (or at least part of a corrupt system) if she supports a bill because of their campaign donations or if he supports a bill while genuinely believing that the bill will be bad for the public at large and good only for his group.

In many cases, private interest, group interest, and public interest can be aligned, and when they are aligned, there is no corruption. For example, Madison, like most of the founders and Montesquieu, believed that men were capable of self-interest and public interest and group interest. They had a flexible view of human nature. They were both pessimistic and optimistic in this sense, gloomy about the possibilities for self-interest dominating yet hopeful that it was not the necessary state of affairs. In the construction of the Constitution they were trying to design institutions to encourage the likelihood of more public interest and less self-interest, and to create structures such that private and public interest would be aligned as frequently as possible.

Conclusion

BENJAMIN FRANKLIN'S WILL gave the king's snuff box portrait to his daughter, Sarah, requesting that "she would not form any of those diamonds into ornaments either for herself or daughters, and thereby introduce or countenance the expensive, vain, and useless fashion of wearing jewels in this country; and those immediately connected with the picture may be preserved with the same."[1] Instead, Sarah sold several of the diamonds and used the proceeds to help pay for a trip to Europe. The present is now dismembered, all the diamonds taken out: the portrait sits at the American Philosophical Society in a barren frame.

Our concept of corruption, too, is corrupted, dismembered, the component parts taken out. Nietzsche described decadence this way: "Word becomes sovereign and leaps out of the sentence, the sentence reaches out and obscures the meaning of the page, the page gains life at the expense of the whole—the whole is no longer a whole."[2] Nietzsche could have been describing the political theory in the Supreme Court. The word *corruption* is removed from sentences in which it was used, the adjectival phrase "quid pro quo" grows so large it obscures meaning itself;

the concept of corruption is no longer part of a coherent whole. Justices of the Supreme Court fixate upon particular words at the cost of history, context, and meaning. The concept of corruption becomes the narrow concept of quid pro quo corruption. The citizen, too, becomes atomized—a set of wants, a "consumer," a "taxpayer"—and government is seen transactionally instead of as part of a social political whole.

The American democratic experiment is in the midst of a political disruption enabled by this conceptual disintegration. We could lose our democracy in the process. Four years after *Citizens United*, wealthy individuals have far more political power than they did, and groups of individuals without money have less. A country founded on political equality and the fight against corruption is burdened by political inequality, corrupting individuals and institutions. Americans don't trust their government, and we feel that the country is going in the wrong direction, not just as a matter of policy but as a democracy. The public—what Montesquieu called the common people—know that there is something deeply wrong about our political culture. In a recent poll, nearly 90 percent of Americans said that reducing corruption in the federal government was high priority.[3]

The dismemberment has also led to divergence. When people in bars and fast food restaurants talk about corruption, they may include violations of the federal bribery statute in their definition, but more likely they mean that their representatives aren't serving them, and they aren't doing so because of some other source of money and power. The public knows there is a deep misalignment where the government is used to serve private ends instead of the public good. Justice Kennedy thinks corruption is defined by quid pro quo. I believe the public sees corruption more as our country's framers did.

A disconnect between meanings of corruption has happened before in culture, if not in law. In the Gilded Age, a prominent railroad lobbyist testified to Congress that "if you have to pay money to get the right thing done, it is only just and fair to do it. . . . If [the politician] has the power to do great evil and won't do right unless he's bribed to do it . . . I think it is a man's duty to go up and bribe him."[4] In our own gilded age, a wealthy venture capitalist recently suggested publicly that people's votes should be proportional to the amount of taxes they pay. He was not clear about whether he was joking or not, but he wanted to be outrageous. Then, as now, the dismemberment of shared meaning and history accompanies the threatened dissolution of self-government.

In American culture, one of the social functions of a word like *corrupt* is to support a system of government where the love of the public and the love of country are celebrated, where citizens do not imagine themselves as solely self-interested. The word *corruption* is itself a bulwark against temptation, separate from any criminal penalties that may attach to it. There are constant temptations to put private interests ahead of public ones—the language of corruption provides social pressure on the other side of that equation.

It is a concept with deep political power, important for its social role and its society-defining role. This differentiates it from other words with related legal roles, like *fiduciary* or *fiduciary duty*. While no one wants to be on a poster that reads, "The CEO of Bank of America violated his fiduciary duty!," it does not carry the same indictment and political power as one that reads, "The CEO of Bank of America is corrupt!" Fiduciary law is law's way of dealing with heightened obligations that derive from intimate and trusting relationships, and it translates emotional complaints into legal forms, whereas corruption law often works the other way—the charge that something is corrupt is highly emotional, but the way the charge works in law is through the violation of a campaign finance law or a conflict-of-interest law. When states passed sprawling but unenforced statutes in the nineteenth century, their broad condemnation played an important role in the public's description of how it wanted public officials and citizens to act. The anticorruption laws expressed a vision of undesirable human behavior and on the other side invoked desirable and possible human political behavior. The ability to call a public official corrupt arguably reveals the authority of the citizen. It suggests that she has the right to claim generalized attention instead of attention toward private interests.

Bribery statutes and constitutional doctrines that use the language of corruption force juries and judges to make decisions about what corruption means. *Corruption* is a tricky word for lawyers because it has different kinds of meanings: some meanings gesture toward the specific (inasmuch as the word is part of a criminal law doctrine), whereas other meanings are inherently broad ranging (inasmuch as it is part of a description of a political culture), and many are in between. In popular culture it is often used in a way that does not specify whether it is being used in a legal sense or a nonlegal sense. The same judge can use the same word in two different ways. *Corruption* is sometimes used like *battery* or *negligence*—a common law word with a specific legal force and imprecise boundaries. Or it can be a constitutional principle that operates like the word "federalism" or the phrases "free speech," "due process," or "cruel and unusual"—an indicator of a foundational commitment.

Because accusations of corruption often accompany specific political scandals, the image conjured up can be quite precise, leading to a sense of precision about the word. However, when it is part of a statute, it is rarely precise, as we've seen. For instance, jurors are sometimes told they must find that the defendant acted "corruptly" to convict under a federal bribery statute and that acting corruptly means "intent to give some advantage inconsistent with official duty and the rights of others." The scope of "official duty and rights of others" is broad. The jury is essentially asked to make a judgment about whether the defendant thought he should not be getting the advantage he was getting. This gives prosecutors, and juries, leeway to determine what constitutes official duty and deviance therefrom.

In this book I have shown how the Constitution was designed in significant part as protection against corruption, broadly conceived, and how courts and legislatures actively relied on this for most of American history. State courts today still treat virtue as the foundation of the republic and favor a broad approach, giving prosecutors the power to charge corrupt intent as the core of a gift crime and giving legislatures the power to pass broad anticorruption statutes that structure private money around elections. The framers' ideas about corruption survived long past the republican era, into the 1970s in the Supreme Court. But since 1976 the Supreme Court has seriously constrained public power to pass anticorruption statutes, and since 2006 it has definitively rejected the traditional concept of corruption.

Corruption, ideally, is understood as an important concept embedded in a basic system that favors self-government. A conception of corruption in a democratic state requires a theory of what democracy is for. The accusation that a state is corrupt includes some idea of a noncorrupt state. A charge that an act, or person, or institution is corrupt implies some conception about what is not a corrupt act, and that in itself includes an imagination of the appropriate relationship of public officer, or citizen, with the state. One cannot use the word coherently in relationship to citizenship, or government, without some vision of good citizenship or good government. The difference between a gift and a bribe depends upon a theory about the appropriate kinds of relationships between those in power and those out of power.

Equally important, a conception of democracy requires a conception of corruption. This is no easy matter. According to legal philosopher Lon Fuller, the "rule of law" exists when law is applied evenly with reference to objective assessments. For the principles of legality to be satisfied, rules must be general, apply to all, and be constant over time, and they must be clear, intelligible, and administered in a way consistent with their language.[5] Laws that include or refer to "corrupt" or "corruptly" threaten to violate some of these requirements because it is not always clear and intelligible what behavior is covered by corruption statutes. The scope of corrupt intent laws depends in large part on a jury determination that a gift was given with intent to influence—a standard that threatens to be unequally administered and is arguably neither clear nor intelligible. On the other hand, structural laws designed to dissuade corruption, like a campaign contribution limit, are clear, intelligible, and less prone to inconsistent administration. However, a court reviewing those laws still needs to make a preliminary determination about whether they were in fact designed to serve anticorruption interests. For both bright-line laws and corrupt intent laws, there are some difficulties at the margins in defining the bounds of what constitutes corruption. It might seem that the concept of corruption is incompatible with requirements of Fuller's rule of law theory.

Yet if corruption is not adequately addressed within law, the absence of such laws threatens the principle that laws must be applied equally to all. For instance, if an attorney general does not prosecute a major campaign donor out of fear of losing her support, the laws are not equally applied. Without anticorruption laws, anyone can donate to any candidate. Political actors using financial power in politics to manipulate government for their own benefit do not lead to a clear, stable, functioning legal system. The quasi-paradox is this: without corruption law, or the concept of corruption, rule of law fails because laws can't be applied equally. Yet with corruption law, and the concept of corruption, we can't always discover the precision that rule of law seems to require.

If you only look at one part of this puzzle, you might conclude that corruption cannot be used in law because its essential imprecision leads to lawlessness. This was the view of Justice Marshall when he concluded that the Yazoo land grant passed by a bribed legislature had to be enforced—he had no clear way to tell the difference between a bribed legislature and an unbribed one. It also comes up when corruption is the reason for a statute, not just when corruption is in the statute. This is the argument used by Justice Scalia in *Citizens United* in concurrence, where he argued that a civic understanding of corruption could lead to "no limit to the Government's censorship power." He worried that corruption could cover too broad a range of activity. Therefore, if corruption is recognized as a justification for statutes that might otherwise violate constitutional restrictions (like the First Amendment), then it will give too great a power to justices to import their own ideas about political processes. If the Court recognizes that an anticorruption principle exists to justify speech-restricting activity, then legislative bodies will be able to pass laws merely by invoking "corruption" and the recognition of the constitutional value of the term will give state and federal legislators too much authority to restrict other rights.

And yet, the rule of law cannot survive without anticorruption measures, some of which will have to reference corruption, others of which will need to be explained by reference to corruption. We should embrace the anticorruption principle's uneasy role, valuing it but recognizing that the concept does not need to be defined in a statute because the most effective anticorruption statutes will go at effects, not the root cause. Courts should recognize that corruption is as important a concept as equality, or free expression, and while it may be a disputed concept at the margins, the commitment to anticorruption principles has a substantive core.

New Structures

Fortunately, the same history that teaches us that corruption was a foundational principle teaches us that structural changes are possible even within the constraints of a misinterpreted Constitution. We can fundamentally rearrange power dynamics and improve representative democracy even without a new Court, or court packing. For instance, states and the federal government can follow the reasoning behind the revolving-door ban of the framers and pass an absolute ban on staffers or members of Congress taking jobs in the influence industry. Any legislature can pass laws banning legislators and staffers from holding stock in companies affected by legislation. Congress can clearly define coordination so that independent corporate spending is actually independent. The public can oppose any Supreme Court nominee that supports the logic of *Buckley, Citizens United,* and *McCutcheon.* To my mind, the two most important solutions that require no Supreme Court blessing are ideas advocated by Teddy Roosevelt: publicly funded elections and trust-busting.

The United States has never designed a system to fund campaigns. Instead, we have outlawed other systems: patronage, direct corporate funding, and unlimited individual funding. Instead of outlawing more systems, we could actively endorse a system that would take away the corrupting threats posed by unlimited independent expenditures and the constant job of fund-raising.

Public financing for presidential elections began in 1976, but not for all federal offices. In 1996 Maine approved the first state-wide "Clean Election Act," which provides public funding for candidates running for all state offices. In the years that followed, Arizona, Massachusetts, North Carolina, New Mexico, New Jersey, Hawaii, and West Virginia all experimented with publicly funded elections. In 2005, after the governor was sentenced to federal prison on corruption charges, Connecticut passed a bill that banned lobbyist contributions to campaigns and allowed candidates to receive public funding once they showed that they had broad-based public support for their campaign. For state Senate, candidates have to raise $15,000 from at least 300 people, in amounts of $5 to $100. To run for state representative, candidates must raise $5,000 from at least 150 residents. Once they have raised that much, they get a fixed grant, sufficient to make them competitive. In New York City, candidates get a six-to-one match, receiving six city dollars for every dollar of the first $175 from any given contributor. That means a $100 contribution is worth $700 to a candidate. The public match applies only for New York City residents, and not PACs, unions, lobbyists, people doing business with the city, or people who live elsewhere. That means three $100 contributions from New York City residents result in $2,100, larger than a $2,000 PAC contribution or out-of-state individual contribution. The experience in both Connecticut and New York is that these systems reduce lobbyist influence and make it harder for lobbyists to get meetings. Candidates spend more time with constituents and less time fund-raising, and different kinds of people run for office, people who would not think they could find donors with $2,000 to support their campaigns. More women and minorities run for office. A voucher system has never been tried, but it is a key element of a law introduced by Congressman John Sarbanes in 2014. Instead of matching funds, it gives voters a tax credit that they can spend on a political campaign of their choice. The basic genius of all these systems is Madisonian: men are not angels, but they can be induced to be more attentive to the public by structure. A system that financially rewards candidates who appeal to large donors has internal moral negative effects: it makes the job of the candidate to serve excessive private interests, when the job of the representative is to serve broader interests. It creates a foundational role contradiction within the job. It institutionalizes corruption. A system that rewards candidates that get tens of thousands of signatures, or tens of thousands of $25 donations, will encourage candidates to spend their intellectual and emotional energies on a broad public. It diffuses the role contradiction and makes it more possible to serve all interests. Instead of institutionalizing corruption, it more closely aligns the job of the candidate with the job of the representative.

Another way of reducing corruption is to fight against monopolies per se. There is a long American tradition of suspicion of concentrated economic power because of its tendency to corrupt government and turn it from a democracy into a plutocracy. In 1906, Taft argued that the Sherman Act had saved the nation from a potential "plutocracy" and described the bill as a protection of economic and political freedoms. The Sherman Act and its later companions—the Clayton Act and the Robinson-Patman Act—played a critical role in maintaining decentralized political and economic power from the late 1930s to the 1970s. After that they were gutted and they now serve only to discipline the most egregious anticompetitive activity. As of 2014 most of the markets for essential goods are governed by monopolies. Retail is governed by Walmart and Amazon; cable is governed by Comcast; finance is governed by four banks; and meat production is governed by four companies. These minigovernments then use their economic power to exercise direct political power. Corruption as understood by the framers flows from monopoly because the monopolists can extract political concessions and subsidies from their role as little autocrats of their individual markets. A return to traditional ideas of political antitrust, strengthened by new laws, would make combination for the sake of concentrating political power more difficult.

When one looks at the reach of world history and human government, self-government appears a rare thing, a small set of remarkable moments when people come together as different but equal and collectively make decisions from a perspective of equality about general rules that all bind themselves to. This scarcity of democracy could be explained either by the spontaneity or by the fact that it may be difficult to achieve and more difficult to maintain. The arc of history has not tended inevitably toward self-government, and there is no reason to believe it is the most natural and stable resting place for human affairs.

Instead, self-government is not easy and requires a blend of commitments, both structural and cultural. The kind of political corruption I have described in this book is a demanding concept. It leads to condemning what seems normal and easy and what we would rather have outside the realm of condemnation. But it may be that persistent self-government requires persistent vigilance against the use of public channels for private ends. We have substantial resources, including the resources of history, to give us the courage—collective courage—to attempt to continue the experiment in liberty.

✦   ✦   ✦

In April 2014, shortly before this book went to press, the Supreme Court decided *McCutcheon v. FEC.* The question before the Court was whether Congress violated the First Amendment by passing a law that limited the total amount of money an individual could give to all federal candidates. Chief Justice John Roberts wrote for the majority, concluding that this aggregate limit violated the First Amendment. The Alabama businessman McCutcheon, he held, could not be restrained in giving as much money to as many candidates and parties as he desired.

The decision in *McCutcheon* relied on *Buckley v. Valeo* in equating all money spent for political campaigns with First Amendment speech. It reinforced earlier decisions holding that political equality is not a legitimate reason for Congress to pass a campaign finance law. But most importantly for our purposes, it defined corruption narrowly as quid pro quo. According to Justice Roberts, gratitude is not corrupting, and the access and influence that campaign contributions create are not corrupting. The opinion signals the real possibility that all contribution limits will be struck down. Throughout the opinion, Roberts shows real skepticism for the idea of the public good. He is also skeptical of the view that representative instruments of government can play a role in protecting us from corrupting tendencies.

Roberts appears confused about the relationship between different types of corruption laws. He defines the constitutional concept of corruption by reference to a particular criminal law case, *McCormick* (the case discussed in Chapter 12). In *McCormick*, the Court was trying not to define corruption in a global sense, but to interpret congressional intent in writing a federal criminal statute. Roberts's use of *McCormick* is like defining the First Amendment by reference to a case interpreting a state statute that uses the word *speech*.

The use of the quid pro quo definition leaves the opinion feeling theoretically thin. Without history or theory, it is unclear why corruption has any special place at all in the constitutional vision. Increasingly, it seems that it does not: the pride of place is mere lip service to *Buckley*. This portends the end of all campaign finance restrictions. Corruption was first stripped of its meaning, and seems likely to be stripped of any power at all.

There are moments when Roberts seems to feel the shakiness of his foundations. Roberts admits that "the line between quid pro quo and general influence may seem vague at times," but, he argues, "the distinction must be respected in order to safeguard basic First Amendment right." In other words, he knows that corruption is not only quid pro quo, and he knows that quid pro quo provides no real clear lines. But if he knows these things, why not take the next natural step and directly engage the foundational questions of the values that anticorruption laws serve and their role in a democracy? As I've intimated elsewhere, it is hard to know whether Roberts, and his colleagues on the Court, genuinely believe that democracy can survive the assault of self-interested money or whether they recognize that we are under assault and simply mistrust Congress more than they mistrust private interests.

My hope is that lawmakers will quickly act to pass public funding systems and anti-monopoly laws to protect our civic culture. I sometimes feel like our country is both young and old, like the eighty-one-year-old Franklin, floating in his hoped-for air balloon. We are in many ways inside his magical experiment, and it has been every bit as extraordinary as imagined. It has brought people to levels often dreamed of, and rarely achieved: where they live together in peace, exercising collective power over their own lives. I have no doubt that this represents one of the greatest achievements in human history. But democracy, without constant vigilance against corruption, is an unstable, unmoored thing, subject to great gusts of whimsy, and likely to collapse. There is no one walking below, holding the string: we need obstacles, restraints, an unbreakable connection between the public and the representatives.

Anticorruption Constitutional Provisions

ARTICLE I, SECTION 2, CLAUSE 1. The House of Representatives shall be composed of Members chosen every second Year by the People of the several States, and the Electors in each State shall have the Qualifications requisite for Electors of the most numerous Branch of the State Legislature.

ARTICLE I, SECTION 2, CLAUSE 2. No Person shall be a Representative who shall not have attained to the Age of twenty five Years, and been seven Years a Citizen of the United States, and who shall not, when elected, be an Inhabitant of that State in which he shall be chosen.

ARTICLE I, SECTION 2, CLAUSE 3. The Number of Representatives shall not exceed one for every thirty Thousand, but each State shall have at Least one Representative.

ARTICLE I, SECTION 2, CLAUSE 3. Representatives and direct Taxes shall be apportioned among the several States which may be included within this Union, according to their respective Numbers, which shall be determined by adding to the whole Number of free Persons, including those bound to Service for a Term of Years, and excluding Indians not taxed, three fifths of all other Persons. The actual Enumeration shall be made within three years after the first Meeting of the Congress of the United States, and within every subsequent Term of ten Years, in such Manner as they shall by Law direct.

The Number of Representatives shall not exceed one for every thirty Thousand, but each State shall have at Least one Representative; and until such enumeration shall be made, the State of New Hampshire shall be entitled to chuse three, Massachusetts eight, Rhode Island and Providence Plantations one, Connecticut five, New York six, New Jersey four, Pennsylvania eight, Delaware one, Maryland six, Virginia ten, North Carolina five, South Carolina five, and Georgia three.

ARTICLE I, SECTION 3, CLAUSE I. The Senate of the United States shall be composed of two Senators from each State, chosen by the Legislature thereof for six Years, and each Senator shall have one Vote.

ARTICLE I, SECTION 3, CLAUSE 3. No Person shall be a Senator who shall not have attained to the Age of thirty Years, and been nine Years a Citizen of the United States, and who shall not, when elected, be an Inhabitant of that State for which he shall be chosen.

ARTICLE I, SECTION 5, CLAUSE 3. Each House shall keep a Journal of its Proceedings, and from time to time publish the same, excepting such Parts as may in their Judgment require Secrecy; and the Yeas and Nays of the Members of either House on any question shall, at the Desire of one fifth of those Present, be entered on the Journal.

ARTICLE I, SECTION 6, CLAUSE I. The Senators and Representatives shall receive a Compensation for their Services, to be ascertained by Law, and paid out of the Treasury of the United States.

ARTICLE I, SECTION 6, CLAUSE 2. No Person holding any Office under the United States, shall be a Member of either House during his Continuance in Office. No Senator or Representative shall, during the Time for which he was elected, be appointed to any civil Office under the Authority of the United States, which shall have been created, or the Emoluments whereof shall have been increased during such time.

ARTICLE I, SECTION 8. Congress shall have the power . . .

Clause 8. To promote the Progress of Science and useful Arts, by securing for limited Times to Authors and Inventors the exclusive Right to their respective Writings and Discoveries.

Clause 12. To raise and support Armies, but no Appropriation of Money to that Use shall be for a longer Term than two Years.

ARTICLE I, SECTION 9.

Clause 7. No money shall be drawn from the Treasury, but in Consequence of Appropriations made by Law; and a regular Statement and Account of Receipts and Expenditures of all public Money shall be published from time to time.

Clause 8. No Title of Nobility shall be granted by the United States: And no Person holding any Office of Profit or Trust under them, shall, without the Consent of the Congress, accept of any present, Emolument, Office, or Title, of any kind whatever, from any King, Prince, or foreign State.

ARTICLE II, SECTION I, CLAUSE I. The executive Power shall be vested in a President of the United States of America. He shall hold his Office during the Term of four Years, and, together with the Vice President, chosen for the same Term, be elected.

ARTICLE II, SECTION I, CLAUSE 7. The President shall, at stated Times, receive for his Services, a Compensation, which shall neither be increased nor diminished during the Period for which he shall have been elected, and he shall not receive within that Period any other Emolument from the United States, or any of them.

ARTICLE II, SECTION 2, CLAUSE 2. He shall have Power, by and with the Advice and Consent of the Senate, to make Treaties, provided two thirds of the Senators present concur.

ARTICLE II, SECTION 2, CLAUSE 2. . . . he shall nominate, and by and with the Advice and Consent of the Senate, shall appoint Ambassadors, other public Ministers and Consuls . . . and all other Officers of the United States, whose Appointments are not herein otherwise provided for, and which shall be established by Law: but the Congress may by Law vest the Appointment of such inferior Officers, as they think proper, in the President alone, in the Courts of Law, or in the Heads of Departments.

ARTICLE II, SECTION 2, CLAUSE 2. [The President] shall have Power, . . . by and with the Advice and Consent of the Senate, [to appoint] Judges of the supreme Court.

ARTICLE II, SECTION 4. The President, Vice President and all civil Officers of the United States, shall be removed from Office on Impeachment for, and Conviction of, Treason, Bribery, or other high Crimes and Misdemeanors.

ARTICLE III, SECTION 1. The Judges, both of the supreme and inferior Courts, shall hold their Offices during good Behaviour, and shall, at stated Times, receive for their Services a Compensation, which shall not be diminished during their Continuance in Office.

AMENDMENT V. . . . nor shall private property be taken for public use, without just compensation.

AMENDMENT XVII. The Senate of the United States shall be composed of two Senators from each State, elected by the people thereof, for six years; and each Senator shall have one vote. The electors in each State shall have the qualifications requisite for electors of the most numerous branch of the State legislatures.

AMENDMENT XXVII. No law, varying the compensation for the services of the Senators and Representatives, shall take effect, until an election of Representatives shall have intervened.

Major Nineteenth- and Twentieth-Century Anticorruption Laws

MAIL FRAUD ACT (1872). Covered state and federal officials, criminalized the use of the mails for fraud, including, controversially, defrauding the public. Interpreted in 1927 to criminalize the theft of honest services.

TILLMAN ACT (1907). Prohibited corporations from contributing money to federal campaigns.

In the 1920s, in response to the Teapot Dome scandal, Congress passed laws requiring disclosure to enable enforcement of the corporate contribution laws.

HATCH ACT (1939). Enacted regulation of primaries by Congress. Limited contributions and expenditures in congressional elections. Prohibited all federal employees from soliciting campaign contributions. Amended in 1940 to place limits on how much an individual could give to a candidate and a limit on how much a national party committee could spend. After the Hatch Act, total campaign spending dipped and did not reach 1936 levels until nearly a quarter century later.

HOBBS ACT (1946). Covered state and federal officials, controversially held to criminalize the use of an official position to extort funds.

TAFT-HARTLEY ACT (1947). Barred both labor unions and corporations from making expenditures and contributions in federal elections.

FEDERAL BRIBERY STATUTE AND FEDERAL GRATUITIES STATUTE (1962). Covered federal officials and criminalized the giving or receiving of something of value in exchange for official action or as a reward for prior official action.

FEDERAL ELECTION CAMPAIGN ACT (1974). Covered federal candidates, limited expenditures (struck down) and contributions around elections, and created public funding system for presidential elections.

FEDERAL PROGRAM BRIBERY STATUTE (1984). Criminalized bribery of state and local officials explicitly.

BIPARTISAN CAMPAIGN REFORM ACT (2002). Prohibited national political party committees from raising or spending funds not subject to federal limits. Defined "electioneering communications" as broadcast ads that name a federal candidate within thirty days of a primary or caucus or within sixty days of a general election.

Notes

Introduction

1. Larry Tise, *The American Counterrevolution: A Retreat from Liberty, 1783–1800* (Mechanicsburg, PA: Stackpole Books, 1998), 59.

2. Letter from William Temple Franklin to Thomas Jefferson, April 27, 1790, in *The Founders' Constitution*, vol. 3, ed. Philip B. Kurland and Ralph Lerner (Chicago: University of Chicago Press, 1987), 385. Picture of the current portrait available at the website of the American Philosophical Society, http://www.amphilsoc.org/exhibits/treasures/louis.htm.

3. Washington correspondent of the *Chicago Press and Tribune*, *New York Times*, March 29, 1860, http://www.nytimes.com/1860/03/29/news/the-newspaper-press-of-washington-and-new-york.html.

4. Robert Penn Warren, *All the King's Men* (San Diego: Harcourt Brace, 1996), chapter 5.

1. Four Snuff Boxes and a Horse

1. Daniel Hays Lowenstein, "For God, for Country, or for Me," *California Law Review* 74 (1986): 1481.

2. Stacy Schiff, *A Great Improvisation: Franklin, France, and the Birth of America* (New York: Henry Holt, 2006).

3. Letter from Thomas Jefferson to William Short, October 3, 1801, in *Memoir, Correspondence and Miscellanies from the Papers of Thomas Jefferson*, vol. 3, ed. Thomas Jefferson Randolph (London: Henry Colburn and Richard Bentley, 1829), 492.

4. Benjamin H. Irvin, *Clothed in Robes of Sovereignty: The Continental Congress and the People Out of Doors* (Oxford: Oxford University Press, 2011), 181.

5. John Bassett Moore and Francis Wharton, *A Digest of International Law* (Washington, DC: U.S. Government Printing Office, 1906), 579.

6. Abraham de Wicquefort, *The Embassador and His Functions*, trans. John Digby (London: Bernard Lintott, 1716), 292.

7. *Plato's Laws*, Book 12, trans. Benjamin Jowett, hosted by the Internet Classics Archive at the Massachusetts Institute of Technology, http://clas sics.mit.edu/Plato/laws.12.xii.html.

8. My accounts of Silas Deane come from Joe R. Paul, *Unlikely Allies: How a Merchant, a Playwright, and a Spy Saved the American Revolution* (New York: Riverhead Books, 2009); Julian P. Boyd, "Silas Deane: Death by a Kindly Teacher of Treason? Part I," *William and Mary Quarterly* 16 (1959): 166; and Thomas Fleming, *The Perils of Peace: America's Struggle for Survival after Yorktown* (Washington, DC: Smithsonian Books, 2008).

9. Schiff, *Great Improvisation*, 153.

10. Fleming, *Perils of Peace*, 58.

11. For various discussions of this particular gift, see Mrs. Elizabeth Duane Gillespie, *A Book of Remembrance* (Philadelphia: J. B. Lippincott, 1901), 27; Faye Strumpf, *Limoge Boxes: A Complete Guide* (Iola, WI: Krause Publications, 2000), 134; and Julie Aronson and Marjorie E. Wiesemen, *Perfect Likeness: European and American Portrait Miniatures from the Cincinnati Art Museum* (New Haven, CT: Yale University Press, 2006), 286. The exact form, aside from the diamonds and the portrait, is uncertain. While some of his contemporaries referred to the present as a box, and many historians have assumed that it was a snuff box, his gift may have been lumped in with the other snuff boxes even though it was dissimilar. It may have been designed to hang from a chain as a pendant or later converted to a pendant (Elle Shushan, personal communication, March 2014).

12. Arthur Lee, *Papers in Relation to the Case of Silas Deane* (Philadelphia: Seventy Six Society, 1855), 182.

13. Benjamin H. Irvin, *Clothed in the Robes of Sovereignty* (Oxford: Oxford University Press, 2011), 181.

14. Lee, *Papers*, 166. Emphasis added.

15. Richard Henry Lee, *The Life of Arthur Lee* (Boston: Wells and Lilly, 1829), 143.

16. Letter from Arthur Lee to the Committee of Foreign Affairs, January 19, 1780, in *The Diplomatic Correspondence of the American Revolution* (Washington, DC: Rives, 1818), 580.

17. Letter from Vergennes to Luzerne, February 5, 1780, in *Emerging Nation: A Documentary History of the Foreign Relations of the United States under the Articles of Confederation*, vol. 1, ed. Mary A. Giunta (Washington, DC: U.S. Independent Agencies and Commissions, 1996), 24, discovered in T. Lawrence Larkin, "A 'Gift' Strategically Solicited and Magnanimously Conferred: The American Congress, the French Monarchy, and the State Portraits of Louis XVI and Marie-Antoinette," *Winterthur Portfolio* 44 (2010): 31.

18. Letter from Arthur Lee, *Diplomatic Correspondence*, 580.

19. *Emerging Nation*, 198.

20. Letter from John Jay to Don Diego de Gardoqui, March 1, 1786, reprinted in *The Diplomatic Correspondence of the United States of America* (Washington, DC: Frances Preston Blair, 1833), 142.

21. Catherine Drinker Bowen, *Miracle at Philadelphia: The Story of the Constitutional Convention, May–September 1787* (Boston: Back Bay Books, 1986), 17.

22. Schiff, *Great Improvisation*, 153.

23. This was discussed in an opinion by the Office of Legal Counsel, "President Reagan's Ability to Receive Retirement Benefits from the State of California," *Opinion of the Office of Legal Counsel* 5 (1981): 188.

24. The other difference is that the "or any of them" is collapsed into the "them" of the clause.

25. See Letter from John Quincy Adams to John Adams, June 7, 1797, in *Writings of John Quincy Adams*, vol. 2, ed. Worthington Chauncey Ford (New York: McMillan, 1913), 180n1.

26. The historical treatment of the "box" as Franklin's comes from this note, which was included in Max Farrand's *Records of the Federal Convention* and therefore has achieved notoriety: "Dr. Franklin is the person alluded to by Randolph. In the winter of 1856, in Philadelphia, under the roof of a venerable granddaughter of Dr. Franklin, I saw the beautiful portrait of Louis XVI, snuff-box size, presented by that king to the doctor. As the portrait is exactly such as is contained in the snuff-boxes presented by Crowned

heads, one of which I have seen, it is probable this portrait of Louis was originally attached to the box in question, which has in the lapse of years been lost or given away by Dr. Franklin." *The Records of the Federal Convention of 1787*, vol. 3, ed. Max Farrand (New Haven, CT: Yale University Press, 1911), 327, citing H. B. Grigsby, *History of the Virginia Federal Convention of 1788*, vol. 9 (Richmond: Virginia Historical Society Collections, 1980), 264. It is of course possible that the snuff box was Lee's or Deane's.

27. See Edmund Randolph, "Remarks at the Virginia Convention Debates," in David Robertson, *Debates and Other Proceedings of the Convention of Virginia of 1788*, 2nd ed. (Richmond, VA: Enquirer Press, 1805), 321–345.

28. A First Amendment written with the same emphatic language would have to be "Congress Shall Make no Law *of any kind whatever . . .*"

29. Merrill D. Peterson, *Thomas F. Jefferson and the New Nation: A Biography* (Oxford: Oxford University Press, 1975), 401.

30. Martha Rojas, in *Old World, New World: America and Europe in the Age of Jefferson*, ed. Leonard Sadowsky (Richmond: University of Virginia Press, 2010), 179.

31. Howard C. Rice Jr., *Thomas Jefferson's Paris* (Princeton, NJ: Princeton University Press, 1976), 123.

32. "To Thomas Jefferson from William Short, 2 May 1791," Founders Online, National Archives, http://founders.archives.gov/documents/Jefferson/01-20-02-0103, source: *The Papers of Thomas Jefferson*, vol. 20, *April 1–August 4, 1791*, ed. Julian P. Boyd (Princeton, NJ: Princeton University Press, 1982), 345–352.

33. John Bassett Moore, *A Digest of International Law*, vol. 5 (Washington, DC: Government Printing Office, 1906), section 651.

2. Changing the Frame

1. "To Benjamin Franklin from Georgiana Shipley," February 11, 1777, Founders Online, National Archives, http://founders.archives.gov/documents/Franklin/01-23-02-0194, source: *The Papers of Benjamin Franklin*, vol. 23, *October 27, 1776, through April 30, 1777*, ed. William B. Willcox (New Haven, CT: Yale University Press, 1983), 303–306.

2. Edward Gibbon, *The History of the Decline and Fall of the Roman Empire*, vol. 3, ed. H. H. Millman (London: John Murray, 1846), 166–167.

3. "Begs the favour from mr. franklin that he Pleases to let him know by the way of the Penny post if he wants more mr. Gibbon's history of the Roman Empire and Garma's teatro de España. Mr. franklin may keep them if not Read as long as he pleases but mr. Sarsfield wants to know it as one of those Books do not belong to him and he desires to be able to give an account of it to the owner." "To Benjamin Franklin from the Comte de Sarsfield," November 7, 1777, Founders Online, National Archives, http://founders.archives.gov /documents/Franklin/01-25-02-0093, source: *The Papers of Benjamin Franklin*, vol. 25, *October 1, 1777, through February 28, 1778*, ed. William B. Willcox (New Haven, CT: Yale University Press, 1986), 143. He asked first in April, then in late fall begged, "Si monsieur franklin n'a plus besoin . . . de l'histoire romaine de M. Gibbons, il fera plaisir a M. de Sarsfield de les lui rapporter mercredi" ("If Mr. Franklin doesn't need M. Gibbon's Roman history, it would please Mr. Sarsfield if you could bring it back Wednesday")."To Benjamin Franklin from Guy-Claude, Comte de Sarsfield," April 4, 1778, Founders Online, National Archives, http://founders.archives.gov/documents/Franklin/01-26-02-0175, source: *The Papers of Benjamin Franklin*, vol. 26, *March 1 through June 30, 1778*, ed. William B. Willcox (New Haven, CT: Yale University Press, 1987), 241.

4. Bernard Bailyn, *The Ideological Origins of the American Revolution* (Cambridge, MA: Belknap Press of Harvard University Press, 1992), 26. "Did not Persia and Macedon distract the councils of Greece by acts of corruption?" (quoting Madison).

5. Ibid., 173.

6. Carl J. Richard, *Greeks and Romans Bearing Gifts: How the Ancients Inspired the Founding Fathers* (Lanham, MD: Roman and Littlefield, 2009), 129.

7. Edmund Burke, "Speech on Conciliation with America," March 22, 1775, reprinted in Edmund Burke, *Selected Writings*, ed. Peter Stanlis (New Brunswick, NJ: Transaction Publishers, 2009), 193.

8. Gordon S. Wood, *The Americanization of Benjamin Franklin* (New York: Penguin, 2005), 96.

9. Patrick Henry, "Speech in the Convention of Virginia on the Expediency of Adopting the Federal Constitution," June 7, 1788, reprinted in E. B. Williston, *Eloquence of the United States*, vol. 1 (Middletown, CT: E. and H. Clark, 1827), 223. Note that Britain is a model and bogeyman—fundamental admiration for British form undergirds design efforts for federalists and

antifederalists alike. See also Gordon S. Wood, *The Creation of the American Republic, 1776–1787* (New York: W. W. Norton, 1969), 32.

10. Notes of Yates, June 22, 1787, in *The Records of the Federal Convention of 1787*, vol. 1, ed. Max Farrand (New Haven, CT: Yale University Press, 1911) (hereafter *Records*).

11. Catherine Drinker Bowen, *Miracle at Philadelphia: The Story of the Constitutional Convention, May–September 1787* (Boston: Back Bay Books, 1986), 17.

12. Notes of Madison, August 14, 1787, in *Records*, vol. 2; Woody Holton develops this idea in *Unruly Americans and the Origins of the Constitution* (New York: Hill and Wang, 2007).

13. J. G. A. Pocock, *The Machiavellian Moment: Florentine Political Thought and the Atlantic Republican Tradition* (Princeton, NJ: Princeton University Press, 1975), 507.

14. Bailyn, *Ideological Origins*, xiii.

15. James D. Savage, "Corruption and Virtue at the Constitutional Convention," *Journal of Politics* 56 (1994): 181.

16. Bailyn, *Ideological Origins*, 131.

17. Notes of Yates, June 22, 1787, in *Records*, vol. 1, quoting Mason.

18. Gordon S. Wood, *Radicalism of the American Revolution* (New York: Knopf, 1992), 109.

19. Ibid., 183.

20. Ibid., 108.

21. Ibid., 176.

22. Ibid., 175.

23. Lance Banning, *The Jeffersonian Persuasion* (Ithaca, NY: Cornell University Press, 1980), 47.

24. Bailyn, *Ideological Origins*, 345; one can also find a discussion in Donald S. Lutz, "The Relative Influence of European Writers on Late Eighteenth-Century American Political Thought," *American Political Science Review* 78 (1984): 189.

25. Aristotle, *Nichomachean Ethics*, Book 8, ch. 10, para. 1 (Minneapolis, MN: Filiquarian Publishing, 2007).

26. Charles de Montesquieu, *The Spirit of Laws* [1748], trans. Melvin Richter (Cambridge: Cambridge University Press, 1991), Book 4.

27. Ibid., Book 5, ch. 3, para. 1.

28. Ibid., Book 5, ch. 2, para. 1.

29. For a full discussion of this, see Simone Goyard-Fabre's discussion of Montesquieu as the anti-Hobbes. Simone Goyard-Fabre, *Montesquieu adversaire de Hobbes* (Paris: Les Lettres Modernes, 1980).

30. "Summer 1759," Founders Online, National Archives, http://founders.archives.gov/documents/Adams/01-01-02-0004-0007-0001, source: *The Adams Papers, Diary and Autobiography of John Adams*, vol. 1, *1755–1770*, ed. L. H. Butterfield (Cambridge, MA: Harvard University Press, 1961), 103–123.

31. "Letter to Frances Gilmer," March 1816, in *Memoir, Correspondence*. For further evidence of Jefferson's rejection of Hobbes, see David Tucke, *Enlightened Republicanism: A Study of Jefferson's Notes on the State of Virginia* (Lanham, MD: Lexington Books, 2008).

32. To be fair, some historians argue that the republicanism of the era has been overstated, and that liberalism is the key to understanding the Constitution. For one example, see Isaac Kramnick, "Republican Revisionism Revisited," *The American Historical Review* 87, no. 3 (June 1982): 629–664.

33. W. M. Spellman, *John Locke* (New York: Palgrave Macmillan, 1997), 139.

34. John Locke, *An Essay Concerning Human Understanding* (Amherst, MA: Prometheus Books, 1995), 19.

35. John Locke, "Of the Dissolution of Government," in *The Second Treatise of Government and A Letter Concerning Toleration* (Mineola, NY: Dover, 2002), 100.

36. Barry Alan Shain, *The Myth of American Individualism* (Princeton, NJ: Princeton University Press, 1994), 24.

37. Samuel Pufendorf, *On the Duty of Man and Citizen according to Natural Law*, Book 2, ch. 17 [1673], trans. Michael Silverthorne, ed. James Tully (Cambridge: Cambridge University Press, 1991).

38. Ibid., Book 2, ch. 8.

39. Noah Webster, *Instructive and Entertaining Lessons for Youth* (New Haven, CT: S. Babcock and Durrie & Peck, 1835), 230.

40. Lance Banning, "Some Second Thoughts on Virtue and the Course of Revolutionary Thinking," in *Conceptual Change and the Constitution*, ed. Terence Ball and J. G. A. Pocock (Lawrence: University Press of Kansas, 1988), 200.

41. Federalist No. 55 (James Madison).

42. Notes of Madison, July 19, 1787, in *Records*, vol. 2.

43. Federalist No. 10 (James Madison).

44. Notes of Madison, July 19, 1787, in *Records*, vol. 2, quoting Gouverneur Morris saying: "The check provided in the 2d. branch was not meant as a check on Legislative usurpations of power, but on the abuse of lawful powers, on the propensity in the 1st. branch to legislate too much to run into projects of paper money & similar expedients."

45. Lawrence Lessig, brief for the government as Amicus Curiae, *McCutcheon v. FEC*, 572 U.S. ___ (2014).

46. Robert G. Natelson, "The General Welfare Clause and the Public Trust: An Essay in Original Understanding," *University of Kansas Law Review* 52 (2003): 48.

47. Bailyn, *Ideological Origins*, 379.

48. Montesquieu, *Laws*, Book 2, ch. 2, para. 26.

49. "Letter from George Washington to the Marquis de Lafayette," February 7, 1788, reprinted in *The Writings of George Washington*, ed. Lawrence Boyd Evans (New York: G. P. Putnam's Sons, 1908), 291.

50. James Madison, "Remarks during the Virginia Debate on the Adoption of the Federal Constitution," June 20, 1788, reprinted in *State Ratification Debates*, vol. 3, 531, 537. See generally Bailyn, *Ideological Origins*, 367–393.

51. Notes of Rufus King, June 1, 1787; Notes of Madison, June 1, 1787, in *Records*, vol. 1.

52. David Hume, *Essays and Treatises on Several Subjects* (London: A. Millar, 1758), 32.

53. Shain, *Myth*, 160–169.

54. St. George Tucker, *Blackstone's Commentaries: With Notes of Reference to the Constitution and Laws, of the Federal Government of the United States; and of the Commonwealth of Virginia* (1803), 119. See also Charles S. Sydnor, *American Revolutionaries in the Making: Political Practices in Washington's Virginia* (New York: Free Press, 1965), 87.

55. Lawrence Lessig, *Republic, Lost: How Money Corrupts Congress and a Plan to Stop It* (New York: Hachette Publishing, 2011).

56. Wood, *Radicalism*, 104.

57. Niccòlo Machiavelli, *Discourses of Livy* [1531] (Oxford: Oxford University Press, 1997), 298–300.

58. Notes of Madison, July 19, 1787, in *Records*, vol. 2.

59. Federalist No. 75 (Alexander Hamilton).

3. Removing Temptations

1. "Letter from Benjamin Franklin to Jean-Baptiste Leroy," in *Memoirs of the Life and Writings of Benjamin Franklin*, vol. 6 (London: Henry Colburn, 1818), 496.

2. Federalist No. 68 (Alexander Hamilton).

3. See James D. Savage, "Corruption and Virtue at the Constitutional Convention," *Journal of Politics* 56 (1994): 181. A review of Madison's and Yates's notes shows that "corruption," and "corrupt" (not including "corruption of blood" and its variants) show up in discussions twice as often as "faction" or "factions" and twice as often as "violent" or "violence." See generally Notes of Madison and Notes of Yates, in *The Records of the Federal Convention of 1787*, vols. 1 and 2, ed. Max Farrand (New Haven, CT: Yale University Press, 1911) (hereafter *Records*).

4. J. G. A. Pocock, *The Machiavellian Moment: Florentine Political Thought and the Atlantic Republican Tradition* (Princeton, NJ: Princeton University Press, 1975), 513.

5. Notes of Madison, June 2, 1787, in *Records*, vol. 1.

6. *Annals of Congress*, vol. 1 (1789–1790), 581, in *Records*, vol. 3.

7. *U.S. Term Limits, Inc. v. Thornton*, 514 U.S. 779, 794 n.11 (1995) (Thomas, J. dissenting, "The Ineligibility Clause was intended to guard against corruption."). See also "Remarks of Alexander Hamilton," in *Records*, vol. 1, 381; *Freytag v. IRS*, 501 U.S. 868, 904 (1991) (Scalia, J. concurring in part and concurring in the judgment, "The Framers' experience with postrevolutionary self-government had taught them that combining the power to create offices with the power to appoint officers was a recipe for legislative corruption.")

8. Notes of Yates, June 22, 1787, in *Records*, vol. 1.

9. Notes of Madison, August 14, 1787, in *Records*, vol. 2.

10. *Selected Works of Thomas Paine & Citizen Tom Paine*, ed. Howard Fast (New York: Modern Library, 1946), 6, 10.

11. Notes of Madison, September 6, 1787, in *Records*, vol. 2.

12. Notes of Yates, June 22, 1787, in *Records*, vol. 1, quoting Mason.

13. Ibid., quoting Butler.

14. *Annals of Congress*, vol. 1 (1798), 905, in *Records*, vol. 3, 375.

15. Ibid.

16. Ibid.

17. "McHenry Speech to the Maryland State House of Delegates," November 29, 1787, in William Hand Browne, *Maryland Historical Magazine* (Louis Henry Dielman Maryland Historical Society, 1909).

18. Notes of Yates, June 22, 1787, in *Records*, vol. 1.

19. Federalist No. 52 (James Madison).

20. Notes of Madison, June 16, 1787, in *Records*, vol. 1. ("Theory & practice both proclaim it. If the Legislative authority be not restrained, there can be neither liberty nor stability; and it can only be restrained by dividing it within itself, into distinct and independent branches. In a single House there is no check, but the inadequate one, of the virtue & good sense of those who compose it.")

21. See Savage, "Corruption," 177. ("In each case, corruption is related to the fear of depedency, where dependency was a function of size.") Savage makes a stronger claim that I would after reading the notes. Size was a frequent topic—and the most startling for a visitor from the present—but certainly not the only context in which corruption was considered.

22. Federalist No. 62 (James Madison).

23. Notes of Madison, July 10, 1787, in *Records*, vol. 1.

24. Notes of Madison, August 17, 1787, in *Records*, vol. 2.

25. Notes of Madison, August 14, 1787, in *Records*, vol. 2.

26. Notes of Madison, July 20, 1787, in *Records*, vol. 2.

27. Savage, "Corruption," 181.

28. "Letter from James Madison to George Hay," August 23, 1823, in *Documentary History of the Constitution of the United States of America, 1787–1870* (Washington, DC: Department of State, 1905), 316.

29. Federalist No. 39.

30. "Mr. Williamson for a six year term: 'The expence will be considerable & ought not to be unnecessarily repeated. If the Elections are too frequent, the best men will not undertake the service and those of an inferior character will be liable to be corrupted.'" Notes of Madison, July 19, 1787, in *Records*, vol. 2.

31. Notes of Yates, June 6, 1787, in *Records*, vol. 1.

32. Federalist No. 66.

33. *Debates in the Several State Conventions*, vol. 2 (New York: Burt Franklin, 1888), 264.

34. Lord John Russell, "Speech on Parliamentary Reform," partially reprinted in *Readings in Modern Europe History: A Collection of Extracts . . . ,*

vol. 2, ed. James Harvey Robinson and Charles Austin Beard (Boston: Ginn & Company, 1909), 240.

35. Speech of John Wilkes, "Debate on Mr. Wilkes Motion for a More Equal Representation," in *The Parliamentary History of England*, vol. 18, *1774–1777* (London: T. C. Hansard, 1803), 1296.

36. Ralph Griffiths, "Review of George Edwards, Royal and Constitutional Regeneration of Great Britain," in *The Monthly Review* (London: T. Becket, January–April 1791), 72.

37. Notes of King Rufus, August 8, 1787 (quoting Mason); Notes of Madison, August 8, 1787, in *Records*, vol. 2.

38. Notes of Madison, August 8, 1787, in *Records*, vol. 2.

39. Akhil Reed Amar, *America's Constitution: A Biography* (New York: Random House, 2005), 70.

40. Notes of Madison, July 20, 1787, in *Records*, vol. 2.

41. See, e.g., Colonel Richard D. Rosen, "Funding 'Non-Traditional' Military Operations: The Alluring Myth of a Presidential Power of the Purse," *Military Law Review* 155 (1998): 25–44 (describing English history that formed the background for the appropriations clause); and Kate Stith, "Congress' Power of the Purse," *Yale Law Journal* 97 (1988): 1352–1353.

42. Adrien Vermeule, "Essay: The Constitutional Law of Official Compensation," *Columbia Law Review* 102 (2002): 509.

43. See *United States v. Richardson*, 418 U.S. 166, 167 n.1 (1974).

44. Malla Pollack, "Purveyance and Power or Over-Priced Free Lunch: The Intellectual Property Clause as an Ally of the Takings Clause in the Public's Control of Government," *Southwestern University Law Review* 30 (2000).

45. Notes of Madison, September 8, 1787, in *Records*, vol. 2.

46. Lawrence Lessig, "A Reply to Professor Hasen," *Harvard Law Review Forum* 26 (2013): 70.

4. *Yazoo*

1. "Report from Congress, January 4," *New York Evening Post*, January 8, 1808, 2.

2. Ibid.; "Tombigbee Celebration of the Declaration of Independence," *Raleigh (NC) Weekly Register*, November 9, 1809, 4.

3. John T. Noonan, *Bribes: The Intellectual History of a Moral Idea* (Collingdale, PA: Diane Publishing Company, 1984), 436. ("Representative Thomas Raburn, for example, was reproached for selling his vote for $600 while others got $1,000. Raburn replied it showed he was easily satisfied and not greedy.")

4. Ibid.

5. Peter C. McGrath, *Yazoo: Law and Politics in the New Republic, the Case of Fletcher v. Peck* (Providence, RI: Brown Unviversity Press, 1966).

6. Albert J. Beveridge, *The Life of John Marshall*, vol. 3 (Boston: Houghton Mifflin, 1919), 551.

7. Joel Chandler Harris, *Stories of Georgia* (New York: American Book Company, 1896), 133–134.

8. Ibid., 134.

9. Tracy Jenkins, "Conflict of Interest in the Yazoo Affair," *James Blair Historical Review* 3 (2012): 49, 58.

10. Henry Adams, *John Randolph* (Boston: Houghton and Mifflin, 1882), 125–126.

11. Ibid., 108–109.

12. Ibid., 107.

13. Thomas H. Palmer, *The Historical Register of the United States* (Philadelphia: T. H. Palmer, 1814), 200.

14. Ibid., 201.

15. Among many other sources discussing this see Noonan, *Bribes*, 440.

16. *American Law Review*, vol. 1 (Boston: Little, Brown, 1867), 278.

17. R. Kent Newmyer, *John Marshall and the Historic Age of the Supreme Court* (Baton Rouge: Louisiana State University Press, 2001), 37.

18. There were other issues in the case that I do not explore because they are not directly relevant to the question of corrupt laws.

19. Francis Hutcheson, *An Inquiry into the Original of Our Ideas of Beauty and Virtue: In Two Treatises* (London: R. Ware, 1725), 296.

20. Richard Price, "Observations on the Nature of Civil Liberty, the Principles of Government, and the Justice and the Policy of the War with America," in *Price: Political Writings*, ed. D. O. Thomas (Cambridge: Cambridge University Press, 1991), 22.

21. John Locke, *Second Treatise of Government*, ed. C. B. Macpherson (Indianapolis, IN: Hackett Publishing, 1980), 68.

22. For a further discussion and arguments that governments are agents of their constituents, see Ethan J. Leib, David L. Ponet, and Michael Serota, "A Fiduciary Theory of Judging," *California Law Review* 101 (2013); Robert G. Natelson, "The Agency Law Origins of the Necessary and Proper Clause," *Case Western Law Review* 55 (2004); and D. Theodore Rave, "Politicians as Fiduciaries," *Harvard Law Review* 126 (2013).

23. Theoretically, if Peck attempted to enforce his contract against the state, he could lose, because in that case it would not be incidental. This leads to two different legal determinations of the validity of a legislative act depending on whether the corruption charges are incidental or central. Probably because of the problems that would arise out of this inconsistency, most commentators and courts have treated this case as standing for a holding he claims he is not making: that corrupt process is irrelevant.

24. For a further discussion of this argument, see Mark Graber, "Naked Land Transfers and American Constitutional Development," *Vanderbilt Law Review* 53 (2000): 79.

25. According to Marshall, "The contract between Georgia and the purchasers was executed by the grant. A contract executed, as well as one which is executory, contains obligations binding on the parties. A grant, in its own nature, amounts to an extinguishment of the right of the grantor, and implies a contract not to reassert that right. A party is, therefore, always estopped by his own grant." However, the changing of the contract to a grant (an executed contract) does not change the obligations of the initial contract. He concluded that "a law annulling conveyances between individuals, and declaring that the grantors should stand seised of their former estates, notwithstanding those grants, would be as repugnant to the constitution as a law discharging the vendors of property from the obligation of executing their contracts by conveyances. It would be strange if a contract to convey was secured by the constitution, while an absolute conveyance remained unprotected. . . . If, under a fair construction of the constitution, grants are comprehended under the term contracts, is a grant from the state excluded from the operation of the provision? Is the clause to be considered as inhibiting the state from impairing the obligation of contracts between two individuals, but as excluding from that inhibition contracts made with itself? The words themselves contain no such distinction. They are general, and are applicable to contracts of every description. If contracts made with the

state are to be exempted from their operation, the exception must arise from the character of the contracting party, not from the words which are employed." Even if it is a contracts case, Mark Graber argues, persuasively, that the bulk of the reasoning in *Fletcher v. Peck* relies on common-law rules about contracts and conveyances, and it is not really a case about the impairment of contracts. Graber, "Naked Land Transfers." It is also, as a historical matter, a weak reading. Forrest McDonald has argued that this clause was not even intended to be there in the first place. Forrest McDonald, *Novus Ordo Seclorum: The Intellectual Origins of the Constitution* (Lawrence: University Press of Kansas, 1985), 273. As David Currie suggested in his classic treaty, the "impairments of contract" clause can be seen in many ways as an early, Marshall Court version of the later "substantive due process." David P. Currie, *The Constitution in the Supreme Court: The First Hundred Years, 1789–1888* (Chicago: University of Chicago Press, 1985). Both were restrictions on the scope of legislative supremacy. See Timothy Sandefur, "Privileges, Immunities, and Substantive Due Process," *New York University Journal of Law and Liberty* 5 (2010) (discussion of the relationship between substantive due process and the impairment of contracts). See also James Oakes, "'Property Rights' in Constitutional Analysis Today," *Washington Law Review* 56 (1981): 590–591. Oakes draws the parallel between the obligations of contracts cases and the substantive due process cases neatly, arguing that the first phase of property rights treatment was from *Fletcher* to 1887, when the contracts clause was used to invalidate dozens of pro-debtor pieces of legislation; the second phase was the substantive due process era.

26. It is also, as a historical matter, a weak reading. Forrest McDonald has argued that this clause was not even intended to be there in the first place. Forrest McDonald, *Novus Ordo Seclorum: The Intellectual Origins of the Constitution* (Lawrence: University Press of Kansas, 1985), 273. As David Currie suggested in his classic treaty, the "impairments of contract" clause can be seen in many ways as an early, Marshall Court version of the later "substantive due process." David P. Currie, *The Constitution in the Supreme Court: The First Hundred Years, 1789–1888* (Chicago: University of Chicago Press, 1985). Both were restrictions on the scope of legislative supremacy. See Timothy Sandefur, "Privileges, Immunities, and Substantive Due Process," *New York University Journal of Law and Liberty* 5 (2010) (discussion of the relationship between substantive due process and the impairments of

contracts). See also James Oakes, "'Property Rights' in Constitutional Analysis Today," *Washington Law Review* 56 (1981): 590–591. Oakes draws the parallel between the obligations of contracts cases and the substantive due process cases neatly, arguing that the first phase of property rights treatment was from *Fletcher* to 1887, when the contracts clause was used to to invalidate dozens of pro-debtor pieces of legislation; the second phase was the substantive due process era.).

27. James W. Ely, *The Guardian of Every Other Right: A Constitutional History of Property Rights*, 3rd ed. (Oxford: Oxford University Press, 2008), 64.

28. "Thomas Jefferson to James Madison," May 25, 1810, Founders Online, National Archives, http://founders.archives.gov/documents/Jefferson/03-02-02-0362, source: *The Papers of Thomas Jefferson*, Retirement Series, vol. 2, *16 November 1809 to 11 August 1810*, ed. J. Jefferson Looney (Princeton, NJ: Princeton University Press, 2005), 416–417.

29. Ibid.

30. "To James Madison from Thomas Jefferson," October 15, 1810, Founders Online, National Archives, http://founders.archives.gov/documents/Madison/03-02-02-0734, source: *The Papers of James Madison*, Presidential Series, vol. 2, *1 October 1809–2 November 1810*, ed. J. C. A. Stagg, Jeanne Kerr Cross, and Susan Holbrook Perdue (Charlottesville: University Press of Virginia, 1992), 580–582.

31. *The Writings of James Madison: 1808–1819* (New York: G. P. Putnam's Sons, 1908), 111–112, fn. 1. Madison is not entirely clear about his own perspective, but he is clearly not inclined to view Granger warmly, calling his political prowess greater than his reason and mentioning his Yazooism as a difficulty at three different points.

32. "Madison's Observations on Jefferson's Draft of a Constitution for Virginia, October 1788," Founders Online, National Archives, http://founders.archives.gov/documents/Jefferson/01-06-02-0255-0005, source: *The Papers of Thomas Jefferson*, vol. 6, *21 May 1781–1 March 1784*, ed. Julian P. Boyd (Princeton, NJ: Princeton University Press, 1952), 308–317.

5. Is Bribery without a Remedy?

1. Sir John Eardley Eardley-Wilmot, *A Tribute to Hydrotherapy*, 3rd ed. (London: Longman, Brown, Green, and Longman's, 1855).

2. Sir John Eardley Eardley-Wilmot, *Is Bribery without a Remedy? A Letter to the Right Honorable Lord John Russell, M.P.* (London: James Kidgway, Picadilly, 1853).

3. Sir Edward Coke, *Institutes of the laws of England, Part Three* (London: E. & R. Brooke, 1797), 145.

4. An Act to Reform the Administration of Justice, June 1385, reprinted in *Select Documents of Constitutional History*, ed. George Burton Adams and Henry Morse Stephens (Norwood, MA: Macmillan, 1901), 147.

5. In 1350 the chief justice of the Supreme Court, William de Thorpe, was put in prison and sentenced to hanging for taking bribes. But he was pardoned the next year. The Thorpe story can be used as evidence of either a weak or a strong rule of law, depending upon whether one focuses on the conviction or the pardon.

6. William Blackstone, *Commentaries on the Laws of England*, vol. 4, chap. 10 (Portland: Thomas B. Waite, 1807), 139–140.

7. Ibid., 140–141 (emphasis added).

8. Moreover, the cases were rare enough that the precise application of corruption statutes to executive officers was ambivalent The mid-eighteenth-century British judge Lord Mansfield was "aggressive," as one biographer put it, in his use of criminal justice, and took an expansive view of bribery when he held that it was a bribe at common law to pay to get a clerkship in Jamaica. "The absence of a statute proscribing a particular activity did not deter him from trying a case if the activity was contrary to good morals." Norman Poser, *Mansfield, Justice in the Age of Reason* (Montreal: McGill–Queens University Press, 2013), 260.

9. A. J. Cella, "The Doctrine of Legislative Privilege of Freedom of Speech and Debate: Its Past, Present and Future as a Bar to Criminal Prosecutions in the Courts," *Suffolk Law Review* 2 (1968): 15.

10. *United States v. Worrall*, 2 U.S. 384 (1798).

11. For a fuller discussion of *Worrall* and its place in the development of Samuel Chase's philosophy, see Stephen Presser, "A Tale of Two Judges . . . ," *Northwestern University Law Review* 73 (March/April 1978).

12. Asher Crosby Hinds, *Hinds' Precedents of the House of Representatives of the United States*, vol. 2 (Washington, DC: Government Printing Office, 1907), 1048–1052, sections 1601–1603.

13. Ibid., 1058–1060.

14. For a fuller discussion of the case's role in contempt proceedings, see Morton Rosenberg, *Congress's Contempt Power: Law, History, Practice, and Procedure* (Washington, DC: Congressional Research Service, 2008), 7–9.

15. The 1797 list of indictable crimes in Delaware included extortion, but not bribery. Just as removal from office was the preferred method of punishment for many bribery statutes, the primary way in which extortion was litigated was in the context of either contract law or "fee bills." Fee bills were statutes that allowed people who had been extorted to get their money back. No intent was required in the fee bill—all someone would have to do is demonstrate that they had paid an officer an amount in excess of what was legally owed. See the discussion of fee bill statutes in *Irons v. Allen*, 169 Pa. 633, 32 A. 655 (PA 1895) and *State v. Andrews*, 51 N.H. 582 (NH 1872).

16. All of these statutes are on file with the author.

17. On file with the author, cited in *State v. Darnall*, 20 Tenn. 290 (1839).

18. This tradition continued for some time. In 1881 Pennsylvania had a law that anyone guilty of election-law violations—including bribery around elections—was not eligible for future public office. *Leonard v. Commonwealth*, 112 Pa. 607 (Pa. 1886).

19. See, e.g., *Commonwealth v. Chapman*, 1 Va. Cas. 138 (1803) (conviction for offering the sheriff money to appoint certain people to a jury).

20. *Newell v. Commonwealth*, 2 Va. 88 (Va. 1795).

21. Thurston Greene, *The Language of the Constitution: A Sourcebook and Guide to the Ideas, Terms, and Vocabulary Used by the Framers of the United States Constitution* (Westport, CT: Greenwood, 1991), 108 (emphasis omitted; quoting New Hampshire); *The constitution of New Hampshire: as altered and amended by a convention of delegates, held at Concord, in said state, approved by the people, and established by the Convention, on the first Wednesday of September, 1792* (Concord: G. Hough, 1792), 67.

22. Supreme Court of Delaware, Definition of Indictable Crimes, 2 Del. Cas. 235 (Del. Supr. 1797).

23. Compare with *State v. Pritchard*, 107 N.C. 921 (1890) and *Leeman v. State*, 35 Ark. 438 (1880). See *Respublica v. Hannum*, 1 Yeates 71, 4 (Pa. 1791), requiring intent, held: "There appear no criminal intentions, passionate expressions, threats, or partiality. It is proved that the prosecutor, believing the bill to be reasonable, actually paid it willingly. We are therefore unanimously

of opinion, that there are no proper grounds for a prosecution by way of information."

24. *Martin v. State*, 1 H. & J. 721 (Md. 1805).

25. *Coates v. Wallace*, 1 Ashm.

26. *Commonwealth v. Shed*, 1 Mass. 227, 229 (Mass. 1804) (emphasis in original).

27. *State v. Dickens*, 2 N.C. 406 (N.C. Super. L&Eq. 1796).

28. *Newell v. Commonwealth*, 2 Va. 88 (1795).

29. A short case addressing whether insolvent debtors' ability to pay shows that there were some prosecutions for bribery. *Commonwealth v. Chapman*, 1 Va. Cas. 138 (Va. Gen. 1803).

30. James Monroe, Inaugural Address, March 4, 1817.

31. *A Digest of the Statute Laws of the State of Georgia*, vol. 2, ed. Thomas Read Rootes Cobb (Athens, GA: Christy, Kelsey, and Burke, 1851), 805 (emphasis added).

32. *The Revised Code of Laws of Illinois*, comp. Samuel Drake Lockwood and Theophilus Washington Smith (Vandalia, IL: Robert Blackwell, 1827), 141.

33. *The Revised Statutes of the State of Michigan* (Detroit: John S. Bagg, Printer to the State, 1838), 639, 640.

34. Statutes on file with the author.

35. *The Revised Statutes of Kentucky: Approved and Adopted by the General Assembly*, comp. C. A. Wickliffe, S. Turner, and S. S. Nicholas (Frankfort, KY: A. G. Hodges, 1852), 273.

36. "An Act to Provide Against Corrupt Legislation," in *General Laws of the State of Minnesota* (Faribault, MN: Orville Brown, State Printer, 1860), 101.

37. *Duke v. Asbee*, 33 N.C. 112 (N.C. 1850).

38. Blackstone, *Commentaries*, vol. 4, chap. 10.

39. *State v. Jackson*, 73 Me. 91 (1881).

40. Act to Prevent Frauds on the Treasury, Act of Feb. 26, 1853, ch. 81, § 6, 10 Stat. 171; see *Cong. Globe*, 32d Cong., 2d Sess. 392 (1853).

41. Act of Feb. 26, 1853; *United States v. Jones*, 5 Utah 552 (Utah. Terr. 1888); *Palliser v. United States*, 136 U.S. 257, 264 (1890).

42. On file with the author.

43. *Revised Laws of Louisiana: Containing the Revised Statutes of the State (Official Edition, 1870) as Amended by Acts of the Legislature, from the Session*

of 1870 to that of 1896 Inclusive, and All Other Acts of a General Nature for the Same Period, comp. and ann. Solomon Wolff (New Orleans: F. F. Hansel, 1897), Act 4, 218.

44. *State v. Ellis*, 33 N.J.L. 102 (N.J. 1868).

45. *Walsh v. People*, 65 Ill. 58 (Ill. 1872). ("At common law, bribery is a grave and serious offense against public justice; and the attempt or offer to bribe is likewise criminal.") See also *Commonwealth v. Brown*, 23 Pa. Super. 470 (1903); *State v. Farris*, 229 S.W. 1100 (Mo. Ct. App. 1921); *State v. Collins*, 210 P. 569, 571 (N.M. 1922).

46. See, e.g., *State v. Ragsdale*, 59 Mo. App. 590 (Mo. App., 1894).

47. Joel Prentiss Bishop, *Commentaries on the Criminal Law* (Boston: Little, Brown, 1882), sections 396–397, 225.

48. Francis Wharton, *A Treatise on the Criminal Law of the United States*, 5th ed., vol. 1 (Philadelphia: Kay and Brother, 1861), 411.

49. *Randall v. Evening News Association*, 97 Mich. 136, 143 (Mich. 1893).

50. *Republic of Hawaii v. Young Hee*, 10 Haw. 114 (Haw. 1895).

51. *Reed v. State*, 43 Tex. 319 (Tex. 1875).

52. Of course there were exceptions, as in *In re Wellcome*, 23 Mont. 450 (Mont. 1899).

53. *People v. Tweed*, 13 Abb. Pr. n.s. 25 (1872).

54. There was a small growth in reported criminal bribery and corruption cases, but even with this growth, the number of extortion and bribery cases was in the hundreds, not thousands. Though presumably this represents just a fraction of the total cases at trial, and differently worded statutes may help account for the low number of cases I identified, the evidence nonetheless signals a paucity of criminal corruption cases. Of those reported cases, a tiny fraction involved legislators at the state or federal levels—a majority of the legislative corruption cases involved school boards or other local officials, typically bribed to vote for a particular candidate for a municipal office. The majority of bribery cases involved a juror, a judge, or a libel charge; the majority of extortion cases involved a sheriff or other local official charging too much in a fee.

55. Even in 1880 there were 20,000 people in American prisons, and federal prisons held just over 1,000 inmates in 1885. Kristofer Allerfeldt, *Crime and the Rise of Modern America: A History from 1865–1941* (London: Routledge, 2011), 75.

56. John T. Noonan, *Bribes: The Intellectual History of a Moral Idea* (Collingdale, PA: Diane Publishing Company, 1984), 565. Parenthetical added by the author.

57. George Haynes, *The Election of Senators* (New York: Henry Holt, 1906), 53.

6. Railroad Ties

1. Gilbert Geis, *White-Collar and Corporate Crime: A Documentary and Reference* (Santa Barbara, CA: Greenwood, 2011), 113.

2. For a full history of this story, see John T. Noonan, *Bribes: The Intellectual History of a Moral Idea* (Collingdale, PA: Diane Publishing Company, 1984), 460–501.

3. "Report of the Select Committee to Investigate the Alleged Credit Mobilier," in *The Congressional Globe, Debates and Proceedings of the 3rd Session of Forty-Second Congress* (Washington, DC: Office of the Congressional Globe, 1873), 1466.

4. Robert Ewing Corlew, Stanley John Folmsbee, and Enoch L. Mitchell, *Tennessee: A Short History* (Knoxville: University of Tennessee Press, 1981), 359.

5. "Tennessee's Credit Redeemed," *New York Times*, April 6, 1881.

6. "Continuance of Testimony before the Bribery Committee," *Louisville Courier-Journal*, December 25, 1881, 1.

7. *Lynn v. Polk*, 76 Tenn. 121, 203 (1881).

8. "Continuance of Testimony," 6.

9. "The Bribery Investigating Committee Meets," *Louisville Courier-Journal*, December 13, 1881, 1.

10. "A State Senator Shot," *New York Times*, December 9, 1881, 1; *Wilmington Morning Star*, December 11, 1881.

11. Ibid.

12. "Bribery Investigating Committee Meets," 1.

13. Sam D. Elliott, "The 200-Page Decision," *Tennessee Bar Journal* 9 (2010): 3.

14. Adam Liptak, "Justices Are Long on Words but Short on Guidance," *New York Times*, November 17, 2010. This article inspired the idea of comparing the length of corruption opinions to great novels.

15. The judge wrote: "For this court to exercise the jurisdiction invoked, would be to assume that the co-ordinate departments of the government are liable to corruption but we are not. If we were to take jurisdiction, and determine that this act was passed by bribery and corruption, the Legislature would have the same right to enquire whether or not our judgment was procured by the same means."

16. This comes from Clifford J. Downey, *Chicago and the Illinois Central Railroad* (Charleston, SC: Arcadia, 2007), a history of the relationship between the railroad and the city.

17. For this, and all the other colorful and useful details behind the history of *Illinois Central*, see Joseph D. Kearney and Thomas W. Merrill, "The Origins of the American Public Trust Doctrine: What Really Happened in *Illinois Central*," *University of Chicago Law Review* 71 (2004): 859.

18. Ibid., 868.

19. Ibid., 888. Kearney and Merrill also uncovered indirect but damning evidence of bribery in some Illinois Central correspondence—but that correspondence was not available at the time to the public.

20. There were two efforts within the backlash to the bill: an effort to investigate corruption in the initial passage of the bill and an effort to repeal the bill. The railroads, according to Merrill and Kearney, put more of their efforts into defeating the investigation than defeating the repeal, although they put substantial resources into each. The bill to have an investigation led to a tie vote. Ibid.

21. *Illinois Central R.R. Co. v. Illinois*, 146 U.S. 387 (1892).

22. Wallace Mendelsohn, "New Light on *Fletcher vs. Peck* and *Gibbon vs. Ogden*," *Yale Law Journal* 58 (1949): 573, fn. 24.

23. Joseph L. Sax, "The Public Trust Doctrine in Natural Resources Law: Effective. Judicial Intervention," 68 *Michigan Law Review* 68 (1970): 471.

24. For a further discussion of this development, see Richard Epstein's argument that the best way to understand *Illinois Central* is as something like a corruption protection: it restrains the legislature from giving away public property for private ends. Richard A. Epstein, "The Public Trust Doctrine," *Cato Journal* 7, no. 2 (Fall 1987): 411–430. He writes, "Well-organized political groups may well be able to obtain net transfers from legislation." Elsewhere, Carol Rose writes, "From quite different directions, Louise

Halper and William Fischel, in their respective investigations of late nineteenth century nuisance law and eminent domain doctrine, have described how the courts drew distinctions in these doctrinal areas to rein in the most egregious legislative giveaways of the day, particularly those that benefitted railway companies." Carol Rose, "Joseph Sax and the Idea of the Public Trust Doctrine," *Ecology Law Quarterly* 25 (1998): 358. See also Louise A. Halper, "Nuisance, Courts, and Market in the New York Court of Appeal, 1850–1915," *Albany Law Review* 54 (1990): 355.

7. The Forgotten Law of Lobbying

1. See, e.g., Richard Briffault, "Lobbying and Campaign Finance: Separate and Together," *Stanford Law and Policy Review* 19 (2008): 107; and Vincent R. Johnson, "Regulating Lobbyists: Law, Ethics, and Public Policy," *Cornell Journal of Law and Public Policy* 16 (2006): 9. ("Though widely vilified, lobbyists representing individuals or groups can make a valuable contribution to informed and effective government. Lobbyists can direct ideas and opinions to appropriate decision makers and clearly express the views of citizens who have too little time or skill to do so personally. Lobbyists also illuminate the practical consequences of proposed government conduct by ensuring that the insights and professional expertise of a particular business or industry become part of the deliberative process.")

2. Briffault, "Lobbying," 107.

3. Johnson, "Regulating Lobbyists," 9. See also Stacie L. Fatka and Jason M. Levien, "Protecting the Right to Petition: Why a Lobbying Contingency Fee Prohibition Violates the Constitution," *Harvard Journal of Legislation* 35 (1998): 566. ("Today, if citizens wish to make their voice heard by their legislator, they must exercise their petition right by employing a lobbyist.")

4. Daniel A. Farber, "Free Speech without Romance," *Harvard Law Review* 105 (1991): 561, includes one of the fuller discussions of this argument. He writes: "Consider, for example, the supply of information about foreign affairs. To the extent that voters seek such information, they can often obtain it secondhand without paying the original producer. The free rider problem is exacerbated in this context because voters also have an incentive to free ride on the activities of other political participants. Because my vote probably will not change the election results, I have little incentive to seek

relevant information. Even if the information were only privately available, I would have little incentive to pay for it. Instead, I might as well sit back and let other people participate in politics. I will obtain whatever benefits exist from a good foreign policy regardless of whether I participate. The result is predictably straightforward: although information in general is likely to be underproduced, political information is even more likely to be underproduced, and underproduced to a greater extent. Furthermore, because information producers will capture only a tiny share of the ultimate benefits of their product in the form of better government, their lobbying activities against censorship similarly will be underfinanced. Therefore, the public good argument for protecting speech applies with particular force to political speech."

5. Samuel White Small, *A Stenographic Report of the Proceedings of the Constitutional Convention by Georgia* (Atlanta: Constitution Publishing Society, 1877), 80–81.

6. Ibid., 101–102.

7. Georgia Constitution of 1877, Articles I and II, para. 5.

8. Statute on file with the author. See also William N. Eskridge Jr., "Federal Lobbying Regulation: History through 1954," in *The Lobbying Manual: A Complete Guide to Federal Lobbying Law and Practice*, 4th ed., ed. William V. Luneberg, Thomas Susman, and Rebecca H. Gordon (Washington, DC: American Bar Association, 2009), 15.

9. *Tool Co. v. Norris*, 69 U.S. 45, 56 (1864).

10. William C. Clark Jr., *The Handbook of the Law of Contracts* (St. Paul, MN: West Publishing Company, 1894), 285.

11. Kenneth Crawford, *The Pressure Boys* (New York: J. Messner, 1939), ix; and Conor McGrath and Phil Harris, "The Creation of the U.S. Lobbying Industry," in *The Routledge Handbook of Political Management*, ed. Dennis W. Johnson (New York: Routledge, 2009).

12. 10 Barb. 489 (1851).

13. See Paul Bond, "Making Champerty Work: An Invitation to State Action," *University of Pennsylvania Law Review* 150 (2002): 1341.

14. Eskridge, "Federal Lobbying Reglation," 5.

15. 57 U.S. 314 (1853).

16. 21 Barb. 361 (1855).

17. 88 U.S. 441 (1874).

18. *Oscanyan v. Arms Co.*, 103 U.S. 261 (1880).

19. Certain financial instruments, debts, or obligations were "not vendible" as a matter of policy. For some examples using this language see *J. M. Chisholm v. Andrews*, 57 Miss. 636 (Miss. 1880); and *Ryan v. Miller*, 236 Mo. 496 (Mo. 1911).

20. *Usher v. McBratney*, 28 F. Cas. 853 (C.C.D. Kan. 1874); and *Rose v. Traux*, 21 Barb. 361 (N.Y. Gen. Term 1855).

21. *Usher*, 28 F. Cas. 853.

22. *Chesebrough v. Conover*, 140 N.Y. 382, 387 (N. Y. 1893).

23. Clark, *Handbook*, 356.

24. *Foltz v. Cogswell*, 86 Cal. 542, 548 (1863); see also *Reclamation Dist. No. 108 v. Hagar*, 66 Cal. 54 (Cal. 1884).

25. *Sweeney v. McLeod*, 15 Or. 330, 335 (1887).

26. *Richardson v. Scott's Bluff County*, 81 N.W. 309, 312 (Neb. 1899).

27. *Houlton v. Nichol*, 67 N.W. 715, 716 (Wis. 1896).

28. *Powers v. Skinner*, 34 Vt. 274, 281 (1861).

29. See, e.g., *Sweeney v. McLeod*, 15 Or. 330 (1887); and *Coquillard's Adm'r v. Bearss*, 21 Ind. 479, 481–482 (1863).

30. *Chippewa Valley, S. R. Co. v. Chicago*, 44 N.W. 17, 24 (Wis. 1889).

31. *Houlton v. Dunn*, 61 N.W. 898, 900 (Minn. 1895).

32. *Powers*, 281.

33. *Mills v. Mills*, 40 N.Y. 543, 546 (1869).

34. Ibid., 546.

35. *McGill's Adm'r v. Burnett*, 7 J.J. Marsh. 640 (Ky. App. 1832).

36. *State v. Miles*, 89 Me. 142 (Me. 1896).

37. *Marshall v. Baltimore & Ohio R.R. Co.*, 57 U.S. 314, 336 (1853).

38. *Brown v. Brown*, 34 Barb. 533, 538 (N.Y. 1861).

39. California Constitution of 1879, Articles IV and XXV (1879).

40. *Herrick v. Barzee*, 190 P. 141, 148 (Or. 1920); *Owens v. Wilkinson*, 20 App. D.C. 51, 71 (1902); and *Trist v. Child*, 88 U.S. 441 (1874).

41. *Trist*, 88 U.S. at 452.

42. *Mills*, 546.

43. Ibid.

44. 424 U.S. 1 (1976).

45. *McGhee v. Lindsay*, 6 Ala. 16, 20 (1844).

46. *Powers*, 280–281, citing *Clippinger v. Hepbaugh*, 5 Watts & Serg. 315 (Pa. 1843).

47. *Powers*, 281.

48. Ibid.

49. *Clippinger*, 321.

50. *Marshall*, 336; *Clippinger*, 315; *Wood v. McCann*, 36 Ky. 366 (1838); *Foltz v. Cogswell*, 25 P. 60 (Cal. 1890); *Rose*; *Frost v. Belmont*, 88 Mass. 152 (1863).

51. *Barber Asphalt Paving Co. v. Botsford*, 44 P. 3, 5 (Kan. 1896).

52. An example is in *McBratney v. Chandler*, 22 Kan. 692 (Kan. 1879).

53. See, for instance, *McDonald v. Buckstaff*, 76 N.W. 476, 481 (1898).

54. Richard Briffault, "Anxiety of Influence," *Election Law Journal* 13, no. 1 (March 2014): 160–193, writes: "Today, however, we would certainly view the efforts of a hired agent to draft a bill, explain it to legislators, and seek the bill's introduction as lobbying."

55. *Steele v. Drummond*, 275 U.S. 199 (1927).

56. *Textile Mills Sec. Corp. v. C.I.R.*, 314 U.S. 326, 337–338 (1941).

57. 345 U.S. 41 (1953).

58. 347 U.S. 612 (1954)

59. *Cammarano v. U.S.*, 358 U.S. 498 (1959).

60. *E. R.R. Presidents Conference v. Noerr Motor Freight, Inc.*, 365 U.S. 127, 135 (1961).

8. The Gilded Age

1. Andrew Jackson's campaigns had been crusades against aristocratic corruption. He was first nominated to the presidency in 1824, in a candidacy based on the theme of a return to the republican principles and a rejection of the corrupt habits of self-serving, wealthy elites. The call for a return to old republicanism had been growing since the early nineteenth century—some of the early Jacksonians had first been involved in John Randolph's breakoff Quid party of fifteen years earlier. His close advocate John Eaton wrote letters circulated as pamphlets signed "Wyoming" that associated Jackson with the virtues of the founding fathers and demanded a return to republican virtue. This was the first presidential campaign in which there were no signers of the Declaration of Independence or the Constitution standing for office, so the candidates had to vie for the spirit of America that

appealed to the public through rhetoric and action, not direct ties to the past. William Nester, *The Age of Jackson and the Art of American Power 1815–1848* (Herndon, VA: Potomac Books, 2013); Sean P. Adams, ed., *A Companion to the Era of Andrew Jackson* (Hoboken, NJ: Wiley-Blackwell, 2013), 260. Jackson won a plurality of votes—over 40 percent—followed by John Quincy Adams with 30 percent of the vote. Because no candidate received the majority of the electoral votes, the House of Representatives, led by Speaker Henry Clay, had the power to appoint the president. They chose Adams. When Adams then appointed Clay to be his secretary of state, Jackson's supporters denounced the decision as a "corrupt bargain" (Adams, *Companion*, p. 280). For the next four years, Jackson's supporters used the corruption theme to bring momentum to his rematch with Adams in 1828. The argument of this second—and successful—campaign was that the country was in a struggle between democracy and corruption, and Jackson represented the former, whereas incumbents and insiders represented the latter. Jackson won in a landslide. The anticorruption rhetoric of the time led to changes in corporate law. In the prior practice of special incorporation, government officials had more discretion to grant or deny, leading to personal relationships being necessary to gain corporate charters. Business entities with directors close to politically powerful legislators sought, and received, the grants of corporate charters from state governments. Jacksonians supported general incorporation—essentially the right to automatically get a corporate charter if one met certain objective criteria. See John Wallis, "Constitutions, Corporations, and Corruption: American States and Constitutional Change, 1842 to 1852," *Journal of Economic History* 65, no. 1 (2005): 211–256; Morton J. Horwitz, "Santa Clara Revisited: The Development of Corporate Theory," *West Virginia Law Review* 88 (1985): 181; Morton Horwitz, *The Transformation of American Law, 1870–1960: The Crisis of Legal Orthodoxy* (Oxford: Oxford Paperbacks 1992), 204. Jackson vetoed the renewed corporate charter of the Second Bank of the United States because of fears of corruption. During the 1832 presidential campaign—one that was almost exclusively about Jackson's bank veto—the theme continued. A leading newspaper patron described Jackson's fight as "the cause of democracy and the people, against a corrupt and abandoned aristocracy," and South Carolina senator Robert Jay Hayne called his victory "the triumph of the people over corruption." Harry L. Watson, *Liberty and Power: The Politics of Jacksonian America* (New York: Hill and Wang, 2006), 168. Unlike some of the founders before him, Jackson rejected the association of virtue with elitism. But like the founders before him, he portrayed corruption as anathema to liberty. His farewell address in 1837 sounded like Franklin fifty years later. If we allowed ourselves to become a corrupt public, he warned, we would become "easier victims to tyranny." His language was that of Madison: "It is from within, among yourselves, from cupidity, from corruption, from disappointed ambition, and inordinate thirst for power, that factions will be formed and liberty endangered." (*Presidential Documents: The Speeches, Proclamations, and Politics That Have Shaped the Nation from Washington to Clinton*, ed. Fred L. Israel and Thomas J. McInerney [New York: Routledge, 2013], 71.)

2. Justus D. Doenecke, *The Presidencies of James A. Garfield and Chester A. Arthur* (Lawrence: Regents Press of Kansas, 1981), 46.

3. Eldon Cobb Evans, *A History of the Australian Ballot System in the United States* (Chicago: University of Chicago Press, 1917), 10.

4. Ibid., 7.

5. Ibid., 8.

6. John Henry Wigmore, *The Australian Ballot System as Embodied in the Legislation of Various Countries*, 2nd ed. (Boston: Charles C. Soule, 1889), 31.

7. Ibid., 32.

8. Mark Twain and Charles Dudley Warner, *The Gilded Age* (New York: Modern Library, 2006), 253.

9. "Funds for the Campaign," *New York Times*, September 27, 1900.

10. "Trusts and Monopolies," in 1896: The Presidential Campaign: Cartoons and Commentary, a Vassar College website, http://projects.vassar.edu/1896/trusts.html.

11. Speech by Teddy Roosevelt at the Centennial Exercises in the New York Avenue Presbyterian Church, Washington, D.C., November 16, 1903, http://www.theodore-roosevelt.com/images/research/txtspeeches/92.txt; "Put Down Corruption, Says the President," *New York Times*, November 16, 1903, http://query.nytimes.com/mem/archive-free/pdf?res=F50E1FF73 F5D11738DDDAE0994D9415B838CF1D3.

9. Two Kinds of Sticks

1. 1903 Annual Message to Congress, December 7, 1903.

2. Jerry O'Callahan, "Senator John H. Mitchell and the Oregon Land Frauds, 1905," *Pacific Historical Review* 21 (August 1952): 255.

3. *Burton v. United States*, 196 U.S. 283 (1905).

4. *Burton v. United States*, 202 U.S. 344 (1906).

5. 40 *Congressional Record* 96.

6. Chap. 420, 34 Stat. 864 (1907), 2 U.S.C. § 441b (2).

7. Robert H. Sitkoff, "Corporate Political Speech, Political Extortion, and the Competition for Corporate Charters," *University of Chicago Law Review* 69 (2002): 1118–1120.

8. Here I am relying on research compiled by Robert Sahr, University of Oregon (2003), available at http://oregonstate.edu/cla/polisci/faculty-re search/sahr/sumcamp.pdf. See also Stephen Ansolabehere, John M. de Figueiredo, and James Snyder Jr., "Why Is There So Little Money in U.S. Politics?," *Journal of Economic Perspectives* 17 (Winter 2003): 105–109. Of course, with few reporting requirements and terrible enforcement, we don't know the actual numbers.

9. 256 U.S. 232 (1921).

10. Brief for Plaintiffs in Error, *Newberry v. United States*, 256 U.S. 232, 234 (1921).

11. Ibid., 236.

12. 313 U.S. 299 (1941).

13. 335 U.S. 106 (1948).

14. 352 U.S. 567 (1957).

10. The Jury Decides

1. *United States v. Bohonus*, 628 F.2d 1167, 1171 (9th Cir. 1980).

2. *United States v. Bush*, 522 F.2d 641 (7th Cir. 1975), *cert. denied*, 47 L. Ed. 2d 748 (1976).

3. Daniel J. Hurson, "Limiting the Federal Mail Fraud Statute—A Legislative Approach," *American Criminal Law Review* 20 (1983): 455–456.

4. *Bush*, 522 F.2d at 647–648.

5. *United States v. George*, 477 F.2d 508, 513 (7th Cir.1973).

6. *Bohonus*, 628 F.2d at 1167, 1171.

7. *Cunningham v. State*, 190 Md. 578, 582 (Md. 1948); see also *Livingston v. Commonwealth*, 184 Va. 830, 36 S.E.2d 561 (Va. 1946); *People v. Gokey*, 9 Ill. App. 3d 675, 678–680 (Ill. App. 1973).

8. See, e.g., *People v. Jackson*, 191 N.Y. 293 (N.Y. 1908).

9. *People v. Lafaro*, 250 N.Y. 336, 342 (N.Y. 1929).

10. *Handley v. State*, 102 P.2d 947, 951 (Okla. Crim. App. 1940).

11. *Republic of Hawaii v. Young Hee*, 10 Haw. 114 (Haw. 1895).

12. *State v. Savoie*, 67 N.J. 439, 341 A.2d 598 (N.J. 1975).

13. *People v. Diedrich*, 31 Cal. 3d 263, 276 (Cal. 1982).

14. *People v. Gaio*, 81 Cal. App. 4th 919, 927 (Cal.App. 2 Dist., 2000) (and cases cited therein).

15. *Martin v. United States*, 166 F.2d 76, 77 (4th Cir. 1948).

16. *In re Crum*, 55 N.D. 876 (1927).

17. *State v. Savoie*, 128 N.J. Super. 329, 345 (N.J. Super. A.D. 1974); *Martin v. United States*, 166 F.2d 76, 79 (4th Cir. 1948).

18. *People v. Esposito*, 146 Misc. 2d 847 (N.Y. Sup. 1990).

19. *People v. Coutu*, 235 Mich. App. 695, 706–707 (Mich. App. 1999).

20. *Barnette v. State*, 855 So. 2d 1129, 1132 (Ala. Crim. App. 2003).

21. Daniel H. Lowenstein, "Political Bribery and the Intermediate Theory of Politics," *UCLA Law Review* 32 (1985): 787.

11. *Operation Gemstone*

1. *Buckley v. Valeo*, 424 U.S. 1, 25 (1976).

2. *FEC. v. Wisconsin Right to Life*, 551 U.S. 449 (2007).

3. See Thomas Burke, "The Concept of Corruption in Campaign Finance Law," *Constitutional Commentary* 14 (1997): 128. See also Justin Sadowsky, "The Transparency Myth: A Conceptual Approach to Corruption and the Impact of Mandatory Disclosure Laws," *Connecticut Public Interest Law Journal* 4 (2005): 310 (corruption is important to understand because of the line of cases beginning with *Buckley*); Dennis Thompson, "Two Concepts of Corruption: Making Campaigns Safe for Democracy," *George Washington Law Review* 73 (2005): 1036–1069.

4. Samuel Issacharoff, Pamela S. Karlan, and Richard H. Pildes, *The Law of the Political Process*, 4th ed. (New York: Foundation Press, 2012).

5. Robert Kaiser, *So Damn Much Money: The Triumph of Lobbying and the Corrosion of American Government* (New York: Vintage, 2009), 291.

6. *McComish v. Bennett*, 131 S. Ct. 2806 (2011).

7. *Buckley v. Valeo*, 424 U.S. 1, 257, 96 S.Ct. 612, 744–745 (1976) (White, J., dissenting) (citing *Ex parte Yarbrough*, 110 U.S. 651, 658 [1884]).

8. 435 U.S. 765 (1978).

9. 494 U.S. 652 (1990).

10. 540 U.S. 93 (2003).

11. Richard Briffault, "Anxiety of Influence," *Election Law Journal* 13, no. 1 (March 2014): 160–193.

12. *A West Virginia State of Mind*

1. See Daniel Hays Lowenstein, "Political Bribery and the Intermediate Theory of Politics," *UCLA Law Review* 32 (1985): 809; Note, "Campaign Contributions and Federal Bribery Law," *Harvard Law Review* 92 (1978): 453–455 ("the potential sweep of the bribery statutes is enormous").

2. Lowenstein, "Political Bribery," 828.

3. Ibid., 787.

4. *In re Crum*, 215 N.W. 682, 688 (N.D. 1927).

5. *State v. London*, 194 Wash. 458, 470, 78 P.2d 548, 554 (Wash. 1938).

6. *State v. Smagula*, 39 N.J. Super. 187, 191, 120 A.2d 621, 623 (N.J. Super. A.D. 1956).

7. *U.S. v. Brewster*, 506 F.2d 62, 77 (C.A.D.C. 1974).

8. *United States v. Shober*, 489 F. Supp. 393 (E.D. Pa. 1979).

9. *People v. Brandstetter*, 103 Ill. App. 3d 259 (1982).

10. *Evans v. United States*, 504 U.S. 255 (1992).

11. *United States v. Cerilli*, 603 F.2d 415, 420 (3d Cir. 1979).

12. *United States v. Dozier*, 672 F.2d 531, 537 (5th Cir. 1982); *United States v. Cerilli*, 603 F.2d 415, 418–419; *United States v. Trotta*, 525 F.2d 1096 (2d Cir. 1975).

13. *United States v. Dozier*, 672 F.2d 531, 537 (5th Cir. 1982).

14. B. Drummond Ayers, "Charleston Journal; Corruption Cases Leave State in Search of Ethics," *New York Times*, September 18, 1989.

15. *Robert L. McCormick, petitioner, v. United States of America*, 1990 WL 10012892 (Appellate Brief) (U.S. October Term 1990), Brief for the United States (No. 89-1918).

16. *United States v. Ring*, 706 F.3d 460 (D.C. Cir. 2013). ("The McCormick Court failed to clarify what it meant by 'explicit,' and subsequent courts have struggled to pin down the definition of an explicit quid pro quo in various contexts.")

17. *Evans v. United States*, 504 U.S. 255, 258 (1992).

18. Ibid., 274 (Kennedy, J., concurring).

19. *United States v. Siegelman*, 640 F.3d 1159, 1171 (11th Cir. 2011), quoting *Evans*. See also *United States v. Whitfield*, 590 F.3d 325, 349 (5th Cir. 2009) (stating that *Evans* "clarified" *McCormick*).

13. Citizens United

1. *United States v. Sun Diamond Growers*, 526 U.S. 398 (1999).

2. 18 U.S.C. § 201(c)(1)(A) (1994).

3. *Citizens United v. FEC*, 558 U.S. 310 (2010).

4. Ibid., quoting *McConnell v. FEC*, 540 U.S. 93 (2003).

5. John M. Murrin, "Escaping Perfidious Albion: Federalism, Fear of Aristocracy, and the Democratization of Corruption in Post-Revolutionary America," in *Virtue, Corruption and Self-Interest: Political Values in the Eighteenth Century*, ed. Richard K. Matthews (Bethlehem, PA: Lehigh University Press, 1994), 120–122.

6. Ibid.

7. William Forbath, "Politics, State Building, and the Courts," in *The Cambridge History of Law in America* (Cambridge: Cambridge University Press, 2008), 643.

8. *Colorado Republican Federal Campaign Committee v. FEC*, 518 U.S. 604, 634 (1996) (Thomas, J., dissenting).

9. *Nixon v. Shrink Missouri Government PAC*, 528 U.S. 377, 423 (2000) (Scalia, J., dissenting) ("The majority today, by contrast, separates 'corruption' from its quid pro quo roots and gives it a new, far-reaching (and speech-suppressing) definition.").

10. *McConnell v. FEC*.

11. *People v. Kohut*, 30 N.Y.2d 183, 187 (N.Y. 1972).

12. *State v. Lopez*, 522 So. 2d 997, 1000 (Fla. App. 3d Dist. 1988).

13. *State v. Ross*, 214 Ariz. 280, 284 (Ariz. App. Div. 1 2007).

14. Ohio Ethics Advisory Opinion No. 2001-04 (Ohio Eth. Com. 2001) at 3.

15. *Barnette v. State*, 855 So. 2d 1129, 1132 (Ala. Crim. App. 2003).

16. *People v. Coutu*, 235 Mich. App. 695, 706–707, 599 N.W.2d 556, 562 (Mich. App. 1999).

17. *Wurster v. State*, 708 N.E.2d 587, 594 (Ind. App. 1999), *aff'd.* 715 N.E.2d 341 (Ind. 1999); *Winn v. State*, 722 N.E.2d 345, 347 (Ind. App. 1999); *Isassi v. State*, 330 S.W.3d 633 (Tex. Crim. App. 2010); *Scaccia v. State Ethics Commission*, 727 N.E.2d 824, 828–829 (Mass. 2000).

18. *United States v. Abbey*, 560 F.3d 513 (6th Cir. 2009). In *Abbey* the court said that quid pro quo did not require "a particular, identifiable act when the illegal gift is given to the official. Instead, it is sufficient if the public official understood that he or she was expected to exercise some influence on the payor's behalf as opportunities arose."

19. *United States v. Rosen*, 716 F.3d 691 (2013).

20. See Richard A. Primus, "Canon, Anti-Canon and Judicial Dissent," *Duke Law Journal* 48 (1998): 250.

21. See Stewart Jay, "The First Amendment: The Creation of the First Amendment Right to Free Expression from the Eighteenth Century to the Mid-Twentieth Century," *William Mitchell Law Review* 34 (2008): 773–782.

22. *Bridges v. California*, 314 U.S. 252, 281 (1941).

23. J. M. Balkin, "Some Realism about Pluralism: Legal Realist Approaches to the First Amendment," *Duke Law Journal* 39, no. 3 (1990): 393. See also *Brandenberg v. Ohio*, 395 U.S. 444 (1969).

24. Ibid., 392.

25. Owen M. Fiss, "State Activism and State Censorship," *Yale Law Journal* 100 (1991): 287.

26. *Palko v. Connecticut*, 302 U.S. 319, 327 (1937).

27. William Chillingworth, *The Religion of Protestants* (Oxford: Leonard Lichfield, 1638).

28. Francis Warton, *The Revolutionary Diplomatic Correspondence of the US*, vol. 6 (Washington, DC: Government Printing Office, 1889), 10.

29. Notes of Yates, June 23, 1787, in *The Records of the Federal Convention of 1787*, vol. 1, ed. Max Farrand (New Haven, CT: Yale University Press, 1911), quoting Mason.

14. The New Snuff Boxes

1. Tim LaPira, "How Much Lobbying Is There in Washington? It's DOUBLE What You Think," http://sunlightfoundation.com/blog/2013/11/25/how-much-lobbying-is-there-in-washington-its-double-what-you-think/.

2. June 14, 1788, Debate in the Virginia Convention, in *The Records of the Federal Convention of 1787*, vol. 3, ed. Max Farrand (New Haven, CT: Yale University Press, 1911), 313.

3. "The Lobbyists Playbook," *60 Minutes*, November 6, 2011 (transcript of a live interview).

4. *The Works of Thomas Jefferson, Federal Edition*, vol. 9 (New York: G. P. Putnam's Sons, 1904–1905).

5. Notes of Yates, June 22, 1787, in *Records*, vol. 1.

6. Howard Ball, *Hugo Black, Cold Steel Warrior* (Oxford: Oxford University Press, 1996), 83.

7. To explore some of the empirical research, see Sanjay Gupta and Charles W. Swenson, "Rent-Seeking by Agents of the Firm," *Journal of Law and Economics* 46 (2003): 260; Nauro F. Campos and Francesco Giovannoni, "Lobbying, Corruption, and Political Influence," *Public Choice* 13 (2007): 1–21.

8. Dennis F. Thompson, *Ethics in Congress: From Individual to Institutional Corruption* (Washington, DC: Brookings Institution Press, 1995), 112.

9. Ray Henry, "Jimmy Carter: Unchecked Political Contributions Are 'Legal Bribery,'" *Huffington Post*, July 17, 2013, http://www.huffingtonpost.com/2013/07/17/jimmy-carter-bribery_n_3611882.html.

10. *United States v. McCormick*, 1992 WL 12132379 (Appellate Brief) (4th Cir., July 22, 1992), Supplemental Brief of Appellant on Remand from the United States Supreme Court (No. 88-5702).

11. Lawrence Lessig, *Republic, Lost: How Money Corrupts Congress and a Plan to Stop It* (New York: Hachette Publishing, 2011).

12. Speech of James Madison, in the *Journals of the American Congress from 1774–1788*, vol. 4 (Washington, DC: Way and Gideon, 1823), 200.

13. Immediately after the case came down, the District of Columbia Circuit Court of Appeals applied the corruption logic of *Citizens United* to hold that political committees could accept unlimited contributions, enabling the structures now known as Super PACs. A few hundred people are responsible for most of the Super PAC funding. So long as they do not make any

explicit deals or coordinate, their activity is treated as "core political speech." None of their activities are considered corrupt under U.S. constitutional law. *SpeechNow.org v. Fed. Election Comm'n,* 599 F.3d 686 (D.C. Cir. 2010).

14. H. A. Washington, ed., *The Writings of Thomas Jefferson: Correspondence, Contin. Reports and Opinions while Secretary of State,* vol. 7 (Washington, DC: Riker, Thorne and Co., 1854), 150.

15. *Randall v. Sorrell,* 548 U.S. 230 (2006).

15. Facts in Exile, Complacency, and Disdain

1. See oral argument in *McCutcheon v. FEC,* The Oyez Project, 572 U.S. ___ (2014), available at: http://www.oyez.org/cases/2010-2019/2013/2013_12_536.

2. Susan Rose-Ackerman, *Corruption and Government: Causes, Consequences, and Reform* (Cambridge: Cambridge University Press, 1999), 2.

3. Susan Rose-Ackerman, *Corruption: Readings in Public Choice and Constitutional Political Economy* (New York: Springer, 2008), 551.

4. J. Peter Euben, "Corruption," in *Political Innovation and Conceptual Change,* ed. Terence Ball, James Farr, and Russell L. Hanson (Cambridge: Cambridge University Press, 1989), 220–246.

5. Ibid., 231–232.

6. Fukuyama must take some blame for the optimistic reading—he did claim that "in the long run" liberal democracy would prevail, that action would follow thought. Francis Fukuyama, *The End of History and the Last Man,* with a new afterword (New York: Avon Books, 2006), 211.

7. Russell Hardin, "Public Choice v. Democracy," in *The Idea of Democracy,* ed. David Copp, Jean Hampton, and John E. Roemer (Cambridge: Cambridge University Press, 1993), 157.

8. *Calder v. Bull,* 3 U.S. 386 (1798).

9. Carrie B. Kerekes, "Government Takings: Determinants of Eminent Domain," *American Law and Economics Review* 13 (2011): 201–219.

10. *Webster v. Doe,* 486 U.S. 592, 608 (1988) (Scalia, J., dissenting).

11. *Caperton v. A. T. Massey Coal Co.,* 556 U.S. 868 (2009).

12. Horace Stern, "Samuel Freeman Miller," in *Great American Lawyers,* vol. 6, ed. William Draper Lewis (Philadelphia: Winston, 1909), 541.

13. 110 U.S. 651, 657–658 (1884).

14. Simon Lazarus, "Stripping the Gears of National Government," *Northwestern University Law Review* 106 (Spring 2012): 817–818 (discussing the contempt for politics).

16. The Anticorruption Principle

1. Jens Chr. Andvig et al., "Research on Corruption: A Policy Oriented Study," survey commissioned by the Norwegian Agency for Development Co-operation, 2000, http://www.icgg.org/downloads/contribution07_andvig.pdf, 8.

2. Bruce E. Gronbeck, "The Rhetoric of Political Corruption," in *Political Corruption: A Handbook*, ed. Arnold J. Heidenheimer, Michael Johnston, and Victor T. Le Vine (New Brunswick, NJ: Transaction Publishers, 1999), 173.

3. The idea of excessiveness that shows up in many of these definitions, and the sense of the range of obligations, is important so as not to make every action in any connection with public life corrupt. There are many trivial moments in a day that one would hardly call corrupt because although they are self-interested, they are not excessive. The idea of excessive self-interest ties the stories that sound corrupt together in a deep way, not accidentally. Interest is excessive when it leads to an actual override of public interest in a significant or meaningful exercise of public power. What constitutes significant may vary from community to community because whether or not an action is corrupt depends upon whether the actor or community sees the action as a significant or meaningful exercise of public power. What constitutes public interest might vary from person to person, but if the person acting perceives that she is putting public interests beneath private ones in the exercise of power, it is corrupt.

4. Citizens, by virtue of their intimate relationship and the necessity of their honest involvement in public affairs, have fiduciary obligations to the public—but only when they engage in public life. Corruption describes the moments when citizens fail those obligations. Presidents, congresspersons, mayors, police officers, and judges have stepped almost entirely into their public role, and so their obligations are more pervasive and opportunities for corruption greater; lobbyists and those who contribute to campaigns

violate their fiduciary obligations only inasmuch as they fail to keep public interests first in the use of public rights; and uninvolved citizens rarely have fiduciary obligations.

5. Laura Underkuffler, *Captured by Evil: The Idea of Corruption in Law* (New Haven, CT: Yale University Press, 2013).

6. Lawrence Lessig, *Republic, Lost: How Money Corrupts Congress and a Plan to Stop It* (New York: Hachette Publishing, 2011).

7. Samuel Issacharoff, "On Political Corruption," *Harvard Law Review* 124 (2010): 118.

8. Deborah Hellman, "Defining Corruption and Constitutionalizing Democracy," *Michigan Law Review* 111 (2013): 1385.

9. Jong-Sung You, "Corruption as Injustice," paper presented at the annual meeting of the American Political Science Association, 2007, http://irps.ucsd.edu/assets/001/503060.pdf.

10. For an exception, see Ronald Dworkin, *Law's Empire* (Cambridge, MA: Harvard University Press, 1986), 174.

11. See John Rawls, *A Theory of Justice* (Cambridge, MA: Harvard University Press, 1971), 235.

12. Lessig, *Republic, Lost*.

13. For a discussion of the fiduciary strain in political thought, see Ethan Leib, David Ponet, and Michael Serota, "A Fiduciary Theory of Judging," *California Law Review* 101 (2013): 699; and D. Theodore Rave, "Politicians as Fiduciaries," *Harvard Law Review* 126 (2013): 671.

14. Bruce Cain, "Moralism and Realism in Campaign Finance Reform," *University of Chicago Legal Forum* 1995 (1996): 112.

15. David A. Strauss, "Corruption, Equality, and Campaign Finance Reform," *Columbia Law Review* 94 (1994): 1369, 1370, 1382.

16. Kathleen M. Sullivan, "Political Money and Freedom of Speech," *University of California at Davis Law Review* 30 (1997): 679.

17. Richard L. Hasen, *The Supreme Court and Election Law: Judging Equality from* Baker v. Carr *to* Bush v. Gore (New York: New York University Press, 2003).

18. Richard Hasen, "Is 'Dependence Corruption' Distinct from a Political Equality Argument for Campaign Finance Reform? A Reply to Professor Lessig," *Election Law Journal* 11 (2013).

19. Baron de Montesquieu, *The Spirit of Laws* [1748], trans. Melvin Richter (Cambridge: Cambridge University Press, 1991).

20. Edward van Roy, "On the Theory of Corruption," *Economic Development and Cultural Change* (October 1970): 86.

21. Stephen Sachs, "Corruption, Clients and Political Machines: A Response to Professor Issacharoff," *Harvard Law Review Forum* 124 (2010): 62.

22. See Underkuffler, *Captured by Evil*, 112.

23. Hellman, "Defining Corruption and Constitutionalizing Democracy," 1385.

24. Hannah Arendt, *The Promise of Politics* (New York: Random House, 2005), 20–21. Another way to express the same idea is that people have different identifications of their personal interest that they might maximize. I might identify as self first and foremost, and spend my energies and attentions on my own private enrichment. Or I might identify as a member of my family first and foremost, and spend my energies to maximize the good of my family. I might identify as a lawyer, or a Vermonter (where I grew up), or a Congregationalist, or a New Yorker (where I live now), or an American. All of these are "groups" with which I can plausibly, psychologically identify and whose interests I can plausibly put before my own. The psychological experience of putting a group interest first is fundamentally different from attempting to maximize one's own interests. Because people are capable of loving different groups (self, family, nation), it is coherent to say that "Peter Thiel put private interests ahead of group interests."

Conclusion

1. Franklin's will, in *The Works of Benjamin Franklin: Containing Several Political and Historical Tracts Not Included in Any Former Edition, and Many Letters, Official and Private, Not Hitherto Published* (Chicago: Townsend MacCoun, 1982), 601.

2. Friedrich Nietzsche, "The Case of Wagner," in *Basic Writings of Nietzsche* (New York: Random House, 2009), 626. I am grateful to Roger Berkowitz for leading me to this passage. See Roger Berkowitz, "The Irony of the Elite," Weekly Read, Hannah Arendt Center, February 21, 2014, http://www.hannaharendtcenter.org/?p=12585.

3. Tim Mak, "Corruption Is Number 2 Issue for 2103," *Politico*, July 30, 2013, http://www.politico.com/.

4. Kristofer Allerfelt, *Crime and Rise of Modern America 1865–1941* (London: Routledge, 2011), 169.

5. Lon Fuller, *The Morality of Law*, rev. ed. (New Haven, CT: Yale University Press, 1969), 33–42.

Cases Cited

Further Reading

Allerfelt, Kristofer. *Crime and Rise of Modern America 1865–1941*. London: Routledge, 2011.

Amar, Akhil Reed. *America's Constitution: A Biography*. New York: Random House, 2005.

Aristotle. *Nichomachean Ethics*. Minneapolis: Filiquarian Publishing, 2007.

Bailyn, Bernard. *The Ideological Origins of the American Revolution*. Cambridge, MA: Belknap Press of Harvard University Press, 1992.

Banning, Lance. *The Jeffersonian Persuasion*. Ithaca, NY: Cornell University Press, 1980.

Currie, David P. *The Constitution in the Supreme Court: The First Hundred Years, 1789–1888*. Chicago: University of Chicago Press, 1985.

Downey, Clifford. *Chicago and the Illinois Central Railroad*. Charleston, SC: Arcadia, 2007.

Euben, J. Peter. "Corruption." In *Political Innovation and Conceptual Change*, edited by Terence Ball, James Farr, and Russell L. Hanson. Cambridge: Cambridge University Press, 1989.

Gibbon, Edward. *The History of the Decline and Fall of the Roman Empire*. Edited by H. H. Millman. London: John Murray, 1846.

Henning, Peter. *The Prosecution and Defense of Public Corruption: The Law and Legal Strategies*. New York: Oxford University Press, 2011.

Holton, Woody. *Unruly Americans and the Origins of the Constitution*. New York: Hill and Wang, 2007.

Kaiser, Robert. *So Damn Much Money: The Triumph of Lobbying and the Corrosion of American Government*. New York: Vintage, 2009.

Lessig, Lawrence. *Republic, Lost: How Money Corrupts Congress and a Plan to Stop It*. New York: Hachette Publishing, 2011.

Locke, John. *The Second Treatise of Government and A Letter Concerning Toleration*. Mineola, NY: Dover, 2002.

Machiavelli, Niccòlo. *Discourses of Livy*. Oxford: Oxford University Press, 1997.

McDonald, Forrest. *Novus Ordo Seclorum: The Intellectual Origins of the Constitution*. Lawrence: University Press of Kansas, 1985.

McGrath, Peter C. *Yazoo: Law and Politics in the New Republic, the Case of Fletcher v. Peck*. Providence: Brown University Press, 1966.

Montesquieu, Baron de. *The Spirit of Laws* [1748]. Translated by Melvin Richter. Cambridge: Cambridge University Press, 1991.

Noonan, John T. *Bribes: The Intellectual History of a Moral Idea*. Collingdale, PA: Diane Publishing, 1984.

Pocock, J. G. A. *The Machiavellian Moment: Florentine Political Thought and the Atlantic Republican Tradition*. Princeton, NJ: Princeton University Press, 1975.

Rose-Ackerman, Susan. *Corruption and Government: Causes, Consequences, and Reform*. Cambridge: Cambridge University Press, 1999.

Schiff, Stacy. *A Great Improvisation: Franklin, France, and the Birth of America*. New York: Henry Holt, 2006.

Shain, Barry Alan. *The Myth of American Individualism*. Princeton, NJ: Princeton University Press, 1994.

Underkuffler, Laura. *Captured by Evil: The Idea of Corruption in Law*. New Haven, CT: Yale University Press, 2013.

Wood, Gordon S. *The Americanization of Benjamin Franklin*. New York: Penguin, 2005.

———. *The Creation of the American Republic, 1776–1787*. New York: W. W. Norton, 1969.

———. *Radicalism of the American Revolution*. New York: Knopf, 1992.

Acknowledgments

Gratitude may be dangerous in the wrong situation, but in the right situation it is among the most glorious of emotions.

There are many friends without whose help I could not have finished this book. Scott Faber, my writing partner, was like a weightlifter's spotter, encouraging me to write while he wrote at the same time on video chat, one brutal Hower of Power at a time over five years. Kelly Jean Kelly, who combines generosity with logic in all of her suggestions, edited early drafts and provided extraordinary advice on connecting, storytelling, and perseverence. Larry Lessig encouraged me from the first e-mail to the last period. His belief in me was such a source of strength. I was blessed to work with two crack research assistants: Margaret Monaghan, who helped me develop, think through, and research early ideas; and Megan Banfield, a wise, careful, and critical-minded research assistant who cheerfully and carefully read every idea, checked my cites (and corrected many of them), and uncovered the early lobbying cases and many old bribery statutes. Thanks to Larry Abraham and Jacob Seward for stellar research; to John Kulka, my wise, kind, and unbelievably patient editor; to Amanda Michel for Russian baths; to Bill Blachly and Ann O'Brien, each for a wonderful place to work in the summer; to Lynn Marie Ruse for dancing; to Alissa Quart for finding magic in the dullest chapters and giving them sparkle; and to Jennifer Dworkin for making me laugh about philosophy, and myself, and protecting me from category mistakes. I had many helpful comments on different ideas, and I thank everyone who contributed. These wonderful people stand out for their thoughtful and deep engagement: Jamie Boyle, Richard Briffault, Nestor Davidson, Jacob Eisler, James Gardner, Paul Haagen, Robert Kaczorowski, Jonathan Mattingly, Robert Post, Jedediah Purdy, Seth Barrett Tilman, and Alex Zakaras. To my parents, Mary and Peter Teachout, thank you for encouraging me to turn toward complications, instead of away from them, and for expecting the most difficult thing: that I say what I mean. Special thanks to Duke Law School and the New America Foundation for their support at the beginning and end of the project, respectively. And great gratitude to the faculty of Fordham Law School. You took a chance on me, and gave me time, freedom, and support.

Finally, to Benjamin Franklin, for giving me hope.

Index